THE SHORTER

# The Shorter Catechism

of the
## Westminster Assembly Explained and Proved from Scripture

## THOMAS VINCENT

THE BANNER OF TRUTH TRUST

THE BANNER OF TRUTH TRUST
3 Murrayfield Road, Edinburgh EH12 6EL
P.O. Box 621, Carlisle, Pennsylvania 17013, USA

★

*First published* 1674
*First Banner of Truth edition* 1980
ISBN 0 85151 314X

★

Reproduced, printed and bound in Great Britain by
Hazell Watson & Viney Ltd, Aylesbury, Bucks

# AN EPISTLE TO THE READER

THAT Popish axiom is long since exploded—That ignorance is the mother of devotion. The world doth now see that without knowledge the mind is not good. And, look, as no knowledge is so necessary as that of the grounds and principles of the Christian religion, so no way is so apt to convey it to the minds of men as that which is called *catechistical*. More knowledge is ordinarily diffused, especially among the ignorant and younger sort, by one hour's catechistical exercise than by many hours' continued discourses. This way helps the understanding, whilst it provokes the attention; many elaborate sermons being lost through the inadvertency of the hearers. Thus, not only ignorance is cured, but error also is prevented; too many being misguided, because they were not at first well-grounded in the principles of the doctrine of Christ. For such reasons as these, we highly approve the labours of this reverend brother, in his "Explanation of the Assembly's Shorter Catechism." And having, to our great satisfaction, perused it ourselves, in whole or in part, do readily recommend it to others: for though he composed it at first for his own particular congregation, yet we judge it may be greatly useful to all Christians in general, especially to private families. The manner

of using it in families must be left to the discretion
of the masters and governors respectively; though yet
we concur with the author, and think it advisable
(as he hints in one of his epistles), that after a question in the Catechism is propounded, and an answer,
without book, returned by one of the family, the
same person, or some other, be called upon to read
(if not to rehearse) the explanation of it, the rest reading along with him in several books; by which means
their thoughts (which are apt to wander) will be the
more intent upon what they are about. To conclude,
though the Assembly's Shorter Catechism itself be
above our recommendation, as having its praises
already in the Churches of Christ, yet we think it
good to give it under our hands, that this Explanation of it is very worthy of acceptation.

(Signed)

| | |
|---|---|
| J. Owen, D.D. | Ben. Needler. |
| Joseph Caryl. | Dan. Bull. |
| G. Griffith. | Cha. Morton. |
| Hen. Stubs. | Willm. Carslake. |
| Edm. Calamy. | Robert Franklin. |
| Mattw. Barker. | Mattw. Sylvester. |
| John Loder. | Nathan Vincent. |
| John Ruyther. | T. Jacomb, D.D. |
| Nicol Blaikie. | T. Case. |
| James Janeway. | T. Watson. |
| H. Vaughan. | T. Doolittle. |
| Willm. Maddocks. | James Innes. |
| John Turner. | Jo. Wells. |
| Will. Thomson. | Richard Mayo. |
| T. Manton, D.D. | John Hicks. |
| Will. Jenkyn. | Edw. Veal. |
| C. Fowler. | Edw. West. |
| T. Lye. | Edw. Lawrence. |
| T. Cawton. | Jo. Chester. |
| Thos. Brooks. | J. Sharp. |

## TO THE MASTERS AND GOVERNORS OF FAMILIES BELONGING TO MY CONGREGATION.

SOME dedicate their books unto lords and ladies, or other great persons; such possibly I might find out, had I a mind to seek; but as my love is most endeared unto you, to whom I stand so nearly related, so my greatest ambition is to be serviceable unto your souls. Your cordial and constant love to me and my labours (in a whiffling age), of which you have given many manifest proofs, deserveth a greater expression of my grateful sense than the dedication of this book unto you. God, by bringing you under my ministry, hath given me the charge of your souls; and God, by bringing persons into your families, hath given you a charge of their souls. Our charge is great, and to be guilty of the ruin of souls is dreadful. Happy shall we be, if we be found faithful to our own and others' souls, in the great day of accounts. Too many, even in our nation and city perish and run blindfold into hell, for want of knowledge; and the most are without knowledge, for want of instruction; and as no way of instruction doth convey clearer light of distinct knowledge in the principles of religion than the way of catechising, so the neglect of this in ministers and masters of families is such a sin of unfaithfulness unto the souls of them that are under their charge, that all of us should take heed we have it not to answer for at the appearance of our Lord. It is not sufficient for you to bring your children and servants to receive public instruction; but it is your duty also to instruct them privately, and at home to examine them in their catechisms. I know no catechism more full of light and sound doctrine than the Shorter Catechism of the late Reverend Assembly; yet, because in many answers there are things not easy to be understood by beginners, therefore, in this my Explanation of it, I have taken pains to take abroad every answer, to open it in several under-questions and answers, and to confirm the truths thereof by reasons and Scripture proofs; which I have endeavoured to do as plainly and familiarly as I could, that everything therein might be the more intelligible and useful unto such as either learn or read it. Some chief controversies in religion I have touched upon, briefly propounding arguments for the backing of the truth, and not left objections wholly unanswered; which I have the rather done, that all of you, especially the more unexperienced young ones under you, might get some armour against everywhere prevailing error. You know that some have committed the whole of the Explanation, so far as we have gone, unto memory (how beneficial they have found this, others besides themselves can speak); yet all have not that strength of memory, neither would I impose this Explanation to be learned without book by all; yet this I advise, that you, who are masters of families, would set apart time, twice, or at least once every week, to examine your children and servants in the Assembly's Catechism, taking Mr Lye's excellent method in the way of asking questions, whom God hath made singularly useful in the diffusing much light amongst young ones. And after they have given you the answers, without book, which are in the Catechism, that then yourselves would read, or cause one of them to read, some part of this Explanation on those answers, so far as you can well go at a time. And if each of them that can read should, both in your families and in our public assembly, have one of these Explanations in their hands, to read along with them that read or publicly answer, they would the better attend and understand what is read or answered: which course, I apprehend, will exceedingly tend to their great profit; and that such as do this with diligence will, through God's blessing, attain in a short time much proficiency in the best knowledge, which is such a jewel, that none, methinks, should be contentedly without, when with less labour than for other jewels of inferior value, it may be obtained. This Explanatory Catechism was chiefly, if not only, intended for you, and the use of such as are of my congregation; which, if it may find acceptation also with, and prove beneficial unto other families, I shall rejoice. The more generally useful my poor endeavours are, as it will tend so much the more to the glory of my great Master, so it will yield to myself the greatest comfort, especially in a dying hour. I shall take my leave of you, though I be not departed from you, with the departing exhortation of the apostle: "And now, brethren, I commend you to God, and to the word of his grace, which is able to build you up, and to give you an inheritance among all them which are sanctified."—Acts xx. 32.—Your earnest souls' well-wisher.

T. VINCENT.

## TO THE YOUNG ONES OF MY CONGREGATION,

### ESPECIALLY THOSE THAT ANSWER THIS EXPLICATORY CATECHISM IN OUR PUBLIC ASSEMBLY.

SHOULD I leave you out in my dedication of this book, I might seem both injurious unto you, for whose sake chiefly the book itself was composed, and injurious to my own love which I have for you, so many ways endeared, whereby also I am strongly obliged to do all the service I can for your souls. Your reciprocal love is a great tie; but the chief obligation of all, is the near relation between us, when I can write to you, not as my hearers only, but to many of you as my children; and that I may say, in the words of the apostle, 1 Cor. iv. 15 (which I desire to speak, not to mine own, but to the praise and glory of God, through whose blessing alone it is that my ministry, so mean comparatively, hath had this effect): "Though ye should have ten thousand instructors in Christ, yet have ye not many fathers; for in Christ Jesus I have begotten you, through the gospel." My endeavours are (as a father to his children), to feed you with knowledge and understanding, and that, of incomparably the most excellent things. Had you as large understanding in the secrets and mysteries of nature as the greatest and most wise philosopher, Solomon himself not excepted—had you skill in all languages under heaven, and could speak with the tongues of men and angels; yet all human knowledge, in the greatest height and improvement of it, would not be worthy to be compared and named the same day with the knowledge of Jesus Christ, and the mysteries of salvation with which I would acquaint you. You have seen the light of the moon, and some brightness in the stars, when the curtains of night have been drawn over the heavens: all which luminaries, upon the rising of the sun, with its more glorious light, have disappeared and shrunk out of sight into darkness?—such is the light of all human knowledge, compared with the beams of divine light, which do issue forth from the Sun of Righteousness. It is the light of the knowledge of the will, and ways, and glory of God in the face of Jesus Christ, that I desire to hold forth unto you. The whole Scripture is full of this light; but as, in the moon, some parts are clearer than others, so in the Holy Scriptures some parts are more full of this light. Such are those parts which contain the chief things to be known and believed, to be done and practised, in order to salvation. These things are excellently reduced by the late Reverend Assembly into questions and answers, in their Shorter Catechism. In this Catechism I have been some years instructing some of you; and that you might the better understand what you there learn, I did, above four years ago, begin this Explanation of it; which at first you had in writing, and upon your desire afterward, I put it sheet after sheet, as you learned it, in the press for you. The often failure of the printer hath caused many interruptions and intercessions in our work. Therefore, having finished the whole, I have now printed the whole together, that we be not broken off upon that account any more; which, as the fruit of much study, and as a token of most dear love, I present unto you. And now, dear young ones, think not much of taking pains in learning that which hath cost me so much pains in composing for you. Such of you as have not time, or strength of memory, for the learning of it, I advise to the frequent reading of it; and where it is not read in your families, that you often read it over alone. How profitable this will prove, experience, through God's blessing, in a short time will show. Hereby you may be able to look over the heads of most of your years in knowledge; which that you may be filled with, as with every grace, is the prayer for you to the Father of lights, from whom cometh every good and perfect gift, of

Yours in the sincerest bonds,

T. VINCENT.

AN

# EXPLANATION

OF THE

# ASSEMBLY'S SHORTER CATECHISM.

---

I. Ques. *What is the chief end of man?*
*Ans.* Man's chief end is to glorify God, and to enjoy him for ever.

Q. 1. What is meant by the chief end of man?
A. The chief end of man, is that which man ought chiefly to aim at or design, to desire, seek after, and endeavour to obtain, as his chief good and happiness; unto which his life and his actions should be referred and directed; which is the glorifying of God, and the enjoying of God for ever.

Q. 2. May men have no other chief end than the glorifying and enjoying of God?
A. Men ought to have no other chief end than the glorifying of God, but they may have subordinate ends. For—
1. Men ought to be diligent in their particular callings, for this end, that they may provide for themselves and their families. " Do your own business, and work with your own hands, that ye may have lack of nothing."—1 Thess. iv. 11, 12. 2. Men may eat, and drink, and sleep, for this end, that they may nourish and refresh their bodies. It is lawful to design, and desire, and seek such things as these in such actions, subordinately, or less principally; but in these and all actions, men ought principally and chiefly

to design and seek the glory of God. " Whether, therefore, ye eat or drink, or whatsoever ye do, do all to the glory of God."—1 Cor x. 31. 3. Men may moderately desire and endeavour after the enjoyment of such a portion of the good things of the world as is needful and useful; but they ought to make choice of God for their chief good, and desire the eternal enjoyment of him as their chief portion. " Whom have I in heaven but thee ? and there is none upon earth that I desire beside thee," or in comparison with thee. " My flesh and my heart faileth : but God is the strength of my heart and my portion for ever."—Ps. lxxiii. 25, 26.

Q. 3. What is it to glorify God?

A. 1. Negatively, to glorify God, is not to give any additional glory to God: it is not to make God more glorious than he is; for God is incapable of receiving the least addition to his essential glory, he being eternally and infinitely perfect and glorious. " Your Father which is in heaven is perfect."—Matt. v. 48. " Thou art my Lord : my goodness extendeth not unto thee."—Ps. xvi. 2.

2. Affirmatively, to glorify God, is to manifest God's glory : not only passively, as all creatures do, which have neither religion nor reason, but also actively, men glorify God, when the design of their life and actions is the glory and honour of God. " That ye should show forth the praises of him who hath called you," &c.—1 Pet. ii. 9. (1.) When inwardly they have the highest estimation of him, the greatest confidence in him, and the strongest affections to him, this is glorifying of God in spirit. " Glorify God in your spirit, which is God's."—1 Cor. vi. 20. (2.) When outwardly they acknowledge God according to the revelations he hath made of himself, when with their lips they show forth God's praise. " He that offereth praise, glorifieth me."—Ps. l. 23. When they sincerely endeavour, in their actions, the exalting of God's name, the promotion of the interest of his kingdom in the world, and to yield that worship and obedience to him which he hath prescribed in his Word. " O magnify the Lord with me, and let us exalt his name together."—Ps. xxiv. 3. " Fear God, and give glory to him; and worship

him that made heaven, and earth, and the sea, and the fountains of waters."—Rev. xiv. 7.

Q. 4. What is it to enjoy God?

A. To enjoy God, is to acquiesce or rest in God as the chief good, with complacency and delight. " Return unto thy rest, O my soul."—Ps. cxvi. 7.

Q. 5. How is God enjoyed here?

A. 1. God is enjoyed here, when people do settle themselves upon and cleave to the Lord by faith. " But cleave unto the Lord your God."—Josh. xxiii. 8. 2. When they taste the Lord's goodness, and delight themselves in the gracious presence and sensible manifestations of God's special love unto them. " O taste and see that the Lord is good."—Ps. xxxiv. 8. " Because the love of God is shed abroad in our hearts by the Holy Ghost."—Rom. v. 5.

Q. 6. How will God be enjoyed by his people hereafter?

A. God will be enjoyed hereafter by his people, when they shall be admitted into his glorious presence, have an immediate sight of his face, and full sense of his love in heaven, and there fully and eternally acquiesce and rest in him with perfect and inconceivable delight and joy. " Now we see through a glass darkly, but then face to face."—1 Cor. xiii. 12. " There remaineth therefore a rest to the people of God."—Heb. iv. 9. " In thy presence there is fulness of joy, at thy right hand are pleasures for evermore."—Ps. xvi. 11.

Q. 7. Why is the glorifying of God and the enjoyment of God joined together as one chief end of man?

A. Because God hath inseparably joined them together, so that men cannot truly design and seek the one without the other. They who enjoy God most in his house on earth, do most glorify and enjoy him. " Blessed are they that dwell in thy house; they will be still praising thee." —Ps. lxxxiv. 4. And when God shall be most fully enjoyed by the saints in heaven, he will be most highly glorified. " He shall come to be glorified in his saints."— 2 Thess. i. 10.

Q. 8. Why ought men chiefly to design the glorifying of God in all their actions?

A. 1. Because God hath made them, and made them

for this end, and given them a soul capable of doing it beyond irrational creatures. "Know ye that the Lord he is God; it is he that made us, and not we ourselves."—Ps. c. 3. "The Lord made all things for himself."—Prov. xvi. 4. "Bless the Lord, O my soul; and all that is within me, bless his holy name."—Ps. ciii. 1. 2. Because God doth preserve them, and makes provision for them, that they might glorify him. "O bless our God, O ye people, which holdeth our soul in life."—Ps. lxvi. 8, 9. "O Come, let us worship before the Lord, for we are the people of his pasture, and the sheep of his hand."—Ps. xcv. 6, 7. 3. Because God hath redeemed them, and bought them with the price of his Son's blood, that they may glorify him. "Ye are not your own; for ye are bought with a price: therefore glorify God in your body, and in your spirit, which are God's."—1 Cor. vi. 19, 20. 4. Because he hath given them his Word to direct, his Spirit to assist, and promiseth his kingdom to encourage them to glorify him. "He showeth his word unto Jacob, his statutes and judgments unto Israel. He hath not dealt so with any nation. Praise ye the Lord."—Ps. cxlvii. 19, 20. "Likewise the Spirit helpeth our infirmities."—Rom. viii. 26. "Heirs of the kingdom which he hath promised to them that love him."—James ii. 1.

Q. 9. Why ought men chiefly to desire and seek the enjoyment of God for ever?

A. 1. Because God is the chief good, and in the enjoyment of God doth consist man's chiefest happiness. "There is none good but one, that is God."—Matt. xix. 17. "There be many that say, Who will show us any good? Lord, lift thou up the light of thy countenance upon us. Thou hast put gladness in my heart, more than in the time that their corn and their wine increased."—Ps. iv. 6, 7. 2. Because God is but imperfectly and inconstantly enjoyed here, and men cannot be perfectly happy until they come to the eternal enjoyment of God in heaven. "We know in part; but when that which is perfect is come, then that which is in part shall be done away."—1 Cor. xiii. 9, 10. "Not as though I had already attained, either were already perfect; but I follow after, if that I may apprehend that for which also I am apprehended."—Phil. iii. 12. "In thy presence there is fulness of joy."—Ps. xvi. 11.

II. Ques. *What rule hath God given to direct us how we may glorify and enjoy him?*

*Ans.* The word of God, which is contained in the scriptures of the Old and New Testaments, is the only rule to direct us how we may glorify and enjoy him.

Q. 1. Why is the word contained in the scriptures of the Old and New Testaments, called the word of God?

A. Because it was not from the invention of the men who wrote the Scriptures, but from the immediate inspiration of the Spirit of God, who indited them. "All Scripture is given by inspiration of God."—2 Tim. ii. 16. "Prophecy of Scriptures came not by the will of men; but holy men of God spake as they were moved by the Holy Ghost."—2 Pet. i. 21.

Q. 2. How do you prove the word in the Scriptures to be the word of God?

A. 1. Because of the majesty of the Scriptures. (I.) God is frequently brought in speaking to and by the prophets, and his majesty set forth in such high expressions as are not to be found in any human writings. "Thus saith the high and lofty One who inhabiteth eternity, whose name is Holy, I dwell in the high and holy place."— Isa. lvii. 15. "Who is the blessed and only Potentate, the King of kings, and Lord of lords; who only hath immortality, dwelling in the light which no man can approach unto."—1 Tim. vi. 15, 16. (2.) The style or way of the Scriptures is with such majesty as is not in other writings; duties are therein prescribed, which none but God can require; sins are therein condemned, which none but God can prohibit; threatenings of punishments are therein denounced, which none but God can inflict; promises of rewards are therein made, which none but God can bestow; and all in such a majestic way, as doth evidence God to be the author of this book of the Scriptures.

2. Because of the holiness and purity of the Scriptures.

"Which God hath promised afore by his prophets in the
Holy Scriptures."—Rom. i. 2.  "The words of the Lord
are pure words, as silver tried in a furnace of earth, and
purified seven times."—Ps. xii. 6.  The Scriptures are
holy from the beginning of them unto the end; they do
not savour at all of anything that is earthly and impure;
especially the laws of the word are holy, commanding
everything that is holy, and forbidding everything that is
impure and unholy; whence it is evident that the Scriptures are the word of the holy God, and that the holy
men which wrote them were acted herein by the Holy
Ghost.

3. Because of the consent and harmony of the Scriptures.  In the Scriptures there is consent between the
Old Testament and the New; a consent between the
types and figures under the law, and the things typified
and prefigured under the gospel—between the prophecies
of the Scriptures, and the fulfilling of those prophecies.
There is in the Scriptures a harmony or agreement of
precepts, and a harmony or agreement of histories, and a
harmony or agreement of design.  Wherefore, since the
Scriptures were written by so many several men, in so
many several ages, and different places, and yet agreeing
so well in their writings, that no irreconcilable difference
is to be found in them, it is evident that they were all
acted by the same Spirit of God; and therefore, that the
Scriptures are the word of God.

4. Because of the high mysteries which are revealed in
the Scriptures.  We read, in the Scriptures, of the
trinity of persons in the Godhead, the incarnation of the
Son of God, the mystical union of Christ and his members.
These, and such like mysteries, were beyond the reach of
the most wise and learned men to invent, much more beyond the reach of unlearned fishermen, by whom they
were revealed; whence it is evident that they spake not
their own words, but what they were taught by the immediate inspiration of the Spirit.

5. Because of the antiquity of the Scriptures.  They
were written, in part, before any other writings of men,
and they contain a history of the most ancient things,

namely, the creation of the old world, the flood, and the like. Such ancient things are there revealed as none but God knew; and therefore God must needs be the author of them.

6. Because of the power and efficacy of the Scriptures. (1.) The Scriptures are powerful to convince, and awaken, and wound the conscience. " The Word of God is quick and powerful, sharper than a two-edged sword."—Heb. iv 12. (2.) The Scriptures are powerful to convert and change the heart. " The law of the Lord is perfect, converting the soul."—Ps. xix. 7. (3.) They are powerful to quicken men out of spiritual death and deadness. " Hear, and your souls shall live."—Isa. lv. 3. " Thy Word hath quickened me."—Ps. cxix. 50. (4.) They are powerful to rejoice and comfort under the deepest distresses. " The statutes of the Lord are right, rejoicing the heart."—Ps. xix. 8. The Scriptures opened and applied are made effectual to produce such powerful effects as do exceed the power of nature, and can be effected only by the power of God; which showeth that God only is the author of the Scriptures, which he would not so far own and honour if they were not his own.

7. Because of the design and contrivement of the Scriptures. (1.) The design of the Scriptures is to give God all the glory; the design is not to exalt any, but to debase and empty all men, and exalt God's name and grace in the world. (2.) The marvellous contrivement of wisdom, in finding out a way for man's recovery and salvation by Jesus Christ, when fallen by sin into such a state of misery, which no mortal brain could have invented; this doth show, not only that this contrivance was from the infinitely wise God, but also that the Scriptures, which have revealed this, are his book.

8. Because the Scriptures were confirmed by miracles. We read of many miracles in the Scriptures, especially those which were wrought by Jesus Christ and his disciples, to confirm their doctrine, that it was from God; such as curing some who were born blind, raising the dead, calming the sea with a word, and many more. Now, these and the like miracles were from the immediate hand

of God; and the relation we have faithfully handed down unto us, as appeareth by the writings still amongst us, of several holy men upon them and concerning them, as also by the several copies of them (which could not be forged, and not be found out) agreeing in the same relation. And as surely as God did effect those miracles, so surely is God the author of the Scriptures, which are confirmed by them.

9. Because the Scriptures were confirmed by the blood of martyrs. There were many thousand Christians in the primitive time, who sealed and gave testimony to the truth of the Scriptures with the loss of their lives. The great faith of the primitive Christians in the truth of the Scriptures, who might easily have found out the deceit, had there been any deceit imposed upon men in them; and the great patience and constancy which they showed in their sufferings, as an evidence of their faith, are a weighty argument, in conjunction with others, to prove the divine authority of the Scriptures.

10. Because of the testimony of the Spirit of God in, and with, and by the Scriptures, upon the hearts of believers. " Ye have an unction from the holy One, and ye know all things;" because " the same anointing teacheth you of all things, and is true, and is no lie."—1 John ii. 20, 27. Without this testimony, and teaching of the Spirit, all other arguments will be ineffectual to persuade unto a saving faith.

Q. 3. Why was the word of God put into scriptures, or writings?

A. 1. That the history and doctrine of the word might be the better conveyed down to posterity; for if the word revealed to holy men so many ages since, had been intrusted only unto the memories of men, by tradition to hand it down from one generation to another (supposing the persons with whom the word was intrusted were faithful), yet the memories of men being weak and unfaithful, many truths, in all likelihood, would have been lost by this time; therefore there was not a more sure way of making known the grace of God unto future ages, than by committing the word of God to writing. " This

second epistle I write unto you in way of remembrance."
—2 Pet. iii. 1. 2. That the gospel made known in the
word, might the better be propagated in several nations.
Reports of others would not so easily have been believed,
as the writings of the prophets and apostles themselves,
unto whom the word was revealed. 3. That there might
be in the Church a standing rule of faith and life, according to which all doctrines might be examined, and all
actions might be ordered; and, by consequence, that corrupt principles and corrupt practices might be prevented,
which the minds and hearts of men are prone unto, and
would have the more seeming pretence for, were there
not express Scripture against both. "To the law and to
the testimony; if they speak not according to this word,
it is because there is no light in them."—Isa. viii. 20.

Q. 4. Which are the scriptures of the Old Testament,
and which are the scriptures of the New Testament?

A. The scriptures of the Old Testament are the scrip-
tures in the former part of the Bible, beginning at
Genesis, and ending with Malachi; the scriptures of the
New Testament are the scriptures in the latter part of
the Bible, beginning at Matthew, and ending with the
Revelation.

Q. 5. Why are the scriptures in the former part of
the Bible called the scriptures of the Old Testament?

A. Because the testament or covenant of grace which
God made with man, is therein revealed in the old dispensation of it; in which Christ, the Testator of the testament, and Mediator of the covenant, is set forth by
types and figures; and many burdensome services and
carnal ordinances of the ceremonial law were required.

Q. 6. Why are the scriptures in the latter part of the
Bible called the scriptures of the New Testament?

A. Because the testament of God or covenant of grace
is therein revealed, in the new dispensation of it, without
types and figures, Christ himself being revealed as come
in the flesh, who before was shadowed under them; who,
having fulfilled the ceremonial law, hath abolished it, and
freed his people from the yoke of bondage, requiring now
more spiritual worship in its room.

Q. 7. Are not the scriptures in the Apocryphal books the word of God?

A. Though there be many true and good things in these books, which may be read profitably, as in other authors, yet they are not to be esteemed as canonical scripture, and part of the Word of God. 1. Because they were not written in the Hebrew tongue, nor acknowledged as canonical by the Jews of old, unto whom the keeping of the oracles of God was then committed. 2. Because in these books there are some things false and disagreeable to the Word of God. 3. Because there is not that power and majesty in those books as in canonical scripture. 4. Because the author of Ecclesiasticus (the choicest of all the Apocryphal books) doth crave pardon, if anything be amiss in that book; which he would not have done had he been guided by the infallible Spirit of God therein.

Q. 8. Have not the Scriptures their authority from the Church, as the Papists affirm?

A. No. 1. Because the Church on whose testimony they say the Scriptures do depend, is an apostate and corrupt Church, and the seat of Antichrist. 2. Because the true Church of Christ doth depend in its being on the Scriptures; and therefore the Scriptures cannot depend upon the Church for their authority. " Ye are fellow-citizens of the saints, and of the household of God, being built upon the foundation of the apostles and prophets, Jesus Christ himself being the chief corner-stone."—Eph. ii. 19, 20. 3. Because if the authority of the Scriptures did depend upon the Church, then the Church in itself, without the Scriptures, must be infallible; otherwise our faith in the Scriptures, from their witness, could not be certain; but the Church in itself, without the Scriptures, is not infallible.

Q. 9. Why are the Scriptures called the rule to direct us how we may glorify and enjoy God?

A. Because all doctrines which we are bound to believe must be measured or judged of; all duties which we are bound to practise as means in order to the attainment of this chief end of man, must be squared or conformed unto this rule. "As many as walk according to this rule, peace be on them."—Gal. vi. 16.

Q. 10. Why are the Scriptures called the only rule?

A. Because the Scriptures, and nothing else, are sufficient to direct us how we may glorify and enjoy God.

Q. 11. Is not natural reason, without the light of the Scriptures, sufficient to direct us?

A. 1. Indeed natural reason may, from the natural impressions of a Deity upon the mind, and the evidences of a Deity in the works of creation and providence, show that there is a God, and that this God is infinite in his being, and power, and wisdom, and goodness: and that he is to be glorified and worshipped by his creatures.

2. But natural reason cannot fully and savingly show what God is. (1.) It cannot reveal his love and mercy to sinners in his Son. (2.) It cannot reveal how he should be glorified and worshipped. (3.) It cannot direct us how we should enjoy him either here or hereafter.

Q. 12. Are not the unwritten traditions of the Church of Rome to be made use of as a rule for our direction, especially since the apostle exhorteth the Thessalonians (2 Thess. ii. 15) to hold fast the traditions which they had been taught, not only by writing, but also by word of mouth; and many of the traditions of the Church of Rome are pretended to be apostolical?

A. The unwritten traditions of the Church of Rome are not to be made use of as a rule for our direction:—
1. Because no unwritten traditions could be conveyed down from the apostles' times unto ours by word of mouth, without danger of mistake and corruption; and therefore we cannot be certain that their traditions, which they call apostolical, are not corrupted, as we must be, if we use them as our rule. 2. Because we have reason to think, the Church of Rome being so much corrupted, that their traditions are corrupted too; especially when historians tell us of the general corruption, ignorance, and viciousness of some generations in their Church, namely, in the ninth and tenth centuries and afterwards; through which sink of times we cannot rationally expect to receive pure traditions. 3. Because several of their traditions are contrary to the express Word of God, like those of the elders amongst the Pharisees, which our Saviour doth condemn,

together with all human impositions. "Ye have made the commandments of God of none effect by your tradition. But in vain do they worship me, teaching for doctrines the commandments of men."—Mat. xv. 6, 9.    4. Because, however the Thessalonians were bound to hold fast some unwritten traditions for a while, because the history of Christ, and much of the gospel, they had for the present only from the mouths and testimony of the apostles; yet afterwards the whole history of Christ, and whatever was necessary to be known, and believed, and practised, in order to salvation, were committed to writing in the books of the New Testament, both for the sake of the present and future generations of the Church, that so the gospel might not be corrupted by unwritten traditions: therefore, all unwritten traditions are to be rejected.

Q. 13. Is not the light within men, and the Spirit of God without the Scriptures (which Quakers and enthusiasts pretend unto), to be made use of as a rule for our direction?

A. The light which is in men, without the Scripture, is not to be used for our rule. 1. Because whatever light any pretend unto without the Word, is but darkness, in which whosoever walketh, he must needs stumble and fall into the ditch. "To the law and to the testimony; if they speak not according to this word, it is because there is no light in them."—Isa. viii. 20.

2. Whatever spirit any have which leadeth them against, or besides the rule of the Scriptures, it is not the Spirit of God and of truth, but a spirit of error and delusion. The Scripture telleth us plainly, that such as hear not the apostles speaking in the Word, are actuated by an erroneous spirit. "Beloved, believe not every spirit, but try the spirits whether they are of God; because many false prophets are gone out into the world. We are of God: he that knoweth God heareth us; he that is not of God heareth us not. Hereby know we the Spirit of truth, and the spirit of error."—1 John iv. 1, 6.

III. Ques. *What do the Scriptures principally teach?*

*Ans.* The Scriptures principally teach what man is to believe concerning God, and what duty God requires of man.

Q. 1. What is it to believe?

A. To believe, is to assent or give credit to truths, because of the authority of another.

Q. 2. What is it to believe what the Scriptures teach?

A. To believe that which the Scriptures teach, is to assent or give credit to the truth thereof, because of the authority of God, whose word the Scriptures are—this is divine faith.

Q. 3. What are implied in the things concerning God which the Scriptures teach?

A. In the things concerning God which the Scriptures teach, are implied all points of faith, as it is divine.

Q. 4. Are Christians to believe nothing as a point of faith, but what the Scriptures teach?

A. No; because no other book in the world is of divine authority but the Scriptures, and therefore not absolutely infallible? 2 Tim 3:16

Q. 5. What is meant by the duty which God requireth of man?

A. By the duty which God requireth of man, we are to understand that which is God's due, or that which we owe to God, and are bound to do, as we are creatures, and subjects, and children.

Q. 6. Are we bound to nothing in point of practice, but what is required in the Scriptures?

A. No; because the laws and commandments of God in the Scriptures are so exceeding large and extensive, that they reach both the inward and outward man, and whole conversation, so that nothing is lawful for us to do, except it be directly or consequentially prescribed in the Word.

Q. 7. How do the Scriptures teach matters of faith and practice?

A. The Scriptures teach the matters of faith and practice, by revealing these things externally; but it is the Spirit of God only, in the Scriptures, which can teach them internally and effectually unto salvation.

Q. 8. Why are the Scriptures said principally to teach what man is to believe concerning God, and what duty God requires of man?

A. Because though all things taught in the Scriptures are alike true, having the stamp of divine authority upon them, yet all things in the Scriptures are not alike necessary and useful. Those things which man is bound to believe and do, as necessary to salvation, are the things which the Scriptures do principally teach.

## IV. Ques. *What is God?*

*Ans.* God is a spirit, infinite, eternal, and unchangeable, in his being, wisdom, power, holiness, justice, goodness, and truth.

Q. 1. What kind of substance is God?

A. God is a spirit. "God is a spirit; and they that worship him, must worship him in spirit and in truth."—John iv. 24.

Q. 2. What is a spirit?

A. A spirit is an immaterial substance, without flesh or bones, or bodily parts. "Behold my hands and my feet, that it is I myself; handle me and see, for a spirit hath not flesh and bones, as ye see me have."—Luke xxiv. 39.

Q. 3 How is God said, then, in Scripture to have eyes, and ears, and mouth, and hands, and other parts? "The eyes of the Lord are upon the righteous, and his ears are open unto their cry."—Ps. xxxiv. 15. "The mouth of the Lord hath spoken it."—Isa. i. 20. "It is a fearful thing to fall into the hands of the living God."—Heb. x. 31.

A. These and the like bodily parts are not in God properly, as they be in men, but figuratively; and after the manner of men, he is pleased to condescend (in expressing himself hereby) to our weak capacities, that we might the more easily conceive of him by such resemblances.

Q. 4. How doth God differ from angels and the souls of men, who also are spiritual and immaterial substances?

A. 1. Angels and the souls of men are created spirits, and depend in their being upon God; but God is an uncreated spirit, and dependeth in his being upon none. 2.

Angels and the souls of men are finite spirits; but God is an infinite spirit.

Q. 5. What is it to be infinite?

A. To be infinite, is to be without measure, bounds, or limits.

Q. 6. In what regard is God infinite?

A. 1. God is infinite, or without bounds, in regard of his being or perfection; and therefore is incomprehensible. "Canst thou by searching find out God? canst thou find out the Almighty unto perfection?"—Job xi. 7. 2. God is infinite, and without measure and bounds, in regard of place; and therefore he is everywhere present. "Can any hide himself in secret places, that I shall not see him? saith the Lord, Do not I fill heaven and earth?"—Jer. xxiii. 24. "And yet neither the earth, nor the heavens, nor the heaven of heavens, is able to contain him."—1 Kings viii. 26. 3. God is infinite, or without measure and bounds, in regard of time; and therefore he is eternal. "Now unto the King eternal, immortal, invisible, the only wise God, be honour and glory, for ever and ever. Amen."—1 Tim. i. 17. 4. God is infinite, or without measure and bounds, in regard of all his communicable attributes.

Q. 7. What is it to be eternal?

A. To be eternal, is to have neither beginning nor ending.

Q. 8. How doth it appear that God is eternal?

A. 1. From Scripture. "Before the mountains were brought forth, or ever thou hadst formed the earth or the world, even from everlasting to everlasting thou art God."—Psal. xc. 2.

2. From reason. (1.) God gave a being to the world, and all things therein, at the beginning of time; therefore he must needs be before the world, and before time, and therefore *from everlasting*. (2.) God is an absolutely necessary Being, because the first Being, because altogether independent, and beyond the reach of any power to put an end to him; therefore he is unchangeable—therefore *to everlasting* he is God.

Q. 9. How doth God differ from his creatures, in regard of his eternity?

A. 1. Some creatures have their beginning with time, and their ending with time, as the heavens and the foundations of the earth. 2. some creatures have their beginning in time, and their ending also in time; as those creatures upon the earth, which are generated and corrupted, which are born, and live for a while, and then die. 3. Some creatures have their beginning in time, yet do not end with or in time, but endure for ever; as angels and the souls of men. 4. But God differeth from all, in that he was from everlasting, before time, and will remain unto everlasting, when time shall be no more.

Q. 10. What is it to be unchangeable?

A. To be unchangeable, is to be always the same, without any alteration.

Q. 11. In what regard is God unchangeable?

A. 1. God is unchangeable in regard of his nature and essence. "Of old thou hast laid the foundation of the earth; and the heavens are the work of thine hands. They shall perish, but thou shalt endure; they shall be changed, but thou art the same."—Ps. cii. 25–27. 2. God is unchangeable in regard of his counsel and purpose. "My counsel shall stand, and I will do all my pleasure."—Isa. xlvi. 10. "Wherein God, willing to show the immutability of his counsel."—Heb. vi. 17. 3. God is unchangeable in regard of his love and special favours. "The gifts and calling of God are without repentance."—Rom. xi. 29. "Every good gift and every perfect gift is from above, and cometh down from the Father of lights, with whom is no variableness, neither shadow of turning."—James i. 17.

Q. 12. How is God said to be infinite, eternal, and unchangeable, in his being, wisdom, power, holiness, justice, goodness, and truth?

A. In that being, wisdom, power, holiness, justice, goodness, and truth, which are communicable unto, and may be in some degree and measure found in the creatures, they are in God infinitely, eternally, unchangeably, and so altogether in an incommunicable manner. (1.) Creatures have a being, but it is a finite being—a being in time, a changeable being; God's being is infinite, eternal, and unchangeable. (2.) Creatures may have wisdom, but it is finite and imperfect wisdom; God's wisdom is infinite and absolutely perfect. (3.) Creatures may have some power, but it is finite and limited power, such as may be taken away—they may have power to do something dependingly upon God; but God is infinite in power—he is omnipotent, and can do all things independently, without the help of any. (4.) Creatures may have some holiness, and justice, and goodness, and truth; but these are qualities in them—they are finite, and in an inferior degree, and they are subject to change; but these things are essence in God—they are infinite and perfect in him; his holiness is infinite, his justice is infinite, his goodness is infinite, his truth is infinite; and all these are eternally in him, without any variableness or possibility of change.

Q. 13. What is the wisdom of God?

A. The wisdom of God is his essential property, whereby, by one simple and eternal act, he knoweth both himself and all possible things perfectly, and according to which he maketh, directeth, and ordereth all future things for his own glory.

Q. 14. Wherein doth the wisdom of God appear?

A. 1. God's wisdom doth appear in his perfect knowledge of all possible things, all past things, all present things, all future things, in their natures, causes, virtues, and operations; and that not by relation, observation, or induction of reason, as men know some things, but by one simple and eternal act of his understanding. " His understanding is infinite."—Ps. clxvii. 5. " O Lord, thou hast searched me, and known me; such knowledge is too wonderful for me; it is high, I cannot attain unto it."—Ps. cxxxix. 1, 6. " Neither is there any creature that is not manifest in his sight, but all things are naked and open unto the eyes of him with whom we have to do."—Heb. iv. 13.

2. God's wisdom doth appear in the beautiful variety of creatures which he hath made, above and below. "O Lord, how manifold are thy works! in wisdom hast thou made them all."—Ps. civ. 24.

3. God's wisdom doth appear in his admirable contrivance of our redemption through his Son, whereby his justice is fully satisfied, and his people are graciously saved.

"Howbeit we speak wisdom among them that are perfect: the wisdom of God in a mystery," &c.—1 Cor. ii. 6, 7. This is that wisdom which was made known by the Church unto the angels. "To the intent that unto the principalities might be known by the Church the manifold wisdom of God."—Eph. iii. 10.

4. God's wisdom doth appear in his excellent government of all his creatures. (1.) In his government of unreasonable creatures—directing them unto their ends, though they have no reason to guide them. (2.) In his government of reasonable creatures that are wicked—overruling all their actions for his own glory, though they be intended by them for his dishonour. "Surely the wrath of man shall praise thee."—Ps. lxxvi. 10. (3.) In his government of his Church and people. The disposal of his special favours to the most unworthy, that he might reap all the glory—his qualifying and making use of instruments in great works beyond their own thoughts and designs—his seasonable provisions for his people—his strange preservation of them from the malice of subtle and powerful enemies—his promoting his own interest in the world, by the means which men use to subvert it, and the like, do evidently declare the infinite wisdom of God.

Q. 15. What is the power of God?

A. The power of God is his essential property, whereby he can do all things. "I am the almighty God."—Gen. xvii. 1.

Q. 16. Wherein doth the power of God show itself?

A. 1. The power of God doth show itself in what he hath done. He hath created all things. "The invisible things of him from the creation of the world are clearly seen, being understood by the things that are made, even his eternal power and Godhead."—Rom. i. 20. He hath effected many miracles, which we read of both in the Old and New Testaments, which exceeded the power of natural causes. He hath raised up to himself, and preserved his Church in all ages, notwithstanding the rage and malice of all the powers of earth and hell, who have endeavoured to extirpate it. "Upon this rock I will build my Church, and the gates of hell shall not prevail against in."—Matt. xvi. 18.

2. The power of God doth show itself in what he doeth. He upholdeth all his creatures in their being and operations. " Upholding all things by the word of his power." —Heb. i. 3. He plucks his chosen people out of the snare of the devil, and powerfully draws them, and joins them by faith unto Jesus Christ. " And what is the exceeding greatness of his power to usward who believe."—Eph. i. 19. He works grace in his people, and maintaineth his work, and enableth them to persevere. " Who are kept by the power of God through faith unto salvation."—1 Pet. i. 5. He restraineth the wicked, and bringeth Satan under the feet of his people. He worketh continually, easily, irresistibly, and indefatigably; all which show his power.

3. The power of God doth show itself in what he *will do*. He will make the kingdoms of the earth to stoop to his Son, and that both of Jew and Gentile. He will ruin Antichrist, though ever so potent at the present. He will raise up the dead out of their graves, and destroy the visible world at the last day. And he will show the power of his anger, in the everlasting punishment of the wicked in hell.

4. The power of God doth show itself in what he *can do*. He can do whatever he pleaseth; he can do whatever is possible to infinite power, whatever doth not imply a contradiction, or argue imperfection.

Q. 17. What is the holiness of God?

A. The holiness of God is his essential property, whereby he is infinitely pure; loveth and delighteth in his own purity, and in all the resemblances of it which any of his creatures have; and is perfectly free from all impurity, and hateth it wherever he seeth it.

Q. 18. How may God be said to be holy?

A. 1. The name of God is holy. " Holy and reverend is his name."—Ps. cxi. 9. 2. The nature of God is holy. "Holy, holy, holy, Lord God almighty."—Rev. iv. 8. 3. The persons of the Godhead are holy. The Father is holy. "Holy Father, keep through thine own name those which thou hast given me."—John xvii. 11. The Son is holy. " Against thy holy child Jesus were they gathered."— Acts iv. 27. The Spirit is holy. " Joy in the Holy Ghost."

—Rom. xiv. 17. 4. The works of God are holy. " The Lord is righteous in all his ways, and holy in all his works." —Ps. cxlv. 17. 5. The word of God is holy. " Which he hath promised afore by his prophets in the Holy Scriptures." —Rom. i. 2. His law is holy. " The law is holy, and the commandment holy, and just, and good."—Rom. vii. 12. And his gospel is holy. " To remember his holy covenant."—Luke i. 72. 6. The worship of God is holy. The matter of it holy. " In every place incense shall be offered unto my name, and a pure offering of righteousness."—Mal. i. 11. The manner of it holy. " God will be worshipped in spirit and in truth."—John iv. 24. The time of it holy. " Remember the Sabbath-day to keep it holy."—Exod. xx. 8. 7. The dwelling-place of God is holy. " Thus saith the high and lofty One, I dwell in the high and holy place."—Isa. lvii. 15. 8. The angels which attend upon God in heaven are holy. " All the holy angels with him."—Matt. xxv. 31. 9. The people of God upon earth are holy. " Thou art a holy people unto the Lord."—Deut. vii. 6. 10. God requireth, worketh, loveth, and delighteth in holiness. " Be ye holy."—1 Pet. i. 15. " This is the will of God, even your sanctification."—1 Thess. iv. 3. 11. God hateth sin and sinners infinitely, and without holiness will not admit any into his kingdom. " Thou hatest all workers of iniquity."—Ps. v. 5. " Follow peace with all men, and holiness, without which no man shall see the Lord."—Heb. xii. 14.

Q. 19. What is the justice of God?

A. The justice of God is his essential property, whereby he is infinitely righteous and equal, both in himself and in all his dealings with his creatures.

Q. 20. Wherein doth the justice of God show itself?

A. 1. In the punishment which he inflicted upon Christ, our Surety, for our sins. " He was wounded for our transgressions, he was bruised for our iniquities."—Isa. liii. 5. 2. In the vengeance he will execute upon unbelievers for their own sins on the day of wrath. " The Lord will be revealed in flaming fire, taking vengeance on them that obey not the gospel, who shall be punished with everlasting destruction."—2 Thess. i. 7–9. 3. In the reward he will give to his people, through the merits of Christ. " Great is your reward in heaven."—Matt. v. 12. " Henceforth there is laid up for me a crown of righteousness."—2 Tim. iv. 8. 4. In those temporal judgments he bringeth upon a people or person for their sins in this world. " O Lord, righteousness belongeth unto thee, but unto us confusion of faces, as at this day."—Dan ix. 7. " Wherefore doth a living man complain, a man for the punishment of his sins?"—Lam. iii. 39.

Q. 21. What is the goodness of God?

A. The goodness of God is his essential property, whereby he is altogether good in himself, and the author of all good. " Thou art good, and doest good."—Ps. cxix. 68.

Q. 22. Wherein doth the goodness of God appear?

A. God's goodness doth appear—1. In the works which he hath made. " And God saw every thing that he had made, and, and, behold, it was very good."—Gen. i. 31. 2. In his bounty and provisions for all his creatures. " The Lord is good to all."—Ps. cxlv. 9. " The eyes of all wait upon thee."—Ver. 15. 3. In his patience and forbearance toward the wicked, and his enemies. " Or despisest thou the riches of his goodness, and forbearance, and long-suffering?"—Rom. ii. 4. 4. And chiefly, God's goodness doth appear in his special love and mercy towards his own people; in choosing them, in redeeming them, in calling them, in pardoning them, in adopting them, in sanctifying them, in all the privileges he bestoweth upon them, and manifestations of his love unto them here, and in his taking them unto, and giving them possession of, his kingdom hereafter. " The Lord God, merciful and gracious, abundant in goodness, keeping mercy for thousands, forgiving iniquity, transgression, and sin," &c.—Exod. xxiv. 6, 7.

Q. 23. What is the truth of God?

A. The truth of God is his essential property, whereby he is sincere and faithful, free from all falsehood and simulation. " In hope of eternal life, which God, who cannot lie, promised before the world began."—Tit. i. 2. " By two immutable things, in which it is impossible for God to lie."—Heb. vi. 18.

Q. 24. Wherein doth the truth of God appear?

A. God's truth doth appear—1. In the soundness of the doctrine which he hath revealed, wherein there is no flaw or corruption. " Hold fast the form of sound words, which thou hast heard of me."—2 Tim. i. 13. 2. In the certainty of the history which he hath recorded, wherein there is no lie or mistake. " It seemed good to me to write to thee, that thou mightest know the certainty of those things wherein thou hast been instructed."—Luke i. 3, 4. 3. In the accomplishment of the prophecies which he hath foretold, wherein there is no failing or falling short. " We have found him of whom Moses and the prophets did write."—John i. 45. " Heaven and earth shall pass away, but my words shall not pass away."—Matt. xxiv. 35. 4. In the fulfilling of the promises which he hath made to his people. " He is faithful that hath promised."—Heb. x. 23. 5. In executing the judgments which he hath threatened against the wicked. " But my words, did they not take hold on your fathers?"—Zech. i. 6. 6. But the great appearance of God's truth will be at the day of Christ's appearance to judgment, when rewards and punishments shall be dispensed according to what he hath foretold us in the book of the Holy Scriptures.

V. Ques. *Are there more Gods than one?*

*Ans.* There is but one only, the living and true God.

Q. 1. Why is God said to be one only?

A. In opposition to many gods. " Hear, O Israel, the Lord our God is one Lord."—Deut. iv. 4. " We know that there is none other God but one. For though there be that are called gods, whether in heaven or in earth (as there be gods many, and lords many), but to us there is but one God."—1 Cor. viii. 4–6.

Q. 2. Why is God said to be the living God?

A. In opposition to dead idols. "Their idols are silver and gold, the work of men's hands. They have mouths, but they speak not; eyes have they, but they see not; they have ears, but they hear not," &c.—Ps. cxv. 4–6. "Ye turned from idols, to serve the living God."—1 Thess. i. 9.

Q. 3. Why is God said to be the true God?

A. In opposition to all false gods. "The Lord is the true God. The gods that have not made the heavens and the earth, shall perish from the earth, and from under these heavens. They are vanity, and the work of errors." —Jer. x. 11, 15.

Q. 4. How doth it appear that God is one only?

A. Because God is infinite, and there cannot be more than one infinite Being, forasmuch as one infinite Being doth set bounds and limits unto all other beings, and nothing that is bounded and limited can be infinite.

Q. 5. How doth it appear that God is living?

A. 1. Because God giveth to and preserveth life in all his creatures. "I give thee charge in the sight of God, who quickeneth all things."—1 Tim. vi. 13. "In him we live, and move, and have our being."—Acts xvii. 28. 2. Because God reigneth for ever. "The Lord is a living God, and an everlasting King."—Jer. x. 10.

Q. 6. How doth it appear that God is true, that he hath a true being, or that there is a God indeed?

A. By several arguments, sufficient to convince all the Atheists in the world, if they would hearken to their own reason.

Q. 7. What is the first argument to prove that there is a God?

A. The first argument to prove that there is a God may be drawn from the being of all things. 1. The being of the heavens, the highest storeys which are there erected, the glorious lights which are there placed, the glittering stars which there move. 2. The being of the earth, whose foundations are sure, and unmoved by storms and tempests, though it hang like a ball in the midst of the air. 3. The being of the vast sea, where there is such abundance of waters, as some think, higher than the earth, which are yet bounded and restrained from overflowing and drowning the land and its inhabitants, as once they did, when their limits were for a while removed. 4. The being of such various creatures above and below, especially of those which have motion and life in themselves. 5. And chiefly, the being of man, the curious workmanship of his body in the womb, especially the being of man's soul, which is immaterial, invisible, rational, immortal, and which cannot arise from the power of the matter (as the sensitive soul of brutes), neither doth depend on the body in some of its operations. These, and all the works which our eye doth see, or mind doth apprehend, do prove that there is a God, who hath given a being to them, and continueth them therein.

Q. 8. Wherein lieth the force of this argument, to prove, from the being of all things, that there is a God?

A. All things that have a being must either—1. Have their being from eternity; or, 2. Must give a being to themselves; or, 3. They must have their being from God. But, (1.) They could not have their being from eternity, for then they would be infinite in duration, and so capable of no measure by time; they would be necessary, and so capable of no alteration or destruction; but both reason and experience do evidence the contrary: therefore they are not eternal. (2.) Things cannot give a being to themselves, for that which giveth a being to a thing must be before it; and hence it would follow that things should be and not be at the same time, which is a contradiction, and absurd. Therefore, (3.) It must necessarily follow that there is a God, who is a necessary, infinite, and eternal being, who is omnipotent, and hath given a being to all creatures.

Q. 9. What is the second argument to prove that there is a God?

A. The second argument to prove that there is a God may be drawn from the government of all things. 1. The beautiful order and constant motion of the heavenly bodies, shedding down light and heat and sweet influence upon the earth; without which all living creatures below would quickly languish and die. 2. The bottling up of waters in the clouds, and sprinkling of rain from thence upon the dry and parched ground; without which it would yield no fruit. 3. The cleansing of the air, and fanning of the earth with the wings of the wind; without which, in some hotter climates, the inhabitants could not live. 4. The subjection of many strong and fierce creatures unto weak and timorous man. 5. The subserviency of irrational and inanimate creatures one to another, and the guiding them, without their own designment, unto their ends. 6. Notwithstanding the various, innumerable, and seeming contrary particular ends which the many creatures in the world have, the directing them, without confusion, unto one common end, in which they do all agree; this doth undeniably prove that there is an infinitely powerful and wise God, who is the supreme Lord and Governor of the world.

Q. 10. What is the third argument to prove that there is a God?

A. The third argument to prove that there is a God, may be drawn from the impressions of a Deity upon the consciences of all men, in all ages and nations; which could not be so deep and universal, were it a fancy only, and groundless conceit. 1. The hellish gripes and lashes, the horrible dreads and tremblings, of guilty consciences upon the commission of some more notorious crimes, which they do not fear punishment for from men, is a witness of a Deity to them, whose future vengeance they are afraid of. 2. The worship which heathens generally give unto false gods, is an evidence that there is a true God, though they be ignorant of him.

Q. 11. What is the fourth argument to prove that there is a God?

A. The fourth argument to prove that there is a God, may be drawn from the revelation of the Scriptures. The majesty, high mysteries, efficiency, and like arguments, which prove that the Scriptures could have no other author but God alone, do more abundantly prove that there is a God, who hath more clearly revealed himself and his will in that book than in the book of his creatures.

Q. 12. What is the fifth argument to prove that there is a God?

A. The fifth argument to prove that there is a God, may be drawn from the image of God on his people—the stamp of holiness upon God's people, which maketh them to differ from all others, and from what themselves were before conversion, doth show (as a picture the man) that there is a God, whose image they bear, and who, by the almighty power of his Spirit, hath thus formed them after his own likeness.

Q. 13. If it be so certain that there is a God, whence is it that there be so many Atheists, who believe there is no God?

A. 1. There are many that live as if there were no God, and wish there were no God, who yet secretly believe that there is a God, and carry a dread of him in their consciences. 2. I hardly think that any who have most of all blotted out the impressions of God, and do endeavour to persuade themselves and others that there is no God, are constantly of that mind, but sometimes, in great dangers, they are under convictions of a Deity. 3. There are none that have wrought up themselves to any measure of persuasion that there is no God, but such whose interest doth sway them, and blind them therein; because, they being so vicious, they know, if there be a God, he will surely take vengeance upon them. 4. The thing is certain that there is a God, whether some believe it or no; as the sun doth shine, though some men be blind, and do not discern its light.

## VI. Ques. *How many persons are there in the Godhead?*

*Ans.* There are three persons in the Godhead, the Father, the Son, and the Holy Ghost; and these three are one God, the same in substance, equal in power and glory.

Q. 1. What is meant by the Godhead?
A. By the Godhead is meant the divine nature or essence.

Q. 2. Are there three divine natures or essences, or are there three Gods?
A. No; for though the three persons be God, the Father God, the Son God, and the Holy Ghost God, yet they are not three Gods, but one God. The essence of God is the same in all the three persons. " There are three that bear record in heaven, the Father, the Word [that is, the

Son], and the Holy Ghost; and these three are one."—1 John v. 7.

Q. 3 What is meant by the three persons in the Godhead?

A. By the three persons in the Godhead, we are to·understand the same nature of God with three ways of subsisting, each person having its distinct personal properties.

Q. 4. What is the personal property of the Father?

A. The personal property of the Father is to beget the Son, and that from all eternity. "Unto which of the angels said he at any time, Thou art my Son, this day have I begotten thee? Unto the Son he saith, Thy throne, O God, is for ever."—Heb. i. 5, 8.

Q. 5. What is the personal property of the Son?

A. The personal property of the Son is to be begotten of the Father. "We beheld his glory, the glory as of the only·begotten of the Father."—John i. 14.

Q. 6. What is the personal property of the Holy Ghost?

A. The personal property of the Holy Ghost is to proceed from the Father and the Son. "But when the Comforter is come, whom I will send unto you from the Father, even the Spirit of truth, which proceedeth from the Father, he shall testify of me."—John xv. 26.

Q. 7. How doth it appear that the Father is God?

A. Because the Father is the original of the other persons, and of every thing else, and because divine attributes and worship are ascribed to him.

Q. 8. How doth it appear that the Son is God?

A. 1. Because he is called God in the Scriptures. "And the Word was God."—John i. 1. "Of whom, as concerning the flesh, Christ came, who is over all, God blessed for ever."—Rom. ix. 5. 2. Because the attributes of God are ascribed unto him. Eternity. "Before Abraham was, I am."—John viii. 58. Omniscience. "Lord, thou knowest all things, thou knowest that I love thee."—John xxi. 17. Omnipresence. "Where two or three are gathered together in my name, there am I in the midst of them."—Matt. xviii. 20. Divine power. "He upholdeth all things by the word of his power."—Heb. i. 3. 3. Because the honour and worship which is due only to God, do belong to him. In him we must believe. "Believe also in me."—John xiv. 1. In his name we must be baptized. "Baptizing them in the name of the Father, and of the Son, and of the Holy Ghost."—Matt. xxviii. 19. Upon his name we must call. "With all that call upon the name of the Lord Jesus Christ."—1 Cor. i. 2. Because if the Son were not God, he could not have been a fit Mediator.

Q. 9. How doth it appear that the Holy Ghost is God?

A. 1. Because the Holy Ghost is called God. "Why hath Satan filled thine heart to lie to the Holy Ghost? Thou hast not lied unto men, but unto God."—Acts v. 3, 4. 2. Because the attributes of God are ascribed unto him. Omnipresence. "Whither shall I go from thy Spirit?"— Ps. cxxxix. 7. Especially, he is present in the hearts of all believers. "He dwelleth in you, and shall be in you." —John xiv. 17. Omniscience. "The Spirit searcheth all things."—1 Cor. ii. 10. 3. Because of the powerful works of the Spirit, which none but God can effect: such as— Regeneration. "Except a man be born of the Spirit, he cannot enter into the kingdom of God."—John iii. 5. Guiding believers into all truth. "Howbeit, when the Spirit of truth is come, he will guide you into all truth."— John xvi. 13. Sanctification. "That the offering up of the Gentiles might be acceptable, being sanctified by the Holy Ghost."—Rom. xv. 16. Comfort, called therefore the Comforter. "But when the Comforter is come, whom I will send unto you from the Father, even the Spirit of truth, which proceedeth from the Father, he shall testify of me."—John xv. 26. Communion. "The communion of the Holy Ghost be with you all."—2 Cor. xiii. 14. 4. Because the honour and worship due only to God, do belong unto the Spirit, we must believe in him. This is an article of the creed (commonly called the Apostles' Creed), "I believe in the Holy Ghost." We must be baptized in his name. "Baptizing them in the name of the Father, and of the Son, and of the Holy Ghost."—Matt. xxviii. 19.

Q. 10. How doth it appear that the Father, the Son, and the Holy Ghost, being one God, are three distinct persons?

A. 1. The Father begetting, is called a person in the Scripture.—Heb. i. 3. Christ is said to be the express image of his person; and by the same reason, the Son begotten of the Father, is a person, and the Holy Ghost proceeding from the Father and the Son is a person. 2. That the Father and the Son are distinct persons, is evident from John viii. 16–18. " I am not alone, but I and the Father that sent me. It is also written in your law, that the testimony of two men is true. I am one that bear witness of myself, and the Father that sent me beareth witness of me." 3. That the Holy Ghost is a dis-}inct person from the Father and the Son, appeareth from John xiv. 16, 17. " I will pray the Father, and he shall give you another Comforter, that he may abide with you for ever, even the Spirit of truth," &c. 4. That the Father, Son, and Holy Ghost are three distinct persons, in one essence, may be gathered from 1 John v. 7. " There are three that bear record in heaven, the Father, the Word, and the Holy Ghost; and these three are one." These three are either three substances, or three manifestations, or three persons, or something else besides persons; but—(1.) They are not three substances, because in the same verse they are called one. (2.) They are not three manifestations, because all the attributes of God are manifestations, and so there would be more than three or thirteen; and then one manifestation would be said to beget and send another, which is absurd. (3.) They are not something else besides persons; therefore, they are three distinct persons, distinguished by their relations and distinct personal properties.

Q. 11. What should we judge of them that deny that there are three distinct persons in one Godhead?

A. 1. We ought to judge them to be blasphemers, because they speak against the ever-glorious God, who hath set forth himself in this distinction in the Scripture. 2. To be damnable heretics; this doctrine of the distinction of persons in the unity of essence being a fundamental truth, denied of old by the Sabellians, Arians, Photineans, and of late by the Socinians, who were against the Godhead of Christ the Son, and of the Holy Ghost; amongst whom the Quakers are also to be numbered, who deny this distinction.

### VII. Ques. *What are the decrees of God?*

*Ans.* The decrees of God are his eternal purpose, according to the counsel of his own will, whereby, for his own glory, he hath fore-ordained whatsoever comes to pass.

Q. 1. What is it for God to decree?

A. For God to decree, is eternally to purpose and fore-ordain, to appoint and determine, what things shall be.

Q. 2. How did God decree things that come to pass?

A. God decreed all things according to the counsel of his will; according to his will, and therefore most freely—according to the counsel of his will, and therefore most wisely. "Being predestinated according to the purpose of him who worketh all things according to the counsel of his own will."—Eph. i. 11.

Q. 3. Wherefore did God decree all things that come to pass?

A. God decreed all things for his own glory.

Q. 4. What sorts are there of God's decrees?

A. There are God's *general* decrees, and God's *special* decrees.

Q. 5. What are God's general decrees?

A. God's general decrees are his eternal purpose, whereby he hath fore-ordained whatever comes to pass; not only the being of all creatures which he doth make, but also all their motions and actions; not only good actions, which he doth effect, but also the permission of all evil actions. "Who worketh all things after the counsel of his own will."—Eph. i. 11. "Against thy holy child Jesus, Herod and Pontius Pilate, with the Gentiles and the people of Israel, were gathered together, for to do whatever thy hand and thy counsel determined before to be done."—Acts iv. 27, 28.

Q. 6. What are God's special decrees?

A. God's special decrees are his decrees of predestination of angels and men, especially his decrees of election and reprobation of men.

Q. 7. What is God's decree of election of men?

A. God's decree of election of men, is his eternal and unchangeable purpose, whereby, out of his mere good pleasure, he hath in Christ chosen some men unto ever-lasting life and happiness, as the end, and unto faith and holiness, as the necessary means in order hereunto, for the praise of his most rich and free grace. " According as he hath chosen us in him, before the foundation of the world, that we should be holy, and without blame before him in love, being predestinated according to the good pleasure of his will, to the praise of the glory of his grace."—Eph. i. 4–6. " God hath from the beginning chosen you to salvation, through sanctification of the Spirit and belief of the truth."—2 Thess. ii. 13.

Q. 8. What is God's decree of reprobation of men?

A. God's decree of reprobation, is his eternal purpose (according to his sovereignty, and the unsearchable counsel of his own will) of passing by all the rest of the children of men who are not elected, and leaving them to perish in their sins, unto the praise of the power of his wrath and infinite justice, in their everlasting punishment. " Hath not the potter power over the clay, of the same lump to make one vessel unto honour, and another unto dishonour? What if God, willing to show his wrath, and to make his power known, endured with much long-suffering the vessels of wrath fitted to destruction?"—Rom ix. 21, 22.

Q. 9. Whence is it that God doth decree the election of some, and the reprobation of others, of the children of men?

A. It was neither the good works foreseen in the one which moved him to choose them, nor the evil works foreseen in the other which moved him to pass them by; but only because he would, he choose some, and because he would not, he did not choose the rest, but decreed to withhold that grace which he was nowise bound to give unto them, and to punish them justly for their sins, as he might have punished all, if he had so pleased. " The children being not yet born, neither having done good nor evil, that the purpose of God, according to election, might stand, not of works, but of him that calleth, it was said,

Jacob have I loved, but Esau have I hated. For he hath mercy on whom he will have mercy, and whom he will, he hardeneth."—Rom. ix. 11, 13, 19.

Q. 10. May any know whether they are elected or reprobated in this life?

A. 1. Those who are elected, may know their election by their effectual calling. "Give diligence to make your calling and election sure."—2 Pet. i. 10. But, 2. None can know certainly in this life (except such as have sinned against the Holy Ghost) that they are reprobated, because the greatest sinners (except such as have committed that sin) may be called. "Neither fornicators, nor idolaters, nor adulterers, nor thieves," &c., "shall inherit the kingdom of God: and such were some of you; but ye are washed, but ye are sanctified, but ye are justified in the name of the Lord Jesus, and by the Spirit of our God."—1 Cor. vi. 9–11. And we read of some called at the eleventh hour.—Matt. xx. 6, 7.

VIII. Ques. *How doth God execute his decrees?*
*Ans.* God executeth his decrees in the works of creation and providence.

Q. 1. What is it for God to execute his decrees?
A. God doth execute his decrees, when he doth what he eternally purposed to do, when he bringeth to pass what he had before ordained should be.

Q. 2. Wherein doth God execute his decrees?
A. God doth execute his decrees in the works of creation, wherein he maketh all things according as he eternally decreed to make them; and in his works of providence, wherein he preserveth and governeth all things, according to his eternal purpose and counsel.

IX. Ques. *What is the work of creation?*
*Ans.* The work of creation is God's making all things. of nothing, by the word of his power, in the space of six days, and all very good.

Q. 1. What is meant by creation?
A. 1. Negatively, by creation is not meant any ordinary

production of creatures, wherein second causes are made use of.

2. Positively, creation is—(1.) A making things of nothing, or giving a being to things which had no being before. Thus the heavens were made of nothing, the earth and waters, and all the matter of inferior bodies were made of nothing; and thus still the souls of men are made of nothing, being immediately infused by God. (2.) Creation is a making things of matter naturally unfit, which could not by any power (put into any second causes) be brought into such a form; thus all beasts and cattle, and creeping things, and the body of man, were at first made of the earth, and the dust of the ground; and the first woman was made of a rib taken out of the man.

Q. 2. Are all things that are made God's creatures?

A. Yes. 1. All things that were made the first six days were most properly and immediately created by God.

2. All the things that are still produced, are God's creatures. (1.) Because the matter of them was at first created by God. (2.) Because the power which one creature hath of producing another is from God. (3.) Because in all productions God doth concur as the first cause, and most principal agent. And lastly, Because the preservation of things by God in their being, is, as it were, a continued creation.

Q. 3. Whereby did God create all things at first?

A. God created all things by the word of his power. It was the infinite power of God which did put forth itself in erecting the glorious frame of the heavens and earth, and that by a word speaking. "God said, Let there be light, and there was light; Let there be a firmament, and the firmament was made," &c.—Gen. i. 3, 6. "By the word of the Lord were the heavens made; and all the host of them by the breath of his mouth. He spake, and it was done; he commanded, and it stood fast."—Ps. xxxiii. 6, 9.

Q. 4. In what time did God create all things?

A. God created all things in the space of six days. He could have created all things together in a moment; but he took six days' time to work in, and rested on the seventh day, that we might the better apprehend the order of the creation, and that we might imitate him in working but six days of the week, and in resting on the seventh.

Q. 5. What was God's work on the first day?

A. On the first day—1. God created heaven; that is, the highest heaven, called the *third heaven*, which is removed above all visible heavens, where the throne of God is, and the seat of the blessed; in which the angels were created, who are called the *hosts of heaven*, and the sons of God, who rejoiced in the view of the other works.—Job xxxviii. 7. 2. God created the earth and the water mingled together, without such distinct, beautiful forms, either of themselves or of the creatures, which afterwards were produced out of them. 3. God created light, which was afterwards placed in the sun and moon, and other stars, when they were made.

Q. 6. What was God's work on the second day?

A. On the second day—1. God created the firmament, which seemeth to include both the heaven, in which afterwards the sun, moon, and stars, were placed, and likewise the air (called often *heaven* in Scripture), where after the birds did fly. 2. God divided the waters which were above part of the firmament of air, from the waters beneath the firmament of air; that is, he placed distinct the waters which were above the clouds from the waters which were mingled with the earth.

Q. 7. What was God's work on the third day?

A. On the third day—1. God gathered the waters which were mingled with the earth into one place, and called them Seas; and the dry land which then appeared, he called Earth. 2. He caused the earth to bring forth all kinds of trees, plants, and herbs, before there was any sun or rain upon the ground.

Q. 8. What was God's work on the fourth day?

A. On the fourth day—1. God made the great lights, the sun and moon; and the lesser lights, namely, the stars; and placed them in the heavens. 2. He appointed these lights their motions, office, and use, to compass the earth, to rule the day and the night, and to be for signs and for seasons, and for days and for years.

Q. 9. What was God's work on the fifth day?

A. On the fifth day—1. God made of the waters, whales, and all kind of great and small fishes, with every living creature which moveth in the sea. 2. God made of the waters, all kind of winged fowls, which fly in the open heaven.

Q. 10. What was God's work on the sixth day?

A. On the sixth day—1. God made of the earth, all beasts, and cattle, and creeping things. 2. God made the first man, his body of the dust of the ground, and immediately created his soul in him, breathing in him the breath of life; and the woman he made of a rib taken out of his side.

Q. 11. Wherefore did God create all things?

A. God created all things for his own glory, that he might make manifest—1. The glory of his power, in effecting so great a work, making every thing of nothing by a word. "Thou art worthy, O Lord, to receive glory, and honour, and power: for thou hast created all things."—Rev. iv. 11. 2. The glory of his wisdom, in the order and variety of his creatures. "O Lord, how manifold are thy works! in wisdom hast thou made them all."—Ps. civ. 24. The glory of his goodness, especially towards man, for whom he provided first a habitation, and every useful creature, before he gave him his being.

Q. 12. In what condition did God create all things at first?

A. God made all things at first very good. "And God saw every thing that he had made, and, behold, it was very good."—Gen. i. 31. All the evil which since hath come into the world, is either sin itself, which is the work of the devil and man, or the fruit and consequence of sin. God made man good and happy; man made himself sinful and miserable.

X. Ques. *How did God create man?*

*Ans.* God created man male and female, after his own image, in knowledge, righteousness, and holiness, with dominion over the creatures.

Q. 1. Why did God create man male and female?

A. God created man male and female, for their mutual

help, and for the propagation of mankind. "And God said, It is not good that the man should be alone : I will make an help meet for him."—Gen. ii. 18. "God created man male and female; and God blessed them, and said unto them, Be fruitful, and multiply, and replenish the earth, and subdue it," &c.—Gen. i. 27, 28.

Q. 2. What is meant by the image of God, after which man was at first created ?

A. By the image of God we are to understand the similitude or likeness of God. "And God said, Let us make man in our image, after our likeness."—Gen. i. 26.

Q. 3. Wherein doth consist the image of God, which was put upon man in his first creation ?

A. 1. Negatively, the image of God doth not consist in any outward visible resemblance of his body to God, as if God had any bodily shape. 2. Positively, the image of God doth consist in the inward resemblance of his soul to God, in knowledge, righteousness, and holiness. "Renewed in knowledge, after the image of Him that created him."—Col. iii. 10. "Put on the new man, which after God is created in righteousness and true holiness."—Eph. iv. 24.

Q. 4. What is included in this image of God, in knowledge, righteousness, and holiness, as man had it at first ?

A. The image of God in man at the first doth include the universal and perfect rectitude of the whole soul : knowledge in his understanding, righteousness in his will, holiness in his affections.

Q. 5. What knowledge had man, when he was created, in his understanding ?

A. Man had, in his first creation, the knowledge of God, and his law, and his creatures, and all things which were necessary to make him happy.

Q. 6. What righteousness had man at first in his will ?

A. Man had at first in his will a disposition, accompanied with an executive power, to every thing which was right, and to give that which was both due to God and also to man, had there been any man besides himself.

Q. What holiness had man at first in his affections ?

A. Man's affections at first were holy and pure, free from

all sin and defilement, free from all disorder and distemper; they were placed upon the most holy, high, and noble objects. Man at first had true and chief love to God; his desires were chiefly after him, and his delight was chiefly in him, and no creature in the world had too great a share. As for grief, and shame, and the like affections, though they were in man radically, yet they were not in man actively, so as to put forth any acts, until he had committed the first sin; then he began to mourn and be ashamed.

Q. 8. What dominion had man at his first creation?

A. Man had dominion, not only over himself and his own affections, but he had also dominion over the inferior creatures, the fish, and the fowls, and the beasts; many of which, since man's disobedience to the command of God, are become disobedient to the command of man. " God said unto them, Have dominion over the fish of the sea, and over the fowl of the air, and over every creature that moveth upon the earth."—Gen. i. 28.

XI. Ques. *What are God's works of providence?*

*Ans.* God's works of providence are his most holy, wise, and powerful preserving and governing all his creatures, and all their actions.

Q. 1. What are the parts of God's providence?

A. The parts of God's providence are—1. His preservation of things. " O Lord, thou preservest man and beast." —Ps. xxxvi. 6. 2. His government of things. " Thou shalt govern the nations upon the earth."—Ps. lxvii. 4.

Q. 2. What is it for God to preserve things?

A. God preserveth things—1. When he continueth and upholdeth them in their being. " O Lord, thy word is settled in heaven; thou hast established the earth, and it abideth; they continue this day according to thine ordinances."—Ps. cxix. 89–91. 2. When he maketh provision of things needful for their preservation. " The eyes of all wait upon thee, and thou givest them their meat in due season. Thou openest thine hand, and satisfiest the desire of every living thing."—Ps. cxlv. 15, 16.

Q. 3. What is it for God to govern things?

A. God governeth things when he ruleth over them, disposeth and directeth them to his and their end. " He ruleth by his power for ever, his eyes behold the nations; let not the rebellious exalt themselves."—Ps. lxvi. 7. " A man's heart deviseth his way, but the Lord directeth his steps."—Prov. xvi. 9.

Q. 4. What is the subject of God's providence?

A. The subject of God's providence is—1. All his creatures, especially his children. " Upholding all things by the word of his power."—Heb. i. 3. " His kingdom ruleth over all."—Ps. ciii. 19. " One sparrow falleth not to the ground without your Father;—ye are of more value than many sparrows."—Mat. x. 29, 31. " Behold the fowls of the air: for they sow not, neither do they reap, nor gather into barns; yet your heavenly Father feedeth them. Are ye not much better than they? Consider the lilies of the field, how they grow; they toil not, neither do they spin: and if God clothe the grass of the field, shall he not much more clothe you?"—Mat. vi. 26, 28, 30. 2. All the actions of his creatures. (1.) All natural actions. " In him we live and move."—Acts xvii. 28. (2.) All morally good actions. " Without me ye can do nothing" (John xv. 5); that is, nothing that is good. (3.) All casual actions. " He that smiteth a man that he die, and lie not in wait, but God deliver him into his hand, I will appoint thee a place whither he shall flee."—Exod. xxi. 12, 13. (4.) All morally evil actions or sins.

Q. 5. How doth God's providence reach sinful actions?

A. 1. God doth permit men to sin. " Who in time past suffered all nations to walk in their own ways."—Acts xiv. 16. " These things hast thou done, and I kept silence." —Ps. l. 21. 2. God doth limit and restrain men in their sins. " The remainder of wrath shalt thou restrain."—Ps. lxxvi. 10. " Because thy rage against me is come up into my ears, therefore I will put my hook into thy nose, and my bridle in thy lips, and I will turn thee back," &c. —2 Kings xix. 28. 3. God doth direct and dispose men's sins to good ends, beyond their own intentions. " O Assyrian, the rod of mine anger, I will send him against an hypocritical nation," (namely, to chastise it for its sin) "howbeit he meaneth not so, neither doth his heart think so," &c.—Isa. x. 5-7. " But as for you, ye thought evil against me; but God meant it unto good, to save much people alive."—Gen. l. 20.

Q. 6. What are the properties of God's providence?

A. 1. God's providence is most holy. " The Lord is righteous in all his ways, and holy in all his works."—Ps. cxlv. 17. 2. God's providence is most wise. " O Lord, how manifold are thy works !" (speaking of the works of providence, as well as creation) " in wisdom hast thou made them all."—Ps. civ. 24. 3. God's providence is most powerful. " He doeth according to his will in the army of heaven, and among the inhabitants of the earth, and none can stay his hand."—Dan. iv. 35. " He ruleth by his power for ever."—Ps. lxvi. 7.

XII. Ques. *What special act of providence did God exercise towards man in the estate wherein he was created?*

*Ans.* When God had created man, he entered into a covenant of life with him, upon condition of perfect obedience; forbidding him to eat of the tree of the knowledge of good and evil, upon the pain of death.

Q. 1. What is a covenant ?

A. A covenant is a mutual agreement and engagement, between two or more parties, to give or do something.

Q. 2. What is God's covenant with man ?

A. God's covenant with man is his engagement, by promise, of giving something, with a stipulation, or requiring something to be done on man's part.

Q. 3. How many covenants hath God made with man ?

A. There are two covenants which God hath made with man—1. A covenant of works; 2. A covenant of grace.

Q. 4. When did God enter into a covenant of works with man ?

A. God did enter into a covenant of works with man immediately after his creation, when he was yet in a state of innocency, and had committed no sin.

Q. 5. What was the promise of the covenant of works which God made with man?

A. The promise of the covenant of works was a promise of *life;* for God's threatening *death* upon man's disobedience (Gen. ii. 17), implieth his promise of life upon man's obedience.

Q. 6. What life was it that God promised to man in the covenant of works?

A. The life that God promised to man in the covenant of works was the continuance of natural and spiritual life, and the donation of eternal life.

Q. 7. Wherein doth natural, spiritual, and eternal life consist?

A. 1. Natural life doth consist in the union of the soul and body. 2. Spiritual life doth consist in the union of God and the soul. 3. Eternal life doth consist in the perfect, immutable, and eternal happiness, both of soul and body, through a perfect likeness unto, and an immediate vision and fruition of God, the chief good.

Q. 8. What was the condition of the first covenant, and that which God required on man's part in the covenant of works?

A. The condition of, and that required by God on man's part, in the covenant of works, was perfect obedience. " The law is not of faith, but, The man that doeth them shall live in them" (Gal. iii. 12); compared with the 10th verse: " As many as are of the works of the law are under the curse; for it is written, Cursed is every one that continueth not in all things which are written in the book of the law to do them."

Q. 9. In what respect was this obedience (required of man in the first covenant) to be perfect?

A. The obedience required of man in the first covenant was to be perfect—1. In respect of the matter of it. All the powers and faculties of the soul, all the parts and members of the body, were to be employed in God's service, and made use of as instruments of righteousness. 2. It was to be perfect in respect of the principle, namely, habitual righteousness, and natural disposition and inclination to do any thing God required, without any indisposition or reluctance, as the angels do obey in heaven. 3. It was to be perfect in respect of the end, which was chiefly to be God's glory, swaying in all actions. 4. It was to be perfect in respect of the manner—it was to be with perfect love and delight, and exactly with all the circumstances required in obedience. 5. It was to be perfect in respect of the time—it was to be constant and perpetual.

Q. 10. What is the prohibition, or the thing forbidden in the covenant of works?

A. The thing forbidden in the covenant of works, is the eating of the tree of knowledge of good and evil. " And the Lord commanded, saying, Of every tree of the garden thou mayest freely eat; but of the tree of knowledge of good and evil, thou shalt not eat of it."—Gen. ii. 16, 17.

Q. 11. Why was this tree called the tree of the knowledge of good and evil?

A. Because man, by eating the fruit of this tree, did know experimentally what good he had fallen from, and had lost, namely, the image and favour of God; and what evil he was fallen into, namely, the evil of sin and misery.

Q. 12. What was the penalty or punishment threatened upon the breach of the covenant of works?

A. The punishment threatened upon the breach of the covenant of works, was death. " In the day thou eatest thereof, thou shalt surely die."—Gen. ii. 17. " The wages of sin is death."—Rom. vi. 23.

Q. 13. What death was it that God threatened as the punishment of sin?

A. The death which God threatened as the punishment of man's sin, was temporal death, spiritual death, and eternal death.

Q. 14. Wherein doth temporal, spiritual, and eternal death consist?

A. 1. Temporal death doth consist in the separation of the soul from the body; this man was liable unto in the day that he did eat of the forbidden fruit, and not before. 2. Spiritual death doth consist in the separation of the soul from God, and the loss of God's image; this death seized upon man in the moment of his first sin. 3. Eternal death doth consist in the exclusion of man from the comfortable and beatifical presence of God in glory for ever, together with the immediate impressions of God's wrath, effecting most horrible anguish in the soul, and in the extreme tortures in every part of the body, eternally in hell ?

XIII. Ques. *Did our first parents continue in the estate wherein they were created?*

*Ans.* Our first parents, being left to the freedom of their own will, fell from the estate wherein they were created, by sinning against God.

Q. 1. What is meant by the freedom of the will ?

A. By the freedom of the will is meant, a liberty in the will of its own accord to choose or refuse; to do or not to do; to do this, or to do that, without any constraint or force from any one.

Q. 2. How many ways may the will be said to be free ?

A. The will may be said to be free three ways. 1. When the will is free only to good; when the will is not compelled or forced, but freely chooseth only such things as are good. Thus, the will of God (to speak after the manner of men) is free only to good; he can neither do nor will any thing that is evil. Such also is the freedom of the wills of angels, and such will be the freedom of all the glorified saints in heaven; there neither is, nor will be, any inclination of the will unto any evil thing for ever, and yet good will be of free choice. 2. The will may be said to be free only unto evil, when the will is not constrained, but freely chooseth such things as are evil and sinful. Thus, the will of the devil is free only unto sin; and thus the wills of all the children of men in the world, whilst in a state of nature, are free only unto sin. 3. The will may be said to be free both unto good and evil, when it sometimes chooseth that which is good, sometimes chooseth that which is evil. Such is the freedom of the wills of all regenerate persons, who have in some measure recovered the image of God; they choose good freely, through a principle of grace wrought in them by the Spirit; yet, through the remainder of corruption, at some times their wills are inclined to that which is sinful.

Q. 3. What freedom of will had man at his first creation?

A. The freedom of will which man had at his first creation, was a freedom both to good and evil. Though the natural inclination and disposition of his will was only to good, yet, being mutable or changeable, through temptation it might be altered, and might become inclinable unto evil.

Q. 4. How were our first parents left to the freedom of their own wills?

A. Our first parents were left by God to the freedom of their own wills, when God withheld that further grace (which he was nowise bound to give unto them) which would have strengthened them against the temptation, and preserved them from falling into sin.

Q. 5. How did our first parents fall, when they were left to the freedom of their own wills?

A. Our first parents, being left to the freedom of their own wills, through the temptation of the devil, who spake unto them in the serpent; through the desirableness of the fruit of the forbidden tree to their sensual appetite; and through the desirableness of being made wise, and like unto God, by eating thereof, under their rational appetite; and through the hopes of escaping the punishment of death threatened by God; they did venture, against the express command of God, to eat of this tree. The woman being first beguiled and perverted by the devil, did eat; and then the man, being persuaded by his wife and the devil too, did eat also. " And the serpent said unto the woman, Ye shall not surely die; for God doth know, that in the day ye eat thereof, then your eyes shall be opened, and ye shall be as gods, knowing good and evil. And when the woman saw that the tree was good for food, and that it was pleasant to the eyes, and a tree to be desired to make one wise, she took of the fruit thereof, and did eat; and gave also unto her husband with her, and he did eat."—Gen. iii. 4-6. " The serpent beguiled Eve, through his subtlety." —2 Cor. xi. 3. " The woman being deceived, was in the transgression."—1 Tim. ii. 14.

Q. 6. What was the state in which our first parents were created, from whence they fell?

A. The state wherein our first parents were created, and from whence they fell, was a state of innocency. "Lo, this only have I found, that God hath made man upright, but they have sought out many inventions."— Eccles. vii. 29.

Q. 7. Whereby did our first parents fall from the state wherein they were created?

A. Our first parents fell from the state wherein they were created, by sinning against God.

XIV. Ques. *What is sin?*

*Ans.* Sin is any want of conformity unto, or transgression of, the law of God.

Q. 1. What is meant by the law of God, which sin is a breach of?

A. By the law of God is meant the commandments which God, the Creator, and Supreme King, and Lawgiver, hath laid upon all the children of men, his creatures and subjects, as the rule of their obedience.

Q. 2. Where is the law of God to be found?

A. The law of God in some part of it, and more darkly, is to be found written upon the hearts of all men (Rom. ii. 15); but most plainly and fully it is to be found written in the Word of God?

Q. 3. How many kinds of laws of God are there in the Word of God?

A. 1. There is the judicial law, which concerned chiefly the nation of the Jews, and in every respect doth not bind all other nations. 2. There is the ceremonial law, which was in no part of it binding upon any, but for a time; namely, before the coming of Christ, who fulfilled this law, and abrogated it. 3. There is the moral law, written at first by God himself, on tables of stone; which is a standing rule of obedience unto the end of the world.

Q. 4. What is meant by want of conformity to the law of God?

A. By want of conformity to God's law, is meant, both

an unsuitableness and disagreeableness to the law, and a not observation, and not obedience to it.

Q. 5. What sins doth want of conformity to the law include?

A. The sins included in the want of conformity to the law of God, are—1. Original sin, and that natural enmity in the heart against the law of God. "The carnal mind is enmity against God; for it is not subject to his law, neither indeed can be."—Rom. viii. 7.    2. All sins of omission. The former is a want of conformity of heart, the latter a want of conformity of life, to God's law.

Q. 6. What is it to transgress the law of God?

A. To transgress the law is to pass the bounds which are set in the law.

Q. 7. How doth it appear that the transgression of the law is sin?

A. It doth appear from 1 John iii. 4 : "Whosoever committeth sin transgresseth the law; for sin is the transgression of the law."

Q. 8. Is nothing a sin, then, but what is against God's law?

A. Nothing is a sin but what God hath either expressly or by consequence forbidden in his law.

XV. Ques. *What was the sin whereby our first parents fell from the estate wherein they were created ?*

*Ans.* The sin whereby our first parents fell from the estate wherein they were created, was their eating the forbidden fruit.

Q. 1. Why did God forbid our first parents to eat of this fruit?

A. Not because there was any intrinsical evil in the fruit of the forbidden tree, it being as indifferent in itself to eat of this tree as any other tree in the garden; but God did forbid them to eat of the fruit of this tree, to try their obedience.

Q. 2. Could this sin, of eating the forbidden fruit, be very heinous, when the thing in itself was indifferent?

A. 1. Though the eating the fruit was indifferent in

itself, yet when so expressly forbidden by God it ceased to be indifferent, but was absolutely unlawful, and a great sin. 2. This sin of eating the forbidden fruit was such a sin as included many other sins, as it was circumstantiated.

Q. 3. What sins did the eating of the forbidden fruit include?

A. The sins included in our first parents' eating the forbidden fruit were—1. Rebellion against God their sovereign, who had expressly forbidden them to eat of this tree. 2. Treason, in conspiring with the devil, God's enemy, against God. 3. Ambition, in aspiring to a higher state, namely, to be as God. 4. Luxury, in indulging so much to please the sense of taste, which did inordinately desire this fruit. 5. Ingratitude to God, who had given them leave to eat of any tree of the garden besides. 6. Unbelief, in not giving credit to the threatening of death, but believing the devil, who said they should not die, rather than God, who told them they should surely die, did they eat of this fruit. 7. Murder, in bringing death, by this sin, upon themselves, and all their posterity. These, and many other sins, were included in this sin of our first parents' eating of the forbidden fruit; which did render it exceeding heinous in the sight of God.

XVI. Ques. *Did all mankind fall in Adam's first transgression?*

*Ans.* The covenant being made with Adam, not only for himself, but for his posterity, all mankind, descending from him by ordinary generation, sinned in him, and fell with him, in his first transgression.

Q. 1. Did all mankind, without any exception, fall in Adam's first transgression?

A. No; for our Lord Jesus Christ, who was one of Adam's posterity, did not fall with Adam, but was perfectly free, both from original and actual sin. " For such an high priest became us, who was holy, harmless, undefiled, separate from sinners."—Heb. vii. 26. " Who did no sin."—1 Pet. ii. 22.

Q. 2. How was it that the Lord Jesus Christ escaped the fall with Adam?

A. Because our Lord Jesus descended from Adam by extraordinary generation, being born of a virgin. " Now the birth of Christ was on this wise: When as his mother Mary was espoused to Joseph, before they came together, she was found with child of the Holy Ghost." —Matt. i 18.

Q. 3. Did all the posterity of Adam, besides Christ, fall in his first sin?

A. All the posterity of Adam, besides Christ, descending from him by ordinary generation, did fall in his first sin. " By one man sin entered into the world, and death by sin; and so death passed upon all men, for that all have sinned."—Rom. v. 12.

Q. 4. How could all the posterity of Adam, being then unborn, fall in his sin?

A. All the posterity of Adam were in him before they were born, and so they sinned in him, and fell with him. " For as in Adam all die, even so in Christ shall all be made alive."—1 Cor. xv. 22.

Q. 5. How were all Adam's posterity in him when he first sinned?

A. 1. They were in him virtually—they were in his loins; and as Levi is said to pay tithes in Abraham, when only in his loins (Heb. vii. 9), so Adam's posterity sinned in his loins. 2. They were in him representatively; Adam was the common head and representative of all mankind.

Q. 6. What reason is there that the posterity of Adam should fall with Adam their representative?

A. Because the covenant of works, wherein life was promised upon condition of obedience, was made with Adam, not only for himself, but also for his posterity; therefore, as if Adam had stood, all his posterity had stood with him; so Adam falling, they all fell with him.

Q. 7. How could Adam be the representative of all his posterity, when there was none of them in being to make choice of him for their representative?

A. 1. It was more fit Adam should be the representative of his posterity than any one else, being the father of them all. 2. Though they did not choose him for their representative, yet God did choose him; and God made as good a choice for them as they could have made for themselves.

**XVII. Ques.** *Into what estate did the fall bring mankind?*

*Ans.* The fall brought mankind into an estate of sin and misery.

**XVIII. Ques.** *Wherein consists the sinfulness of that estate whereinto man fell?*

*Ans.* The sinfulness of that estate whereinto man fell, consists in the guilt of Adam's first sin, the want of original righteousness, and the corruption of his whole nature, which is commonly called original sin, together with all actual transgressions which proceed from it.

Q. 1. How many sorts of sin are there which denote the sinfulness of the estate of man by the fall?

A. There are two sorts of sin, namely, original sin and actual sin.

Q. 2. Wherein doth original sin consist?

A. Original sin doth consist in three things. 1. In the guilt of Adam's first sin. 2. In the want of original righteousness. 3. In the corruption of the whole nature.

Q. 3. How are all the children of men guilty of Adam's first sin?

A. All the children of men are guilty of Adam's first sin by imputation: as the righteousness of Christ, the second Adam, is imputed unto all the spiritual seed, namely, to all believers; so the sin of the first Adam is imputed to all the natural seed which came forth of his loins. "For as by one man's disobedience many were made sinners; so by the obedience of one shall many be made righteous."—Rom. v. 19.

Q. 4. What is included in the want of original righteousness?

A. The want of original righteousness doth include— 1. Want of true spiritual knowledge in the mind. "The natural man receiveth not the things of the Spirit of God;

neither can he know them, because they are spiritually discerned."—1 Cor. ii. 14. 2. Want of inclination and power to do good; and want of all spiritual affections in the will and heart. " In me (that is, in my flesh) dwelleth no good thing; . . . . .but how to perform that which is good I find not."—Rom. vii. 18.

Q. 5. Is the want of original righteousness a sin ?

A. Yes; because it is a want of conformity to the law of God, which requireth original and habitual righteousness, as well as actual.

Q. 6. If God withhold this original righteousness, is not he the author of sin ?

A. No; because though man be bound to have it, yet God is not bound to restore it when man hath lost it; and it is not a sin, but a punishment of the first sin, as God doth withhold it.

Q. 7. How could the souls of Adam's posterity, not yet created, nor having relation to Adam, be justly deprived of original righteousness ?

A. The souls of Adam's posterity never had a being without relation of Adam; they being created in the infusion and conjunction of them to their body, and, through their relation to the common head, partake justly of the common punishment.

Q. 8. Wherein doth consist the corruption of the whole nature of man ?

A. The corruption of the nature of man doth consist in the universal depravation which is in every part of man since the fall. 1. In the darkness and defilement of the mind. " For ye were sometimes darkness, but now are ye light in the Lord."—Eph. v. 8. And, " The minds and consciences of the unbelieving are defiled."—Tit. i. 15. 2. In the crookedness and enmity of the heart and will against God and his law. " The carnal mind" (that is, the carnal heart) " is enmity against God; for it is not subject to the law of God, neither indeed can be."—Rom. viii. 7. As also in the inclination of the heart unto sin, and the worst of sins, there being the seed of all manner of sins in the heart, as it is corrupted with original sin. " Out of the heart proceed evil thoughts, murders, adulteries, for-

nications, thefts, false witness, blasphemies."—Matt. xv.
19. 3. In the disorder and distemper of the affections,
all of them being naturally set upon wrong objects through
this inherent corruption. 4. The members also of the
body are infected, being ready weapons and instruments
of unrighteousness.—Rom. vi. 13.

Q. 9. How is the corruption of nature conveyed, then, to
all the children of men?

A. 1. It is not from God, who is the author of all good,
but of no evil; for though he withhold original righteousness, yet he doth not infuse original corruption. 2. It is
conveyed by natural generation, in the union and conjunction of soul and body; the soul, being destitute or void
of original righteousness, is infected with this corruption,
as liquor is tainted which is put into a tainted vessel: but
the way of its conveyance is one of the most difficult
things in divinity to understand.

Q. 10. Have we reason to deny this original corruption,
because we have not reason clearly to understand the way
of its conveyance?

A. No; because—1. The Scripture doth assert that our
natures, since the fall, are corrupt. " Adam" (though made
after the likeness of God) " begat a son after his own likeness" (Gen. v. 3); that is, with a corrupt nature. " That
which is born of the flesh is flesh."—John iii. 6. " Behold, I was shapen in iniquity; and in sin did my mother
conceive me."—Ps. li. 5. " You hath he quickened, who
were dead in trespasses and sins."—Eph. iii. 1. 2. Experience doth tell us, that in every one there is a natural
antipathy to good, and proneness to evil: therefore, as
when a man's house is on fire, it is greater wisdom to
endeavour to quench it than to inquire how it was set on
fire; so it is greater wisdom to endeavour the removal of
this natural corruption, than to inquire how it was conveyed.

Q. 11. Do not sanctified persons beget children without
natural corruption?

A. No; because parents that are sanctified are sanctified
but in part, their nature remaining in part corrupt; and
they beget children according to their nature, and not

according to their grace; as the winnowed corn that is sown groweth up with husks upon it, or as the circumcised Jews did beget uncircumcised children in the flesh as well as the heart.

Q. 12. Why is this sin called original sin?

A. Because we have it from our birth or original, and because all our actual transgressions do proceed from it.

Q. 13. What is actual sin?

A. Actual sin is any breach of God's law, either of omission or commission; either in thought, heart, speech, or action. Of which more in the commandments.

XIX. Ques. *What is the misery of that estate whereinto man fell?*

*Ans.* All mankind by their fall lost communion with God, are under his wrath and curse, and so made liable to all the miseries in this life, to death itself, and to the pains of hell for ever.

Q. 1. Wherein doth man's misery by the fall consist?

A. Man's misery by the fall doth consist in three things. 1. In what man hath lost. 2. In what man is brought under. 3. In what man is liable unto.

Q. 2. What hath man lost by the fall?

A. Man by the fall hath lost communion with God.

Q. 3. Wherein did the communion with God consist which man by the fall hath lost?

A. The communion with God which man by the fall hath lost consisted in the gracious presence and favour, together with the sweet fellowship and enjoyment, of God in the garden of Eden. This, man by the fall was deprived of; and all his posterity, whilst in their fallen estate, are without. "And Adam and his wife hid themselves from the presence of the Lord. And the Lord God sent him forth from the garden of Eden; and so drove out the man." —Gen. iii. 8, 23, 24. "At that time we were without Christ, having no hope, and without God in the world."— Eph. ii. 12.

Q. 4. Is the loss of communion with God a great misery and loss?

A. Yes; because God is our chief good, and in communion with him doth consist man's chiefest happiness; therefore the loss of communion with God is man's greatest loss.

Q. 5. What is man brought under by the fall?

A. By the fall, man is brought under God's wrath and curse. "And were by nature the children of wrath, even as others."—Eph. ii. 3. "As many as are of the works of the law" (that is, all who are under the covenant of works, as all unbelievers are), "are under the curse."—Gal. iii. 10.

Q. 6. Is it a great misery to be under God's wrath and curse?

A. Yes; because as his favour is better than life, so his wrath and displeasure is worse than death. His blessing maketh man blessed and happy; his curse maketh man wretched and miserable.

Q. 7. What is that punishment which man is liable unto by the fall?

A. Man is liable, by the fall—1. Unto all miseries in this life. 2. To death itself. 3. To the pains of hell for ever.

Q. 8. What are the miseries in this life which man is liable unto by the fall.

A. The miseries in this life which man is liable unto by the fall, are either external, or internal and spiritual.

Q. 9. What are the external miseries of this life which the fall hath brought upon mankind?

A. All the external miseries which either are or have been in the world, are the effects of the fall; and sin doth expose men to all sorts of miseries. 1. To more public and general calamities; such as pestilence, famine, sword, captivity, and the like. "I will send upon you famine and pestilence, and bring the sword upon thee."—Ezek. v. 17. 2. Sin doth expose men unto more private and particular miseries, such as—(1.) All sorts of sickness in their bodies. "The Lord shall smite thee with a consumption, and with a fever, and with an inflammation, and with an extreme burning," &c.—Deut. xxviii. 22. (2.) Losses of their estates. "Thou shalt build an house, but thou shalt not dwell therein; thou shalt plant a vineyard, and shalt not gather the grapes thereof."—Deut. xxviii. 30. (3.) Reproach and disgrace on their names. "Thou shalt become a proverb and a by-word."—Verse 27. (4.) Losses of relations, and every other external affliction and misery men are liable unto in this life for their sins.

Q. 10. What are the internal and spiritual miseries which men are liable unto in this life by the fall?

A. Men by the fall are liable—1. To the thraldom of the devil, to be led about by him at his will. "And that they may recover themselves out of the snare of the devil, who are taken captive by him at his will."—2 Tim. ii. 26. 2. To judiciary blindness of mind, and a reprobate sense. "God hath given them the spirit of slumber, eyes that they should not see, and ears that they should not hear."—Rom. xi. 8. "Because they liked not to retain God in their knowledge, God gave them over to a reprobate mind."—Rom. i. 8. 3. To judiciary hardness of heart, and searedness and benumbedness of conscience. "Whom he will he hardeneth."—Rom. ix. 18. "Having their conscience seared as with a hot iron."—1 Tim. iv. 2. "Who being past feeling, have given themselves over unto lasciviousness, to work all uncleanness with greediness.—Eph. iv. 19. 4. To vile actions. "For this cause God gave them up unto vile affections: and they burned in their lust one towards another, working that which is unseemly."—Rom. i. 26, 27. 5. To strong delusions, and belief of damnable errors. "God shall send them strong delusions, to believe a lie; that they all might be damned that believed not the truth, but had pleasure in unrighteousness."—2 Thess. ii. 11, 12. 6. To distress and perplexity of mind, dread and horror of spirit, and despairful agonies, through the apprehension of certain future wrath. "There remaineth nothing but a certain fearful looking for of judgment, and fiery indignation, which shall devour the adversary."—Heb. x. 27.

Q. 11. What is the punishment which man by the fall is liable unto at the end of his life?

A. Man by the fall at the end of his life, is liable unto death itself. "Death passed upon all, for that all have sinned."—Rom. v. 12. "The wages of sin is death."—Rom. vi. 23.

Q. 12. Is death a punishment unto all upon whom it is inflicted?

A. 1: Though death be the consequent of sin in all, yet to believers, through Christ, it is unstinged, and it is an outlet from misery, and an inlet to glory. 2. Death, to the wicked and unbelievers, is a dreadful punishment, being a king of terrors, and grim sergeant, that is sent by God to arrest the wicked, and convey them into future misery.

Q. 13. What is the punishment which man by the fall is liable unto in the other world?

A. The punishment which man by the fall is liable unto in the other world, is the punishment of hell for ever.

Q. 14. Wherein doth consist the punishment of hell?

A. The punishment of hell doth consist—1. In the punishment of loss. 2. In the punishment of sense.

Q. 15. What will be the punishment of loss in hell?

A. The punishment of loss in hell, will be a banishment from the comfortable presence of God, and an exclusion or shutting out from heaven; where the saints will have a fulness and eternity of joy and happiness. "Depart from me, ye cursed."—Matt. xxv. 41. "Ye shall see Abraham, and Isaac, and Jacob, and all the prophets, in the kingdom of God, and you yourselves thrust out."—Luke xiii. 28. "In thy presence is fulness of joy, and at thy right hand there are pleasures for evermore."—Ps. xvi. 11.

Q. 16. What will be the punishment of sense in hell?

A. The punishment of sense in hell, will be both on the soul and on the body. 1. The souls of the wicked in hell will be filled with horror and anguish through the strokes of God's immediate vengeance, and the bitings of the never-dying worm of conscience. "It is a fearful thing to fall into the hands of the living God."—Heb. x. 31. "Where their worm dieth not, and the fire is not quenched."—Mark ix. 44. 2. The bodies of the wicked in hell will be most grievously tormented in every part and member, and that both in extremity and to eternity. "Depart from me, ye cursed, into everlasting fire, prepared for the devil and his angels."—Matt. xxv. 41. "The Son of man shall send forth his angels, and they shall gather out of his kingdom all them that do iniquity, and shall cast them into a furnace of fire: there shall be wailing and gnashing of teeth."—Matt. xiii. 41, 42.

**XX. Ques.** *Did God leave all mankind to perish in the estate of sin and misery?*

*Ans.* God having, out of his mere good pleasure, from all eternity, elected some to everlasting life, did enter into a covenant of grace, to deliver them out of the estate of sin and misery, and to bring them into an estate of salvation by a Redeemer.

Q. 1. Do all mankind perish in the estate of sin and misery into which they are fallen?

A. No; for some God doth bring out of this estate of sin and misery into an estate of salvation. "Being in nothing terrified by your adversaries, which to them is an evident token of perdition, but to you of salvation, and that of God."—Phil. i. 28.

Q. 2. Whom doth God bring into an estate of salvation?

A. God doth bring all his elect people into an estate of salvation, unto which he hath chosen them. "God hath from the beginning chosen you to salvation."—2 Thess. ii. 3.

Q. 3. Who are the elect people of God?

A. The elect people of God are those whom, from all eternity, out of his mere good pleasure, he hath chosen unto everlasting life. "According as he hath chosen us in him before the foundation of the world; having predestinated us unto the adoption of children, according to the good pleasure of his will."—Eph. i. 4, 5. "As many as were ordained to eternal life believed."—Acts xiii. 48.

Q. 4. By whom doth God bring his elect into an estate of salvation?

A. God doth bring his elect into an estate of salvation by a Redeemer. "Neither is there salvation in any other; for there is none other name under heaven given among men, whereby we must be saved?"—Acts iv. 12.

Q. 5. In what way doth God bring his elect into an estate of salvation?

A. God doth bring his elect into an estate of salvation in the way of his covenant.

Q. 6. By virtue of which covenant of God is it that his elect are saved?

A. 1. Not by virtue of the covenant of works. "As many as are of the works of the law are under the curse. If there had been a law given which could have given life, verily righteousness should have been by the law."—Gal. iii. 10, 21.   2. It is by virtue of the covenant of grace that the elect are saved.

Q. 7. With whom was the covenant of grace made?

A. As the covenant of works was made with the first Adam, and all his posterity, so the covenant of grace was made with Christ, the second Adam, and in him with all the elect, as his seed, which are the Israel of God. "Now to Abraham and his seed were the promises made," (that is, not the promises of making all nations blessed.) "He saith not, Unto seeds; as of many but as of one, To thy seed, which is Christ."—Gal. iii. 16. " This is the covenant that I will make with the house of Israel."—Heb. viii. 10.

Q. 8. Was it the same covenant which was made with Christ and the elect?

A. No; for there was a covenant which God made with Christ as Mediator, and the representative of the elect, which was the foundation of all that grace which was afterwards promised in that covenant of grace which he made with ourselves in and through Christ.

Q. 9. What was the covenant which God made with Christ as the head and representative of the elect?

A. God did covenant and promise to Christ, as the representative of the elect, that, upon condition he would submit to the penalty which the sins of the elect did deserve, and undertake in all things the office of a Mediator, he should be successful, so as to justify and save them. "When thou shalt make his soul an offering for sin, he shall see his seed, and the pleasure of the Lord shall prosper in his hand.   And by his knowledge shall my righteous servant justify many."—Isa. liii. 10, 11.

Q. 10. Was this a covenant of grace which God made with Christ, when it required perfect obedience?

A. It was a covenant of grace in reference to the elect, whom Christ did represent; since hereby the obedience was accepted at the hands of their representative which the covenant of works required of themselves. "Who hath saved us, according to his own purpose and grace, which was given us in Christ Jesus before the world began."—2 Tim. i. 9.

Q. 11. What are the promises of the covenant of grace which God hath made with the elect through Christ?

A. The promises of the covenant of grace, which God hath made with the elect, through Christ, are either more general or more particular. 1. More generally, God hath promised to the elect, through Christ, "that he will be to them a God, and they shall be to him a people."—Heb. viii. 10. These two promises are so general and comprehensive, that they include all the rest. The promise that "he will be to them a God," doth include his special favour and affection, together with all the expressions of it, in taking care of them, and making provision of all temporal and spiritual good things for them here, and giving them eternal life and happiness in the other world. The promise that "they shall be to him a people," doth include the giving them all those gifts and qualifications which are requisite to that estate and relation. 2. More particularly, God, in the covenant of grace, hath promised to the elect through Christ—(1.) Illumination; that he will teach them the knowledge of himself, and that more fully and clearly than they had been, or could be, taught one by another. "They shall not teach every man his neighbour, and every man his brother, saying, Know the Lord: for all shall know me, from the least to the greatest."—Heb. viii. 11. (2.) Remission; that he will forgive their sins. "For I will be merciful to their unrighteousness, and their sins and iniquities will I remember no more."—Verse 12. (3.) Sanctification. "I will put my laws into their mind, and write them in their heart."—Verse 10. There are also other promises of sanctification which belong to this covenant. "Then will I sprinkle clean water upon you, and ye shall be clean; a new heart also will I give you, and a new spirit will I put within you: and I will take away the stony heart out of your flesh, and I will give you an heart of flesh ; and I will put my Spirit within you, and cause you to walk in my statutes; and ye shall keep my judgments, and do them."—Ezek. xxxvi. 25–27.

Q. 12. What is the condition of the covenant of grace ?

A. The condition of the covenant of grace, whereby the elect have an actual interest in the things promised, is faith; by which they have an interest in Christ. "Whosoever believeth in him shall not perish, but have everlasting life."—John iii. 16. "Believe on the Lord Jesus Christ, and thou shalt be saved."—Acts xvi. 31.

Q. 13. Why is the covenant with the elect called the covenant of grace?

A. Because not only the things promised to the elect are grace, or the free gifts of God, which they do not in the least deserve; but also because faith (the condition of this covenant, whereby the promises are made theirs) is God's gift and work, wrought in them by his Spirit, which in his covenant he promiseth unto them. "By grace are ye saved, through faith; and that not of yourselves: it is the gift of God."—Eph. ii. 8. "You are risen through the faith of the operation of God."—Col. ii. 12.

Q. 14. Was the covenant which God made with the children of Israel of old a covenant of works, or a covenant of grace ?

A. The covenant which God made of old with the children of Israel was not a covenant of works, but the same covenant of grace, as to the substance of it, which is made known in the gospel. For—1. It was impossible that any of the fallen children of Adam should be justified and saved by the covenant of works. "By the works of the law shall no flesh be justified."—Gal. ii. 16. 2. The children of Israel had the same Mediator of the covenant, and Redeemer, which the people of God have now, namely, the Lord Jesus Christ, who was typified by Moses, and by the sacrifices under the law. 3. They had the same promises of remission and salvation. 4. They had the same condition of faith required to enable them to look to and lay hold on Christ, held forth to them in types and figures.

Q. 15. Wherein doth the dispensation of the covenant

of grace under the gospel differ from the dispensation of it under the law?

A. The dispensation of the covenant of grace under the gospel doth differ from the dispensation of it under the law—1. In regard of the easiness of the covenant under the gospel. Under the law it was burdensome; and ceremonial rites and services required are called a "yoke of bondage" (Gal. v. 1); which yoke is now removed. 2. In regard of the clearness of the dispensation under the gospel. Under the law, Christ was not yet come, but was held forth in types, and figures, and dark shadows—and the promises, especially of eternal life, were more obscure; but now the shadows are fled, Christ the substance being come, and life and immortality are brought more clearly to light by the gospel.—2 Tim. i. 10. 3. In regard of the power and efficacy. There was a weakness in the legal dispensation, and therefore a disannulling of it.—Heb. vii. 18. Under the gospel there is a more powerful influence of the Spirit, which is promised more plentifully.—Acts ii. 17. 4. In regard of the extent of it. The legal dispensation was confined to the nation of the Jews; whereas the gospel dispensation doth extend to the Gentiles, and every nation. " Go ye into all the world, and preach the gospel to every creature."—Mark xvi. 15.

XXI. Ques. *Who is the Redeemer of God's elect?*
*Ans.* The only Redeemer of God's elect is the Lord Jesus Christ, who, being the eternal Son of God, became man, and so was, and continueth to be, God and man in two distinct natures, and one person for ever.

Q. 1. What is he called that is the Redeemer of God's elect?.

A. The Redeemer of God's elect is called the Lord Jesus Christ.

Q. 2. Why is he called the Lord.

A. Because of his univeral sovereignty and dominion. " He is Lord of all."—Acts x. 36.

Q. 3. Why is he called Jesus?

A. Because he is the Saviour of his people. " Thou

shalt call his name Jesus; for he shall save his people from their sins."—Matt. i. 21.

Q. 4. Why is he called Christ?

A. Because he is anointed by the Father unto his office with the Holy Ghost, which was given to him without measure. "God anointed Jesus of Nazareth with the Holy Ghost, and with power."—Acts x. 38. "God giveth not the Spirit by measure unto him."—John iii. 34.

Q. 5. How doth the Lord Jesus Christ redeem the elect of God."

A. The Lord Jesus Christ doth redeem the elect of God—1. By purchase, paying the price of his blood for them. "Ye were not redeemed with corruptible things, as silver and gold, but with the precious blood of Christ, as of a lamb without blemish and without spot."—1 Pet. i. 18, 19. "Who gave himself a ransom."—1 Tim. ii. 6. 2. By conquest, rescuing them, through his almighty power, out of the snare of the devil, who before led them captive. "He led captivity captive."—Eph. iv. 3. "And having spoiled principalities and powers, he made a show of them openly, triumphing over them."—Col. ii. 15.

Q. 6. Whose Son is the Lord Jesus Christ?

A. The Lord Jesus Christ is the eternal Son of God.

Q. 7. How doth the Lord Jesus Christ differ from other sons of God?

A. 1. Angels are called the sons of God; but they are sons of God by creation. "All the sons of God shouted for joy."—Job xxxviii. 7. 2. Saints are called the sons of God, by adoption and regeneration. "That we might receive the adoption of sons."—Gal. iv. 5. "Every one that loveth is born of God."—1 John iv. 7. 3. The Lord Jesus Christ is the natural Son of God by eternal generation. "Unto which of the angels said he at any time, Thou art my Son, this day have I begotten thee?"—Heb. i. 5.

Q. 8. What did Christ, the eternal Son of God, become, that he might redeem the elect?

A. Christ, that he might redeem the elect, being the eternal Son of God, became man. "And the Word was made flesh, and dwelt among us (and we beheld his glory, the glory as of the only begotten of the Father), full of grace and truth."—John i. 14. "When the fulness of time was come, God sent forth his Son made of a woman," &c.—Gal. iv. 4.

Q. 9. How was it necessary in order to the redemption of the elect, that Christ should become man?

A. It was necessary, in order to the redemption of the elect, that Christ should become man—(1.) That he might be capable of suffering death for them, which, as God, he was incapable of: without which suffering of death there could have been no remission or salvation. "Without shedding of blood there is no remission."—Heb. ix. 22. (2.) That he might be their high priest to reconcile them unto God. "For verily he took not on him the nature of angels, but the seed of Abraham; wherefore in all things it behoved him to be made like unto his brethren, that he might be a merciful and faithful high priest in things pertaining to God, to make reconciliation for the sins of the people."—Heb. ii. 16, 17.

Q. 10. Was it necessary that the Redeemer of the elect should be God as well as man?

A. Yes; because if he had not been God as well as man, —1. He could not have borne up under, nor have got loose from, the weight of wrath which was laid upon him for the sins of men. 2. His sufferings would have been of finite extent, and so could not have made satisfaction to God's infinite justice, which was offended by sin.

Q. 11. How is Christ God and man?

A. Christ is God and man by an hypostatical or personal union, both his natures, divine and human, remaining distinct without composition or confusion, in one and the same person.

Q. 12. Will this union of the divine and human natures in Christ ever be dissolved?

A. No; for he was, and continueth to be, God and man in two distinct natures, and one person for ever. "Because he continueth for ever, he hath an unchangeable priesthood."—Heb. vii. 24.

Q. 13. May the properties of the divine nature be ascribed to the human nature, or the properties of the human nature be ascribed to the divine nature of Christ?

A. Though it be improper to ascribe the properties of the one nature to the other nature, yet, by virtue of this near union of both natures in one person, there is a communication of the properties of each nature to the person of Christ.

**XXII. Ques.** *How did Christ, being the Son of God, become man?*

*Ans.* Christ, the Son of God, became man, by taking to himself a true body and a reasonable soul, being conceived by the power of the Holy Ghost, in the womb of the Virgin Mary, and born of her, yet without sin.

Q. 1. Was it a voluntary act in Christ, the Son of God, to become man?

A. Yes; because he took on him the human nature, that he might be thereby fitted to be our Redeemer. " In burnt-offerings and sacrifices for sin, thou hast no pleasure. Then said I, Lo, I come."—Heb. x. 6, 7. " He took on him the seed of Abraham."—Heb. iii. 16.

Q. 2. Was Christ, the Son of God, a real man, like unto other men?

A. Christ, the Son of God, was a real man, taking to himself the two essential parts of man. 1. He had a real body of flesh, and blood, and bones; not a phantastical body, which is a body only in appearance. " Behold my hands and my feet: handle me, and see; for a spirit hath not flesh and bones, as ye see me have."—Luke xxiv. 39. 2. He had a real rational soul, and his divine nature did not supply the place of the soul. " Thou shalt make his soul an offering for sin."—Isa. liii. 10. " My soul is exceeding sorrowful, even unto death."—Matt. xxvi. 3.

Q. 3. Was the birth of Christ like unto the birth of other men?

A. No; for Christ was born of a virgin, namely, the Virgin Mary. " Behold, a virgin shall conceive, and bear a son."—Isa. vii. 14. "And Joseph took unto him Mary his wife; and knew her not till she had brought forth her first born son; and he called his name Jesus."—Matt. i. 24, 25.

Q. 4. How could Christ be born of a virgin?

A. It was a miraculous conception, by the power of the Holy Ghost, in the womb of the Virgin Mary. "And Mary said to the angel, How shall this be, seeing I know not a man? And the angel said unto her, The Holy Ghost shall come upon thee, and the power of the Highest shall overshadow thee; therefore also that holy thing which shall be born of thee shall be called the Son of God."— Luke i. 34, 35.

Q. 5. Was Christ born in sin like other men?

A. No; for however Christ took upon him the nature of man, and many human infirmities, yet he was perfectly free from sinful infirmities. "We have not a high priest which cannot be touched with the feeling of our infirmities, but was in all points tempted like as we are, yet without sin.—Heb. iv. 15.

XXIII. Ques. *What offices doth Christ execute as our Redeemer?*

*Ans.* Christ, as our Redeemer, executeth the offices of a prophet, of a priest, and of a king, both in his estate of humiliation and exaltation.

Q. 1. What is it to execute an office?

A. To execute an office, is to do or perform what belongeth to the office.

Q. 2. How many offices doth Christ execute as our Redeemer?

A. There are three offices Christ doth execute as our Redeemer—1. The office of a prophet: "Moses truly said unto the fathers, A prophet shall the Lord your God raise up unto you, of your brethren, like unto me; him shall ye hear in all things whatsoever he shall say unto you." —Acts iii. 22. 2. The office of a priest: "Thou art a priest for ever, after the order of Melchizedek."—Heb. v. 6. 3. The office of a king: "Yet have I set my King upon my holy hill of Zion."—Ps. ii. 6.

Q. 3. In what estate doth Christ execute these offices?

A. 1. Christ doth execute these offices in his estate of

humiliation here on earth.  2. Christ doth execute these offices in his estate of exaltation now in heaven.

**XXIV.** Ques. *How doth Christ execute the office of a prophet?*

*Ans.* Christ executeth the office of a prophet, in revealing to us, by his word and Spirit, the will of God for our salvation.

Q. 1. What doth Christ reveal to us as a prophet?

A. Christ, as a prophet, doth reveal unto us the will of God for our salvation.

Q. 2. What is meant by the will of God which Christ doth reveal?

A. By the will of God which Christ doth reveal, is meant the whole counsel of God, or whatever God would have us to know, believe, and do, in order to salvation.

Q. 3. Whereby doth Christ reveal unto us the will of God for our salvation?

A. Christ doth reveal unto us the will of God for our salvation—1. By his word: "These things are written that ye might believe that Jesus is the Christ, the Son of God; and that, believing, ye might have life through his name." —John xx. 31.  2. By his Spirit: "But the Comforter, which is the Holy Ghost, whom the Father will send in my name, he shall teach you all things."—John xiv. 26.

Q. 4. Which is the word of Christ, whereby he doth reveal to us the will of God?

A. The whole book of the Scriptures of the Old, and especially of the New Testament, is the word of Christ. "Let the word of Christ dwell in you richly."—Col. iii. 16.

Q. 5. How are the whole Scriptures the word of Christ, when but a small part of them was spoken by his own mouth?

A. The whole Scriptures are the word of Christ, forasmuch as the prophets and apostles, and other penmen of the Scriptures wrote not their own word, but the word which they had from the Spirit of Christ.  "Of which salvation the prophets have inquired, searching what or what manner of time the Spirit of Christ, which was in them, did signify, when it testified beforehand the sufferings of Christ," &c.—1 Pet. i. 10, 11.

Q. 6. Is the word of Christ, without his Spirit, sufficient to teach us the will of God for our salvation?

A. The word, without the Spirit of Christ, is insufficient to teach us the will of God for our salvation, because it is by the Spirit of Christ only that we are enabled to discern and receive the things which are necessary to salvation. "The natural man receiveth not the things of the Spirit of God, for they are foolishness unto him; neither can he know them, because they are spiritually discerned."—1 Cor. ii. 14.

Q. 7. Is the Spirit of Christ without his word, sufficient to teach us the will of God for our salvation?

A. Christ, by his Spirit without his word, could teach us the will of God; but he doth not, neither hath promised now to do it, since the whole will of God necessary to our salvation is revealed in his word: the word of Christ without his Spirit cannot, the Spirit of Christ without his word will not, teach us the will of God for our salvation.

XXV. Ques. *How doth Christ execute the office of a priest?*

*Ans.* Christ executeth the office of a priest, in his once offering up of himself a sacrifice to satisfy divine justice, and reconcile us to God, and in making continual intercession for us.

Q. 1. What is the first part of Christ's priestly office?

A. The first part of Christ's priestly office is, his offering up sacrifice to God for us. "Every high priest is ordained to offer gifts and sacrifices, wherefore it is of necessity that this man have somewhat to offer."—Heb. viii. 3.

Q. 2. What is a sacrifice?

A. A sacrifice is a holy offering rendered to God by a priest of God's appointment.

Q. 3. Was Christ a priest of God's appointment?

A. Yes; for he was called and anointed by God to this office. "No man taketh this honour unto himself, but he that is called of God, as was Aaron: so also Christ glorified not himself to be made an high priest, but he that said, Thou art a priest for ever, after the order of Melchizedek."—Heb. v. 4–6.

Q. 4. What sacrifice did Christ offer to God for us?

A. Christ did offer unto God for us the sacrifice of himself. " But now once in the end of the world hath he appeared to put away sin by the sacrifice of himself."—Heb. ix. 26.

Q. 5. Did Christ offer the sacrifice of himself often?

A. No; but he offered the sacrifice of himself once only, this being sufficient for our sins. " Christ was once offered to bear the sins of many."—Heb. ix. 28.

Q. 6. Wherefore was it that Christ did offer the sacrifice of himself unto God for us?

A. Christ did offer the sacrifice of himself unto God for us—1. That hereby he might satisfy God's justice for us. 2. And that hereby he might reconcile us unto God.

Q. 7. How doth it appear that Christ did satisfy God's justice by the sacrifice of himself?

A. 1. Because Christ's sacrifice of himself was of sufficient worth to satisfy God's justice, infinitely offended by our sins, being the sacrifice of him who, as God, was of infinite dignity. 2. Because this sacrifice of Christ was accepted by God in behalf of sinners. " Christ hath loved us, and hath given himself for us, an offering and sacrifice to God for a sweet-smelling savour."—Eph. v. 2. 3. It doth further appear, because Christ in his death, who was our sacrifice, did bear our sins, or the punishment due for our sins; and wherefore did he bear them, but for the satisfaction of God's justice? " Who his own self bare our sins in his own body on the tree."—1 Pet. ii. 24. And he is said to give his life a ransom for many (Matt. xx. 28); which ransom was God's satisfaction.

Q. 8. What is the consequent of the satisfaction Christ hath given to God by the sacrifice of himself?

A. The consequent of Christ's satisfaction by this sacrifice is, our reconciliation unto God. " That he might reconcile both unto God in one body by the cross."—Eph. ii. 16.

Q. 9. What is the second part of Christ's priestly office?

A. The second part of Christ's priestly office is, his making intercession for us. " He bare the sins of many, and made intercession for the transgressors."—Isa. liii. 2.

Q. 10. What doth Christ do for us in his intercession?

A. Christ, in his intercession, doth pray unto and plead with God, as our advocate, that through the merit of his death we might be actually reconciled, our persons accepted, our sins pardoned, our consciences quieted, our prayers answered, and at last our souls saved. " If any man sin, we have an advocate with the Father, Jesus Christ the righteous."—1 John ii. 1. " If ye shall ask any thing in my name, I will do it."—John xiv. 14.

Q. 11. Where doth Christ make intercession for us?

A. Christ doth make intercession for us at the right hand of God in heaven. "It is Christ that died, yea, rather that is risen again, who is even at the right hand of God, who also maketh intercession for us."—Rom. viii. 34.

Q. 12. Doth Christ make intercession for us only for a time?

A. Christ maketh intercession for us continually and for ever. " He is able to save them to the uttermost that come unto God by him, seeing he ever liveth to make intercession for them."—Heb. vii. 25.

Q. 13. Wherein doth Christ's priestly office differ from the priestly office under the ceremonial law ?

A. 1. The priests under the law were priests after the order of Aaron; but Christ is a priest after the order of Melchizedek, without father as man, without mother as God, &c. Heb. vii. 1–20. 2. The priests under the law were sinful; but Christ is holy, and perfectly free from sin. " Such an high priest became us, who is holy, harmless, undefiled, separate from sinners."—Heb. vii. 26. 3. The priests under the law were many, because mortal; but Christ is the one only high priest of his order, and abideth continually. " They truly were many priests, because they were not suffered to continue by reason of death; but this man continueth ever."—Heb. vii. 23, 24. 4. The priests under the law were consecrated and settled in their office without an oath; but Christ with an oath. "For those priests were made without an oath; but this with an oath, by him that said unto him, The Lord sware, and will not repent, Thou art a priest for ever," &c.—Heb. vii. 21. 5. The priesthood under the law was changeable ; but Christ's priesthood is unchangeable. " For the priesthood being changed, there is made of necessity a change also of the law; but this man hath an unchangeable priesthood."—Heb. vii. 12, 24.   6. The priests under the law offered up many sacrifices, and those of bulls and goats, and the blood of others; but Christ offered up but once one sacrifice, and that the sacrifice of himself, and his own blood.  " Nor yet that he should offer himself often, as the high priest entereth into the holy place every year with the blood of others."—Heb. ix. 25.   "He offered one sacrifice for sins for ever."—Heb. x. 12.   7. The priests under the law offered sacrifice for themselves, for their own sins as well as for the sins of the people; but Christ offered sacrifice only for others, being himself without sin. " Who needeth not daily, as those high priests, to offer up sacrifice, first for his own sins, and then for the people's." —Heb. vii. 27.   8. The sacrifices which the priests under the law did offer were types of Christ's sacrifice, not being sufficient in themselves to take away sin, nor accepted by God any further than Christ was eyed in them; but Christ's sacrifice of himself was the thing typified, and is efficacious in itself for remission, and for itself is accepted. " The law having a shadow of good things to come, can never with those sacrifices make the comers thereunto perfect.  For it is not possible that the blood of bulls and goats should take away sins.  Christ, by one offering, hath perfected for ever them that are sanctified." —Heb. x. 1, 4, 14.   9. The priests under the law appeared in the behalf of the people before God in the temple, the holy place made with hands; but Christ appeareth before God in heaven for us.  "Christ is not entered into the holy places made with hands, which are the figures of the true; but into heaven itself, now to appear in the presence of God for us."—Heb. ix. 14.   10. The priests under the law had only the office of priesthood; but Christ is priest, prophet, and king.

XXVI. Ques. *How doth Christ execute the office of a king?*

*Ans.* Christ executeth the office of a king, in subduing us to himself, in ruling and defending us, and in restraining and conquering all his and our enemies.

Q. 1. Over whom doth Christ exercise his kingly office?

A. Christ doth exercise his kingly office—1. Over his elect people. " Thou art the Son of God, thou art the King of Israel."—John i. 49. 2. Over his and their enemies. " Rule thou in the midst of thine enemies"— Ps. cx. 2.

Q. 2. How doth Christ exercise his kingly office over his elect people?

A. Christ doth exercise his kingly office over his elect people—1. In his subduing them to himself. 2. In his ruling them. 3. In his defending them.

Q. 3. What doth Christ's subduing his elect people to himself suppose?

A. Christ's subduing his elect people to himself doth suppose that at first they are stubborn and disobedient, rebellious, and enemies unto him. "For we ourselves were sometimes foolish, disobedient, serving divers lusts."— Tit. iii. 3. " You were sometimes alienated, and enemies in your mind by wicked works."—Col. i. 21.

Q. 4. What doth Christ's subduing his elect people to himself imply?

A. Christ's subduing his elect people to himself doth imply his effectual calling of them, and bringing them under his government, wherein, by his word and Spirit, he doth conquer their stubbornness and enmity, and make them a willing people to himself. " Thy people shall be willing in the day of thy power."—Ps. cx. 3.

Q. 5. How doth Christ rule his people?

A. Christ doth rule his people—1. By giving them laws, unto which they are to conform their hearts and lives. "The Lord is our lawgiver, the Lord is our king."—Isa. xxxiii. 22. 2. By annexing or adding to his laws threatenings of punishing the disobedient, and promises of rewarding the obedient. "I will kill her children with death; and all the Churches shall know that I am he which searcheth the reins and hearts; and I will give to every one of you according to your works."—Rev. ii. 23. 3. By appointing Church officers, not only for declaring and publishing his laws, but also for the execution of some threatenings, who, having the key of discipline as well as the key of doctrine committed to them, are to rule under him in the Church, and have power of binding and loosing, of administering Church censures, and relaxing or taking them off. "And I will give unto thee the keys of the kingdom of heaven; and whatsoever thou shalt bind on earth shall be bound in heaven, and whatsoever thou shalt loose on earth shall be loosed in heaven."—Matt. xvi. 19. 4. And chiefly, Christ doth rule his people inwardly by his Spirit, whereby he doth write his laws in their hearts, working in them a disposition and strength to yield to him that obedience which he requireth. "I will put my laws into their mind, and write them in their hearts."—Heb. viii. 10. "Ye are the epistle of Christ, written not with ink, but with the Spirit of the living God; not in tables of stone, but in fleshy tables of the heart."— 2 Cor. iii. 3.

Q. 6. How doth Christ defend his people?

A. Christ doth defend his people—1. By hiding them under his wings. "How often would I have gathered thy children together, even as a hen gathereth her chickens under her wings!"—Matt. xxiii. 37. "He shall cover thee with his feathers, and under his wings shalt thou trust; his truth shall be thy shield and buckler."—Ps. xci. 4. 2. By restraining and conquering all his and our enemies.

Q. 7. Who are the enemies of Christ and his people?

A. The enemies of Christ and his people, are the devil, the flesh, the world, and death.

Q. 8. What is it for Christ to restrain his and his people's enemies?

A. Christ doth restrain his and his people's enemies, when (their power remaining) he doth set bounds and limits to them, over which he doth not suffer them to pass.

Q. 9. What is it for Christ to conquer his and his people's enemies?

A. Christ doth conquer his and his people's enemies, when he taketh away their power in part, that they have not dominion over his people; but then he doth completely conquer them, when he doth bring all enemies under his feet, and utterly abolish and destroy them. "Nay, in all these things we are more than conquerors through him that loved us."—Rom. viii. 37. "For he must reign till he hath put all enemies under his feet."—1 Cor. xv. 25.

**XXVII. Ques.** *Wherein did Christ's humiliation consist?*

*Ans.* Christ's humiliation consisted in his being born, and that in a low condition, made under the law, undergoing the miseries of this life, the wrath of God, and the cursed death of the cross; in being buried, and continuing under the power of death for a time.

Q. 1. In what things did Christ humble himself?

A. Christ did humble himself—1. In his birth. 2. In his life. 3. In his death.

Q. 2. How did Christ humble himself in his birth?

A. Christ humbled himself in his birth, in that he, being the eternal Son of God, in time became man, and was born, not of a great princess, but of a mean virgin; not in a stately palace, but in the stable of an inn; and instead of a cradle, was laid in a manger. "He hath regarded the low estate of his hand-maiden."—Luke i. 48. "And she brought forth her first-born son, and wrapped him in swaddling clothes, and laid him in a manger, because there was no room for him in the inn."—Luke ii. 7.

Q. 3. How did Christ humble himself in his life?

A. Christ did humble himself in his life, in that—1. He subjected himself to the law. "God sent forth his Son, made of a woman, made under the law."—Gal. iv. 4. 2. He conflicted with the temptation of the devil. "Then was Jesus led up of the spirit into the wilderness, to be tempted of the devil."—Matt. iv. 1. 3. He endured the contradictions, reproaches, and indignities of wicked men. "Consider him who endured such contradiction of sinners against himself."—Heb. xii. 3. "If they have called the Master of the house Beelzebub, how much more them of his household?"—Matt. x. 25. 4. He underwent the sinless infirmities of the flesh, such as weariness, hunger, thirst, and the like, in regard to his body; and grief and sorrow in regard to his soul. "Jesus being wearied with his journey, sat on the well."—John iv. 6. "When he had fasted forty days and forty nights, he was afterwards an hungered."—Matt. iv. 2. "He is a man of sorrows, and acquainted with grief."—Isa. liii. 3.

Q. 4. How did Christ humble himself in his death?

A. Christ humbled himself in his death—1. In regard of the antecedents of it. 2. In regard of his death itself. 3. In regard of the consequences of it.

Q. 5. How did Christ humble himself in regard of the antecedents of his death?

A. Christ humbled himself in regard of the antecedents of his death—1. In permitting Judas to betray him. 2. In submitting himself to the officers to take him. 3. In hearing Peter deny him. 4. In suffering the people to mock him, spit on him, buffet him, and Pilate to scourge and condemn him; with many affronts and indignities which were offered to him.—Matt. xxvi., xxvii.

Q. 6. How did Christ humble himself in regard of his death itself?

A. Christ humbled himself in regard of his death itself, in that—1. The kind of his death was an accursed and disgraceful death, as also a lingering and painful death, being the death of the cross. "He humbled himself, and became obedient unto death, even the death of the cross." Phil. ii. 8. "Christ was made a curse for us; as it is written, Cursed is every one that hangeth on a tree."—Gal. iii. 13. 2. He, together with the pain of his body on the cross, endured the wrath of God due for man's sin in his soul. "About the ninth hour, Jesus cried with a loud voice, My God, my God, why hast thou forsaken me?"—Matt. xxvii. 46.

Q. 7. How did Christ humble himself in regard of the consequents of his death?

A. Christ humbled himself in regard of the consequents of his death, in that—1. He was buried. "And when Joseph had taken the body, he wrapped it in a clean linen cloth, and laid it in his own new tomb."—Matt. xxvii. 59, 60. 2. He continued under the power of death for a time, namely, until the third day. "As Jonah was three days and three nights in the whale's belly, so shall the Son of man be three days and three nights in the heart of the earth."—Matt. xii. 40.

Q. 8. What doth Christ's humiliation assure us of?

A. Christ's humiliation doth assure us of our redemption, through the merits of his sufferings. "In whom we have redemption through his blood, even the forgiveness of sins."—Eph. i. 7.

Q. 9. What doth Christ's humiliation, especially his death, teach us?

A. Christ's humbling himself unto death doth teach us —1. To humble ourselves and be lowly, like unto our Master. "Learn of me, for I am meek and lowly in heart."—Matt. xi. 29. 2. That as Christ died for our sins, so we should die to sin, and not be unwilling to suffer and to die for his sake, if called thereunto. "If we be dead with Christ, we shall also live with him. Reckon yourselves to be dead indeed unto sin."—Rom. vi. 8, 11. "Forasmuch as Christ hath suffered for us, arm yourselves likewise with the same mind."—1 Pet. iv. 1.

## XXVIII. Quest. *Wherein consisteth Christ's exaltation?*

*Ans.* Christ's exaltation consisteth in his rising again from the dead on the third day, in ascending up to heaven, in sitting at the right hand of God the Father, and in coming to judge the world at the last day.

Q. 1. What is the first part of Christ's exaltation?

A. The first part of Christ's exaltation is his resurrection from the dead.

Q. 2. How do you prove that Christ rose again from the dead?

A. 1. By the many witnesses who saw him, and conversed with him after his resurrection. "He was seen of Cephas, then of the twelve; after that, he was seen of above five hundred brethren at once."—1 Cor. xv. 5, 6. 2. Because otherwise our faith would be in vain, the guilt of sin would still remain upon us, and there would be no hope for us. "If Christ be not raised, your faith is vain; ye are yet in your sins."—1 Cor. xv. 17.

Q. 3. By whom was Christ raised from the dead?

A. Christ was raised from the dead by his own power and Spirit, whereby he was declared to be the Son of God. " I lay down my life, that I might take it again. I have power to lay it down, and I have power to take it again." —John x. 17, 18. " Declared to be the Son of God with power, according to the Spirit of holiness, by the resurrection from the dead."—Rom. i. 4.

Q. 4. How soon did Christ rise after his death?

A. Christ rose again from the dead on the third day. " He was buried, and rose again the third day, according to the Scriptures."—1 Cor. xv. 4.

Q. 5. Did Christ rise again with the same body which was buried?

A. Christ did rise again with the same body, for he bore the print of the nails in his hands and his feet, and of the spear in his side. " Reach hither thy finger, and behold my hands; and reach hither thy hand, and thrust it into my side."—John xx. 27.

Q. 6. Was not Christ's body corrupted in the grave, like the bodies of others?

A. No; for God did not suffer him to see corruption. " He whom God raised again saw no corruption."—Acts xiii. 37.

Q. 7. Was not Christ's body mortal after his resurrection?

A. No; for then his body did put on immortality. "Christ, being raised from the dead, dieth no more; death hath no more dominion over him."—Rom. vi. 9.

Q. 8. What doth the resurrection of Christ teach us?

A. The resurrection of Christ doth teach us to walk in newness of life. " Like as Christ was raised up from the dead by the glory of his Father, even so we also should walk in newness of life."—Rom. vi. 4.

Q. 9. What doth the resurrection of Christ assure us of?

A. The resurrection of Christ doth assure us, that our bodies shall be raised again from the dead on the last day. " Now is Christ raised from the dead, and become the first fruits of them that slept."—1 Cor. xv. 20.

Q. 10. What is the second part of Christ's exaltation?

A. The second part of Christ's exaltation is his ascension into heaven.

Q. 11. How do you prove that Christ ascended into heaven?

A. By the Scripture record of the witnesses who saw him. "And he led them out as far as Bethany; and he lifted up his hands, and blessed them. And while he blessed them, he was parted from them, and carried up into heaven."—Luke xxiv. 50, 51.

Q. 12. How long after Christ's resurrection was his ascension?

A. Christ's ascension was forty days after his resurrection. "Until the day in which he was taken up, after he had given commandments unto the apostles whom he had chosen; to whom he showed himself alive after his passion, by many infallible proofs, being seen of them forty days."—Acts i. 2, 3.

Q. 13. Wherefore did Christ ascend into heaven?

A. Christ ascended into heaven—1. That his person (God-man) might be glorified there with that glory which (as God) he had with the Father before the world. "And now, O Father, glorify thou me with thine own self, with the glory which I had with thee before the world was."—John xvii. 5. 2. That he might (as Head of the Church) take possession of heaven for all his members. "Whither the forerunner is for us entered."—Heb. vi. 20.

Q. 14. What doth Christ's ascension into heaven teach us?

A. Christ's ascension into heaven doth teach us to set our affections on things above, where Christ is. "Set your affections on things above, not on things on the earth."—Col. iii. 2.

Q. 15. What is the third part of Christ's exaltation?

A. The third part of Christ's exaltation, is his sitting at the right hand of God the Father.

Q. 16. What is meant by Christ's sitting at the right hand of God?

A. By Christ's sitting at the right hand of God is meant, his being exalted unto the highest honour, and power, and favour in heaven.

Q. 17. What doth Christ do for his people which are on the earth, at the right hand of God in heaven?

A. Christ, at the right hand of God in heaven—1. Doth make continual intercession for his people. "Who is even at the right hand of God, who also maketh intercession for us."—Rom. viii. 34. 2. He is preparing a place in heaven for them. "In my Father's house are many mansions: I go to prepare a place for you."—John xiv. 2.

Q. 18. What is the fourth part of Christ's exaltation?

A. The fourth part of Christ's exaltation, is his coming to judge the world. "When the Son of man shall come in his glory, and all the holy angels with him, then shall he sit upon the throne of his glory; and before him shall be gathered all nations," &c.—Matt. xxv. 31, 32, &c.

Q. 19. When is it that Christ will come to judge the world?

A. Christ will come to judge the world at the last day; then the world shall be at an end, and all things shall be dissolved. "But the day of the Lord will come, in the which the heavens shall pass away with a great noise, and the elements shall melt with fervent heat; the earth also, and the works that are therein, shall be burnt up."—2 Pet. iii. 10.

Q. 20. In what glory will Christ come to judge the world at the last day?

A. Christ will come to judge the world with his own glory, and his Father's, and the holy angels'. "He shall come in his own glory, and in his Father's, and of the holy angels."—Luke ix. 26.

Q. 21. How will Christ judge the world at this his glorious appearance?

A. Christ will judge the world at his glorious appearance, in righteousness, rendering to every one according to his deserts. "He hath appointed a day, in the which he will judge the world in righteousness."—Acts xvii. 35. "We must all appear before the judgment-seat of Christ, that every one may receive the things done in his body, according to that he hath done, whether it be good or bad."—2 Cor. v. 10.

**XXIX.** Ques. *How are we made partakers of the redemption purchased by Christ?*

*Ans.* We are made partakers of the redemption purchased by Christ, by the effectual application of it to us by his Holy Spirit.

Q. 1. By whom was our redemption purchased?

A. Our redemption was purchased for us by the blood of Christ. " By his own blood he entered in once into the holy place, having obtained eternal redemption for us." —Heb. ix. 12.

Q. 2. By whom is our redemption applied?

A. Our redemption is applied by the Holy Spirit, in his effectual operation upon us. " Not by works of righteousness which we have done, but according to his mercy he saved us, by the washing of regeneration, and renewing of the Holy Ghost; which he shed on us abundantly, through Jesus Christ our Saviour."—Tit. iii. 5, 6.

**XXX.** Ques. *How doth the Spirit apply to us the redemption purchased by Christ?*

*Ans.* The Spirit applieth to us the redemption purchased by Christ, by working faith in us, and thereby uniting us to Christ in our effectual calling.

Q. 1. Whence is it that the redemption purchased by Christ is applied to us, or that we have an interest therein?

A. We have an interest in the redemption purchased by Christ, through our union to him in our effectual calling. " Of him are ye in Christ Jesus, who of God is made unto us wisdom, and righteousness, and sanctification, and redemption."—1 Cor. i. 30. " Whom he called, them he also justified."—Rom. viii. 30.

Q. 2. What is the union between Christ and us?

A. The union between Christ and us is that whereby Christ and we are joined together, and made one. " He that is joined unto the Lord, is one spirit."—1 Cor. vi. 17.

Q. 3. Whence is it that we are united unto Christ?

A. We are united unto Christ—1. By the Spirit on

God's part, whereby he draws us, and joins us unto Christ. " No man can come unto me, except the Father, which hath sent me, draw him."—John vi. 44. 2. By faith on our part, whereby we come unto Christ, and lay hold upon him. " He that cometh unto me shall never hunger, and he that believeth on me shall never thirst."—John vi. 35. " That Christ may dwell in your hearts by faith."—Eph. iii. 17.

Q. 4. Is faith from ourselves, or from God?

A. Though faith be our act, yet it is God's gift, and the work of his Spirit. " By grace are ye saved, through faith; and that not of yourselves; it is the gift of God."—Eph. ii. 8. " Ye are risen with him through the faith of the operation of God."—Col. ii. 12.

## XXXI. Ques. *What is effectual calling?*

*Ans.* Effectual calling is the work of God's Spirit, whereby, convincing us of our sin and misery, enlightening our minds in the knowledge of Christ, and renewing our wills, he doth persuade and enable us to embrace Jesus Christ, freely offered to us in the Gospel.

Q. 1. What is the difference between effectual calling and ineffectual calling?

A. 1. Ineffectual calling is the bare external call of the word, whereby all sinners are freely invited unto Christ, that they may have life and salvation by him, but in itself is insufficient to persuade and enable them to come unto him. " Many be called, but few chosen."—Matt. xx. 16. " Ye will not come unto me, that ye might have life."— John v. 40. 2. Effectual calling is the internal call of the Spirit accompanying the external call of the word, whereby we are not only invited unto Christ, but also enabled and persuaded to embrace him as he is freely offered to us in the gospel. " Every one that hath heard, and hath learned of the Father, cometh unto me."—John vi. 45.

Q. 2. What is the work of the Spirit of God in our effectual calling?

A. The work of the Spirit of God in our effectual calling, is twofold—1. Upon our minds. 2. Upon our wills.

Q. 3. What is the work of the Spirit of God in our effectual calling upon our minds?

A. The work of the Spirit of God in our effectual calling upon our minds is—1. A convincing us of our sin and misery. 2. An enlightening us in the knowledge of Christ.

Q. 4. What is it for the Spirit to convince our mind of our sin and misery?

A. The Spirit worketh in our mind a conviction of our sin and misery, when he giveth us a clear sight and full persuasion of the guilt of our sins, and a feeling apprehension of the dreadful wrath of God, and the endless miseries of hell which we have deserved for sin, and every hour are exposed unto : which doth wound our hearts and consciences and filleth us with perplexing care what to do to be saved. "And when he is come, he will reprove (or convince) the world of sin."—John xvi. 8. "Now when they heard this, they were pricked in their hearts, and said unto Peter and the rest of the apostles, Men and brethren, what shall we do ?"—Acts ii. 37.

Q. 5. Whereby doth the Spirit convince us of our sin and misery?

A. The Spirit convinceth us of our sin and misery by the law, and threatenings thereof. "By the law is the knowledge of sin."—Rom. iii. 20. "Cursed is every one that continueth not in all things which are written in the book of the law to do them."—Gal. iii. 10.

Q. 6. What knowledge of Christ doth the Spirit enlighten our minds withal, after the conviction of our sin and misery?

A. The Spirit doth enlighten our minds, after conviction of our sin and misery, with the knowledge—1. That Christ only can save, and that he is all-sufficient to do it. "Neither is there salvation in any other: for there is none other name under heaven, given among men, whereby we must be saved."—Acts iv. 12. "Wherefore he is able also to save them to the uttermost that come unto God by him."—Heb. vii. 25. 2. That Christ is willing to save all that come unto him. "Him that cometh unto me I will in no wise cast out."—John vi. 37. 3. That Christ hath undertaken to save us, and is faithful to perform it. "That he might be a merciful high priest, in things pertaining to God, to make reconciliation for the sins of the people."—Heb. ii. 17.

Q. 7. Whereby doth the Spirit enlighten us with the knowledge of Christ?

A. The Spirit doth enlighten us with the knowledge of Christ, by the discoveries of Christ in the Gospel, opening our eyes to discern him there discovered. "To whom I send thee, to open their eyes, and to turn them from darkness unto light," &c.—Acts xxvi. 17, 18.

Q. 8. What is the work of the Spirit of God in our effectual calling upon our wills?

A. The work of the Spirit of God in our effectual calling upon our wills, is to renew them.

Q. 9. What is it for our wills to be renewed?

A. Our wills are renewed when the Spirit doth put new inclinations and dispositions into them. "A new heart also will I give you, and a new spirit will I put within you; and I will take away the stony heart out of your flesh, and I will give you an heart of flesh."—Ezek. xxxvi. 26.

Q. 10. Are not we able to renew our own will, and to turn from sin unto Christ ourselves?

A. No; it is the almighty power of the Spirit of God that doth persuade and enable us to embrace Jesus Christ by faith. "And what is the exceeding greatness of his power to us-ward who believe, according to the working of his mighty power, which he wrought in Christ, when he raised him from the dead."—Eph. i. 19, 20.

XXXII. Ques. *What benefits do they that are effectually called partake of in this life?*

*Ans.* They that are effectually called, do in this life partake of justification, adoption, and sanctification, and the several benefits which in this life do either accompany or flow from them.

XXXIII. Ques. *What is justification?*

*Ans.* Justification is an act of God's free grace, wherein he pardoneth all our sins, and accepteth us as righteous in his sight, only for the righteousness of Christ imputed to us, and received by faith alone.

Q. 1. Wherein doth our justification consist?

A. Our justification doth consist in two things. 1. In the pardon of our sins. 2. In the acceptation of us as righteous.

Q. 2. Who is the author of our justification?

A. God is the author of our justification, whose act it is. "Who shall lay anything to the charge of God's elect? It is God that justifieth."—Rom. viii. 33.

Q. 3. Doth God justify us freely, or because of some merit in ourselves.

A. God doth justify us by an act of free grace. "Being justified freely by his grace."—Rom. iii. 24.

Q. 4. Through whose righteousness is it that we are justified?

A. We are justified through the righteousness of Christ. "Being justified freely by his grace, through the redemption which is in Christ."—Rom. iii. 24.

Q. 5. How is the righteousness of Christ made ours?

A. The righteousness of Christ is made ours by imputation. "David also describeth the blessedness of the man unto whom the Lord imputeth righteousness without works."—Rom. iv. 6.

Q. 6. What is it for the righteousness of Christ to be imputed to us?

A. The righteousness of Christ is imputed to us, when, though it be subjectively in Christ, or the righteousness which he wrought, yet by God it is accounted ours, as if we wrought it ourselves in our own persons.

Q. 7. What is that righteousness of Christ which is imputed to us for our justification?

A. The righteousness of Christ, which is imputed to us for our justification, is his whole obedience to the law in our stead, and that both his passive obedience in all his sufferings, especially in his death, whereby we have the pardon of all our sins ("In whom we have redemption through his blood, the forgiveness of sins;"—Eph. i. 7); and his active obedience also, whereby we are accepted as righteous in God's sight: " For as by one man's disobedience many were made sinners; so by the obedience of one shall many be made righteous."—Rom. v. 19.

Q. 8. Whereby do we receive and apply this righteousness of Christ.

A. We receive and apply this righteousness of Christ by faith. " Even the righteousness of God which is by faith of Jesus Christ unto all and upon all them that believe."—Rom. iii. 22.

Q. 9. Are we justified by faith only, and not by works, at least in part?

A. We are justified only by faith, and neither in whole nor in part by works. " Knowing that a man is not justified by the works of the law, but by the faith of Jesus Christ : even we have believed in Jesus Christ, that we might be justified by the faith of Christ."—Gal. ii. 16.

Q. 10. How is it then said, " Ye see, then, how that by works a man is justified, and not by faith only?"—James ii. 24.

A. 1. The apostle Paul doth plainly and positively affirm, and by many arguments prove, justification by faith without works, in his Epistles to the Romans and the Galatians ; and be sure the apostle James, being inspired by the same Spirit in writing his Epistle, doth not really contradict this doctrine. 2. The apostle James doth not in this chapter treat of the justification of our faith in the sight of God, but of the justification of our faith in the sight of men; and thus he doth assert that justification is by works. " I will show thee my faith by my works."—Verse 18. Faith justifieth our persons, but works justify our faith, and declare us to be justified before men, who cannot see nor know our faith but by our works.

Q. 11. How do you prove that we are not justified by works?

A. 1. Because the whole world is guilty of sin, and those that are guilty of sin cannot have a perfect righteousness of works, and those that have not a perfect righteousness cannot be justified in the sight of God. Thus the apostle convicted both Jew and Gentile of sin in the 1st and 2d chapters to the Romans, and this "that every mouth may be stopped, and the whole world may become guilty before God" (chap. iii. 19): and therefore inferreth, " By the deeds of the law no flesh living shall be justified."— Verse 20.   2. Because, if we were justified by works, the reward would be of debt, and not of grace.  "Now to him that worketh is the reward not reckoned of grace, but of debt."—Rom. iv. 4.   But the reward is not of debt, but of grace ; and they that are justified, are not justified as righteous, with a righteousness of works, but as ungodly. " He justifieth the ungodly."—Verse 5.   3. Because Abraham, the father of the faithful, though he had a righteousness of works, yea, works wrought in faith, yet he was not justified by his works ; and if he were justified without his works, so are all others that are justified, justified without works.   " For if Abraham were justified by works, he hath whereof to glory."—Rom. iv. 2.   But Abraham had not whereof to glory before God, therefore he was not justified by works.

Q. 12.  How do you prove that we are justified by faith only ?

A.  1. It is positively asserted and concluded from several arguments by the apostle.  "Therefore we conclude that a man is justified by faith, without the deeds of the law."—Rom. iii. 28.   2. There being such a thing as justification—and justification cannot be by works, as hath been proved—and there being no other way of justification but by faith, it must be by faith.   3. The righteousness of Christ is perfect, and sufficient for our justification; and by faith his righteousness is received and made ours in the account of God: therefore we are justified by faith.   4. Justification by faith doth give God all the glory, and excludeth all boasting in man; therefore it is by faith. " Where is boasting, then ?  It is excluded.  By what law ? By the law of works ?  Nay; but by the law of faith."— Rom. iii. 27.   5. Abraham was justified by faith, and all others are justified the same way.

Q. 13.  How doth faith justify ?

A.  Faith doth not justify as a work in us, but as an instrument which applieth the perfect righteousness of Christ without us, whereby we are justified.

Q. 14. May we be justified by faith in Christ's righteousness without us, although we have no righteousness within us?

A. We are justified only by faith in Christ's righteousness without us, but this justification is always accompanied with sanctification, in which a righteousness is wrought within us, without which our justification cannot be true. By the same faith whereby our persons are justified our hearts also are purified. "Purifying their hearts by faith." —Acts xv. 9.

### XXXIV. Ques. *What is adoption?*

*Ans.* Adoption is an act of God's free grace, whereby we are received into the number, and have a right to all the privileges of the sons of God.

Q. 1. How many ways may we be said to be the children of God?

A. We are the children of God—1. By regeneration. 2. By adoption, whereby we differ, (1.) From Christ, who is God's Son by eternal generation; (2.) From the angels, who are God's sons by creation.

Q. 2. What is it for men to adopt children?

A. Men adopt children, when they take strangers, or such as are none of their own children, into their families, and account them their children; and accordingly do take care for them as if they were their own.

Q. 3. What is it for God to adopt children?

A. God doth adopt children, when he taketh them which are strangers, and by nature children of wrath, into his family, and receiveth them into the number, and giveth them a right to all the privileges of the sons and daughters of God. "And were by nature the children of wrath, even as others. Now, therefore, ye are no more strangers and foreigners, but fellow-citizens with the saints, and of the household of God."—Eph. ii. 3, 19. "And I will be a father unto you, and ye shall be my sons and daughters, saith the Lord Almighty."—2 Cor. vi. 18.

Q. 4. Is there any motive in any of the children of men, to induce God to adopt them, as there is in those that are adopted by men?

A. There is neither beauty, nor any lovely qualification, nor anything in the least, to move and incline God to adopt any whom he doth adopt, but it is an act only of his free grace and love. "Behold, what manner of love the Father hath bestowed upon us, that we should be called the sons of God."—1 John iii. 4.

Q. 5. Are all the children of men the adopted children of God?

A. No; only such persons are adopted as do believe in Christ. "As many as received him, to them gave he power to become the sons of God, even to them that believe on his name."—John i. 12. "For ye are all the children of God by faith in Jesus Christ."—Gal. iii. 26.

Q. 6. What are those privileges which the adopted children of God have a right unto?

A. The privileges which the adopted children of God have a right unto are—1. God's fatherly protection of them from temporal and spiritual evils. "The Lord shall preserve them from all evil."—Ps. cxxi. 7. 2. God's fatherly provision of all needful things, both for their soul and body. "They that seek the Lord shall not want any good thing."—Ps. xxxiv. 10. 3. God's fatherly correction of them. "For whom he loveth he chasteneth, and scourgeth every son whom he receiveth."—Heb. xii. 6. 4. God's audience and return to their prayers. "And this is the confidence which we have in him, that if we ask anything according to his will, he heareth us; and if we know that he heareth us, whatever we ask, we know that we have the petitions we desired of him."—1 John v. 14, 15. 5. A sure title to the inheritance of the kingdom of heaven. "And if children, then heirs; heirs of God, and joint-heirs with Christ."—Rom. viii. 17.

XXXV. Ques. *What is sanctification?*

*Ans.* Sanctification is the work of God's free grace, whereby we are renewed in the whole man, after the image of God, and are enabled more and more to die unto sin, and live unto righteousness.

Q. 1. Wherein doth sanctification differ from justification and adoption ?

A. Sanctification doth differ from justification and adoption, in that—1. Justification and adoption are acts of God without us; sanctification is a work of God within us. 2. Justification and adoption do make only a relative change; sanctification doth make in us a real change. 3. Justification and adoption are perfect at first; sanctification is carried on by degrees unto perfection.

Q. 2. Whose work is the work of sanctification ?

A. 1. Though we be the subjects of sanctification, yet we are not the authors and efficient causes of our sanctification; we can defile ourselves, but we cannot cleanse and renew ourselves. 2. Sanctification is the work of God, which is wrought by his Spirit. " God hath from the beginning chosen you to salvation, through sanctification of the Spirit."—2 Thess. ii. 13.

Q. 3. Is there no desert of the grace of sanctification in any of the children of men before they are sanctified ?

A. No; for all the children of men are by nature wholly polluted with sin, and it is wholly of God's free grace that any of them are sanctified.

Q. 4. Wherein doth our sanctification consist ?

A. Our sanctification doth consist in our renovation after the image of God, in knowledge, righteousness, and holiness. " Put on the new man, which is renewed in knowledge, after the image of him that created him."— Col. iii. 10. " And that ye put on the new man, which after God is created in righteousness and true holiness." —Eph. iv. 24.

Q. 5. What is the subject of our sanctification ?

A. The subject of our sanctification is our whole man, understanding, will, conscience, memory, affections, which are all renewed and changed in regard of their qualifications; and all the members of our body, which are changed in regard of their use, being made instruments of righteousness.

Q. 6. Wherein is our sanctification begun?

A. Our sanctification is begun in our regeneration and effectual calling; wherein our minds are first enlightened, and our wills renewed, and the habits of all graces are infused.

Q. 7. How is our sanctification carried on?

A. Our sanctification is carried on by degrees, as God doth bless his providences, especially his ordinances, through them to communicate further measures of his Spirit and grace.

Q. 8. Wherein is our sanctification perfected?

A. Our sanctification is perfected in our glorification, when we shall be made perfectly free from sin, and fully conformable unto the image of God.

Q. 9. What are the parts of sanctification?

A. There are two parts of sanctification—1. Mortification, whereby we are enabled to die more and more unto sin. "Reckon ye yourselves to be dead indeed unto sin." —Rom. vi. 11. 2. Vivification, whereby we are enabled to live unto righteousness. "Yield yourselves unto God, as those that are alive from the dead, and your members as instruments of righteousness unto God."—Rom. vi. 13.

XXXVI. Ques. *What are the benefits which in this life do accompany or flow from justification, adoption, and sanctification?*

*Ans.* The benefits which in this life do accompany or flow from justification, adoption, and sanctification, are, assurance of God's love, peace of conscience, joy in the Holy Ghost, increase of grace, and perseverance therein to the end.

Q. 1. How many sorts of benefits are there which do belong to those who are justified, adopted, and sanctified?

A. There are three sorts of benefits which do belong unto those who are justified, adopted, and sanctified, namely—1. Benefits in this life. 2. Benefits at death. 3. Benefits at the resurrection.

Q. 2. What are the benefits which belong to justified, adopted, and sanctified persons in this life?

A. The benefits which belong to justified persons in this life are five. 1. Assurance of God's love. 2. Peace of conscience. 3. Joy in the Holy Ghost. 4. Increase of grace. 5. Perseverance in grace to the end. "Being justified by faith, we have peace with God, through our Lord Jesus Christ. By whom also we have access by faith into this grace wherein we stand, and rejoice in the hope of the glory of God. And hope maketh not ashamed, because the love of God is shed abroad in our hearts by the Holy Ghost which is given unto us."—Rom. v. 1, 2, 5. "Being confident of this very thing, that he which hath begun a good work in you, will perform it until the day of Jesus Christ."—Phil. i. 6.

Q. 3. What are the benefits that do accompany and flow from the sight and sense of justification, adoption, and sanctification?

A. The benefits which do accompany and flow from the sight and sense of justification, adoption, and sanctification, are, assurance of God's love, peace of conscience, joy in the Holy Ghost.

Q. 4. May not unjustified and unsanctified persons attain any of these benefits?

A. Unjustified persons may some of them have a presumptuous confidence of God's love, but not real assurance; they may have a carnal security, and false peace, but no true spiritual peace; they may have a carnal joy, or ungrounded spiritual joy, but no sound spiritual and heavenly joy of the Holy Ghost; these benefits are given only unto such as are truly justified, adopted, and sanctified.

Q. 5. Whence is it that all that are justified, adopted, and sanctified, do not attain these benefits?

A. Because all have not a sight and sense of their justification, adoption, and sanctification, but are under doubts, and therefore fear that God doth hate them, and not love them; therefore they have troubles of conscience instead of peace, and sorrow in spirit instead of the joys of the Holy Ghost.

Q. 6. How may a child of God get a sure evidence of his justification and adoption?

A. A child of God may get a sure evidence of his justification and adoption by his sanctification.

Q. 7. What is a sure evidence of sanctification?

A. A sure evidence of sanctification is increase of grace.

Q. 8. What are the benefits which accompany and flow from the being of justification, adoption, and sanctification?

A. The benefits which accompany and flow from the being of justification, adoption, and sanctification, are, increase of grace, and perseverance therein to the end.

Q. 9. Do all truly justified, adopted, and sanctified persons increase in grace?

A. 1. All truly justified, adopted, and sanctified persons do not at all times actually increase in grace, for some of them may at some times be under declining and decays of grace. 2. They are always of a growing disposition, and desirous to grow in grace; and at some time or other they do grow, when they do not perceive themselves to grow, but fear that they do decline.

Q. 10. Do all truly justified, adopted, and sanctified persons persevere in grace to the end?

A. All truly justified, adopted, and sanctified persons do persevere in grace to the end, and shall assuredly attain the heavenly inheritance.

Q. 11. How do you prove this?

A. 1. From God's everlasting, unchangeable love, and his faithfulness in his promises of perseverance, as well as of heaven, which he hath made unto them. 2. From their union and relation to Christ, and his undertaking for them. 3. From the constant abode and indwelling of the Spirit of God in them. 4. From the nature of grace; which is an abiding seed, which can never be totally extirpated.

Q. 12. May not any believer, by falling into sin, fall from grace?

A. Some believers may, through the remainder of corruption in them, and the violence of Satan's tempting of them, fall into sin foully, and so fall from some degrees and measures of grace; but they will never fall totally nor finally from grace. And when we see any fall totally and finally from the profession which they formerly made, we may know they were never in that sincerity which they professed themselves to be. "They went out from

us, but they were not of us; for if they had been of us, no
doubt they would have continued with us; but they went
out, that they might be made manifest that they were not
all of us."—1 John ii. 19.

XXXVII. Ques. *What benefits do believers receive
from Christ at death ?*

*Ans.* The souls of believers are at their death
made perfect in holiness, and do immediately pass
into glory; and their bodies, being still united to
Christ, do rest in their graves till the resurrection.

Q. 1. How manifold are the benefits of believers at their
death?

A. The benefits of believers at their death are twofold
—1. In regard of their souls.   2. In regard of their bodies.

Q. 2. What is the benefit of believers at their death, in
regard of their souls?

A. The souls of believers at their death—1. Are made
perfect in holiness.   "And to the spirits of just men made
perfect."—Heb. xii. 23.   2. They do immediately pass
into glory.   "Having a desire to depart, and to be with
Christ."—Phil. i. 23.

Q. 3. Wherein doth consist the perfect holiness which
the souls of believers shall have at their death?

A. The perfect holiness of believers' souls at their death
doth consist—1. In their perfect freedom from the stain
and pollution, from the being, or any inclination unto sin.
"There shall in no wise enter into it any thing that defileth."—Rev. xxi. 27.   2. In their perfect rectitude of soul,
and full conformity unto the image of Christ.   "Till we
all come in the unity of the faith, and of the knowledge of
the Son of God, unto a perfect man, unto the measure of
the stature of the fulness of Christ."—Eph. iv. 13.

Q. 4. What is that glory which the souls of believers, at
death, do immediately pass into?

A. The souls of believers at death do immediately pass
into—1. A glorious place.   2. A glorious company.   3. A
glorious state.

Q. 5. What is that glorious place which the souls of believers, at death, do immediately pass into?

A. The glorious place which believers' souls do immediately pass into, is their Father's house in heaven, where there are mansions prepared for them by Christ. " In my Father's house are many mansions; if it were not so, I would have told you. I go to prepare a place for you."—John xiv. 2.

Q. 6. What is the glorious company which the souls of believers do immediately pass into?

A. The glorious company which the souls of believers do immediately pass into, is the company of God, and Christ in his glory, as also the company of angels, and the souls of other saints in their glory. " Therefore we are always confident, knowing that whilst we are at home in the body, we are absent from the Lord (for we walk by faith, not by sight). We are confident, I say, and willing rather to be absent from the body, and to be present with the Lord."—2 Cor. v. 6–8. " Ye are come to the heavenly Jerusalem, to an innumerable company of angels, to the general assembly, and to God the Judge of all, and to the spirits of just men made perfect, and to Jesus the Mediator of the new covenant."—Heb. xii. 22–24.

Q. 7. What is that glorious state which the souls of believers at death do immediately pass into?

A. The glorious state of the souls of believers immediately after their death, is a state of blessed rest. " There remaineth therefore a rest to the people of God."—Heb. iv. 9. " And I heard a voice from heaven, saying, Blessed are the dead that die in the Lord, from henceforth : Yea, saith the Spirit, that they may rest from their labours; and their works do follow them."—Rev. xiv. 13.

Q. 8. What is the benefit of believers at their death, in regard of their bodies?

A. 1. The bodies of believers at their death are still united unto Christ; for though death doth for a while separate their souls from their bodies, yet death cannot separate Christ from either. But as, when Christ died, his hypostatical or personal union still remained, his divine nature being united both to his soul in heaven and to his body in the tomb on earth, so, when believers die, their mystical union unto Christ still remaineth, and Christ is united both unto their souls with him in glory, and to their bodies, which are his members, even when they are rotting in the grave. " Know ye not that your bodies are the members of Christ ?"—1 Cor. vi. 15. " Them also which sleep in Jesus will God bring with him."—1 Thess. iv. 14. 2. The bodies of believers do rest in their graves as in beds, until the resurrection. " He shall enter into peace; they shall rest in their beds, each one walking in his uprightness."—Isa. lvii. 2.

Q. 9. What is that resurrection here spoken of ?

A. The resurrection here spoken of is the last and general resurrection of all the dead that have lived in all ages, from the beginning of the creation—which will be, first of the righteous, and then of the wicked—at the last day. " The hour is coming, in the which all that are in the graves shall hear his voice, and shall come forth, they that have done good unto the resurrection of life, and they that have done evil unto the resurrection of damnation."—John v. 28, 29. " The dead in Christ shall rise first."—1 Thess. vi. 16.

Q. 10. How do you prove that there shall be such a general resurrection ?

A. It may be undeniably proved from the power of God, and the revelation of the Word. If God be of infinite power, and therefore can raise all the dead, and infinitely true, and in his Word hath revealed that he will raise all the dead, then there shall be a general resurrection. But God is infinitely powerful, and can raise all the dead, and infinitely true, and in his Word hath revealed that he will raise all the dead; therefore there shall be a general resurrection. The ground of the Sadducees' error, who denied the resurrection, was their ignorance of these two great foundations of this doctrine, namely, the power of God, and the Scriptures. " Do ye not therefore err, because ye know not the Scriptures, neither the power of God ?"—Mark xii. 24.

Q. 11. Shall the dead be raised with the same bodies which they had when alive before ?

A. The dead shall be raised with the same bodies. " And though after my skin worms destroy this body, yet in my flesh shall I see God."—Job xix. 26.

Q. 12. How do you prove that the dead shall be raised with the same body?

A. 1. Because if the dead were not raised with the same body, it could in no proper sense be called a resurrection, but a new creation. 2. Because the first body was an instrument of righteousness or sin, and therefore shall share in the reward or punishment.

Q. 13. Will not the bodies, when they are raised, differ from what they are now?

A. The bodies which shall be raised will not differ from what they are now, in regard of their substance and essence; but they will exceedingly differ in regard of their qualities.

Q. 14. Wherein do unbelievers differ from believers at their death?

A. The bodies of unbelievers are at their death shut up in the prison of the grave; and the souls of unbelievers are shut down in the prison of hell, where they are filled with horror and anguish in the company of devils, and other damned spirits, and there reserved in chains of darkness until the judgment of the great day. " By which also he went and preached unto the spirits in prison; which sometime were disobedient."—1 Pet. iii. 19, 20. " God spared not the angels that sinned, but cast them down into hell, and delivered them into chains of darkness, to be reserved unto judgment."—2 Pet. ii. 4.

XXXVIII. Ques. *What benefits do believers receive from Christ at the resurrection?*

*Ans.* At the resurrection, believers being raised up in glory, shall be openly acknowledged and acquitted in the day of judgment, and made perfectly blessed in the full enjoying of God to all eternity.

Q. 1. How many ways may the benefits which believers receive from Christ at the resurrection be considered?

A. The benefits which believers receive from Christ at

the resurrection may be considered in three respects—1. In respect of their resurrection itself. 2. In respect of the day of judgment, after their resurrection. 3. In respect of heaven, after the day of judgment.

Q. 2. What is the benefit of believers in respect of their resurrection itself?

A. The benefit of believers in respect of their resurrection itself is, that they shall be raised in glory.

Q. 3. What glory doth this refer unto?

A. It doth refer unto the glory which shall be put upon the bodies of believers at their resurrection, which were vile bodies, both whilst they were putrefied in the grave, and whilst alive before, as they were instruments of sin, and subject to diseases and death. "Who shall change our vile body."—Phil. iii. 21.

Q. 4. What is that glory which shall be put upon the bodies of believers at the resurrection?

A. The bodies of believers, at the resurrection, shall be made most healthful, strong, spiritual, incorruptible, immortal, most beautiful, and glorious, like unto Christ's most glorious body. "Who shall change our vile body, that it may be fashioned like unto his glorious body, according to the working whereby he is able to subdue all things unto himself."—Phil. iii. 21. "So also is the resurrection of the dead. It is sown in corruption, it is raised in incorruption ; it is sown in dishonour, it is raised in glory; it is sown in weakness, it is raised in power; it is sown a natural body, it is raised a spiritual body. For this corruptible must put on incorruption, and this mortal must put on immortality. So when this corruptible shall have put on incorruption, and this mortal shall have put on immortality, then shall be brought to pass the saying that is written, Death is swallowed up in victory."—1 Cor. xv. 42–44, 53, 54.

Q. 5. What benefits shall believers have after their resurrection, at the day of judgment?

A. At the day of judgment—1. Believers shall be gathered together from all the corners of the earth by the angels. "And he shall send his angels with a great sound of a trumpet, and they shall gather together his elect from the

four winds, from one end of heaven to the other."—Matt.
xxiv. 31. 2. Believers shall be all caught up together in
the clouds, to meet the Lord Jesus, who will come down
with a shout from heaven. " For the Lord himself shall
descend from heaven with a shout, with the voice of the
archangel, and with the trump of God; and the dead in
Christ shall rise first; then we which are alive and remain,
shall be caught up together with them in the clouds, to
meet the Lord in the air."—1 Thess. iv. 16, 17. 3. Believers shall be placed on the right hand of Jesus Christ.
" And he shall set the sheep on his right hand."—Matt.
xxv. 33. 4. Believers shall be openly acknowledged by
Christ to be his, and acquitted from false aspersions which
had been cast upon them, and from the real guilt of all
sins which had been committed by them, because of their
interest in Christ and his righteousness. " Whosoever
shall confess me before men, him will I confess also before
my Father which is in heaven."—Matt. x. 32. " Who
shall lay any thing to the charge of God's elect? It is
God that justifieth. Who is he that condemneth? It is
Christ that died."—Rom. viii. 33, 34. 5. Believers shall
be entertained and invited by Christ to take possession of
the glorious inheritance prepared for them. " Then shall
the King say unto them on his right hand, Come, ye
blessed of my Father, inherit the kingdom prepared for
you from the foundation of the world."—Matt. xxv. 34.
6. Believers shall sit with Christ as assessors in judgment
of the wicked angels and wicked men. " Do ye not know
that the saints shall judge the world? Know ye not that
we shall judge angels?"—1 Cor. vi. 2, 3.

Q. 6. What benefits shall believers receive after the
day of judgment in heaven?

A. Believers in heaven shall be made perfectly blessed
in their full enjoyment of God to all eternity.

Q. 7. Wherein will consist the perfect blessedness of
believers in heaven?

A. The perfect blessedness of believers in heaven will
consist—1. In their perfect immunity or freedom from all
evil, and that both of sin and misery. " That he might
present it to himself a glorious Church, not having spot or

wrinkle, or any such thing; but that it should be holy and without blemish."—Eph. v. 27. "And God shall wipe away all tears from their eyes; and there shall be no more death, neither sorrow, nor crying, neither shall there be any more pain."—Rev. xxi. 4. 2. In their full enjoyment of God, the chiefest good.

Q. 8. What doth the full enjoyment of God in heaven imply?

A. The full enjoyment of God which believers shall have in heaven, doth imply—1. That they shall have the glorious presence of God with them. "Behold, the tabernacle of God is with men, and he will dwell with them."—Rev. xxi. 3. 2. That they shall have the immediate and beatifical vision of his face. "And they shall see his face, and his name shall be in their foreheads."— Rev. xxii. 4. "For now we see through a glass darkly, but then face to face."—1 Cor. xiii. 12. "We shall see him as he is."—1 John iii. 2. 3. That they shall have both a full persuasion and sense of God's love unto them, and perfect love in their hearts towards him, which doth necessarily result or arise from the vision of God in heaven. 4. That they shall have fulness and exceeding joy. "In thy presence is fulness of joy."—Ps. xvi. 11. "Now to him that is able to present you faultless before the presence of his glory with exceeding joy."—Jude 24.

Q. 9. What is it that will sweeten the happiness of believers in the full enjoyment of God in heaven?

A. That which will sweeten the happiness of believers in their full enjoyment of God in heaven, will be the eternity thereof—that it shall be without any interruption, and without any end. "And so shall we ever be with the Lord."—1 Thess. iv. 17.

Q. 10. Wherein will differ the condition of unbelievers and all the wicked world, from that of believers, at the last day?

A. The condition of unbelievers, and all the wicked world, will be miserable beyond expression at the last day of judgment: For—1. Their bodies shall arise, and come forth like prisoners out of the grave, and whatsoever strength and immortality shall be put upon them, will be only to make them capable of eternal torments and misery. 2. They shall, with horror and dreadful shriekings, see Christ coming in flaming fire, to take vengeance upon them. " Behold, he cometh with clouds, and every eye shall see him, and they also which pierced him; and all kindreds of the earth shall wail because of him."—Rev. i. 7. " The Lord Jesus shall be revealed from heaven with his mighty angels, in flaming fire, taking vengeance on them that know not God, and obey not the gospel."— 2 Thess. i. 7, 8. 3. They shall stand before the throne and judgment-seat of Christ, where the books shall be opened wherein all their sins are recorded—according to which they shall be judged, and sentenced to everlasting punishment. " And I saw a great white throne, and him that sat on it, from whose face the earth and the heaven fled away, and there was found no place for them. And I saw the dead, small and great, stand before God; and the books were opened, and the dead were judged out of those things which were written in the books, according to their works."—Rev. xx. 11, 12. " Then shall he say unto them on the left hand, Depart from me, ye cursed, into everlasting fire, prepared for the devil and his angels."—Matt. xxv. 41. 4. They shall then be driven away from the presence of the Lord into hell, where they shall be punished with extremity of anguish, and torment in soul and body, without any alleviation or intermission, unto all eternity. " And these shall go away into everlasting punishment."—Matt. xxv. 46. " Indignation and wrath, tribulation and anguish, (shall be) upon every soul of man that doeth evil, of the Jew first, and also of the Gentile." —Rom. ii. 8, 9. " And the smoke of their torment ascendeth up for ever and ever : and they have no rest day nor night."—Rev. xiv. 11.

XXXIX. Ques. *What is the duty which God requireth of man?*

*Ans.* The duty which God requireth of man is obedience to his revealed will.

Q. 1. Upon what account is obedience unto God the duty of man?

A. Obedience unto God is the duty of man, because God is his Creator, and Benefactor, and supreme Sovereign Lord and King.

Q. 2. Is there any other Lord over the conscience, who can require obedience of men for their own sake chiefly, besides God?

A. God is the only Lord of the conscience; and though we are to obey magistrates, and parents, and masters, yet we are chiefly to do this because God requireth us so to do; and if they command us to do anything which God doth forbid, we are to refuse obedience, being to obey God rather than any man in the world. "Whether it be right in the sight of God to hearken unto you rather than unto God, judge ye."—Acts iv. 19.

Q. 3. What rule hath God given us, according to which our whole obedience must be guided?

A. The only rule which God hath given us, according to which our whole obedience unto him must be guided, is his revealed will.

Q. 4. Hath God any other will than that which he hath revealed?

A. God hath a secret will of his counsel concerning all things which come to pass, and this cannot be known as to most things beforehand, and therefore is no rule for our obedience.

Q. 5. What is the difference between God's secret will and God's revealed will?

A. God's secret will is concerning all things that are done, and shall be done; and doth extend even unto sinful actions, which he doth will to permit, and determine, and direct beyond man's will and intention, to his own glory. But God's revealed will is concerning those things which may and ought to be done, and doth extend only unto those things which are duty, and which in themselves do tend to God's glory; and this revealed will is the rule of man's obedience.

Q. 6. Where is the revealed will of God to be found?

A. The revealed will of God is to be found in the Scriptures, where the whole duty of man to God is made known. "He hath showed thee, O man, what is good; and what doth the Lord require of thee, but to do justly, and to love mercy, and to walk humbly with thy God?"—Micah vi. 8.

XL. Ques. *What did God at first reveal to man for the rule of his obedience?*

*Ans.* The rule which God at first revealed to man for his obedience, was the moral law.

Q. 1. Are there any other laws which God hath given unto man?

A. The Lord gave other positive laws to the people of the Jews, which they were bound to yield obedience unto, such as the ceremonial laws; but these laws were not intended as a standing rule of obedience for all nations, in all ages, and therefore were, after a time, abrogated or disannulled; and the not yielding obedience to them by us at this time is no sin.

Q. 2. Doth the moral law continue to be a rule of obedience in the days of the gospel?

A. As the moral law was at first revealed that it might be a rule of man's obedience, so it doth continue so to be unto all men in every nation, unto the end of the world.

Q. 3. How can the moral law be a rule of obedience unto the heathen and infidel world, who are without the light of the Scriptures to make it known unto them?

A. Though without the light of the Scriptures there cannot be so clear a discovery of the moral law, yet by the light of nature it is made known unto all nations in some measure, sufficient to leave the very heathen without excuse for their disobedience. " For when the Gentiles, which have not the law, do by nature the things contained in the law, these having not the law, are a law unto themselves; which show the work of the law written in their hearts."—Rom. ii. 14, 15.

Q. 4. Can any man attain life by obedience unto the moral law?

A. If any man could yield perfect obedience unto the moral law, he might attain life thereby; but all being guilty of sin, perfect obedience is impossible, and life thereby is unattainable; therefore the law was not given unto man after his fall that it might give life. " The law is not of faith; but, The man that doeth them shall live in them."—Gal. iii. 12. " Now we know that what things soever the law saith, it saith to them who are under the law, that every mouth may be stopped, and all the world may become guilty before God."—Rom. iii. 19. " If there had been a law given which could have given life, verily righteousness should have been by the law. But the Scripture hath concluded all under sin."—Gal. iii. 21, 22.

Q. 5. Wherefore, then, was the law given, when righteousness and life were not attainable thereby?

A. The law was given to be a schoolmaster to bring men unto Christ, that they might attain life by faith in him. " Wherefore the law was our schoolmaster to bring us unto Christ, that we might be justified by faith."—Gal. iii. 24.

Q. 6. How doth the law bring men unto Christ?

A. The law bringeth men unto Christ—1. By convincing men of sin. The prohibitions of the law convince them of their sins of commission; the injunctions of the law convince them of their sins of omission. " For by the law is the knowledge of sin."—Rom. iii. 20. 2. By discovering unto them the curse of God which is due to them for sin, which all guilty sinners do lie under. " Cursed is every one that continueth not in all things which are written in the book of the law to do them."—Gal. iii. 10. 3. By awakening the consciences of the guilty, begetting bondage and fear in them; the Spirit working with the law as a spirit of bondage, doth show them their danger and future wrath, because of their disobedience. " These are the two covenants; the one from the Mount Sinai, which gendereth to bondage."—Gal iv. 24. And thus men are brought unto a sight of their need of Christ, and his perfect righteousness, without which there can be no life and salvation.

Q. 7. When men are brought, and by faith joined unto Christ, doth the moral law cease to be of any further use unto them?

A. Though believers, through their interest in Christ, are delivered from the curse and condemnation, the rigour and irritation, of the moral law, which, whilst out of Christ, they are under, yet the moral law is still of singular use unto believers, to provoke them unto thankfulness for Christ, who hath fulfilled the law in their stead; and to be a rule according to which they ought to endeavour, as much as may be, to order their hearts and lives, however in this life perfection of obedience thereunto is unattainable. " But now we are delivered from the law, that being dead wherein we were held. The law is holy, and the commandment holy, and just, and good."—Rom. vii. 6, 12. " The grace of God that bringeth salvation hath appeared to all men; teaching us, that denying ungodliness and worldly lusts, we should live soberly, righteously, and godly in this present world."—Tit. ii. 11, 12.

## XLI. Ques. *Where is the moral law summarily comprehended?*

*Ans.* The moral law is summarily comprehended in the ten commandments.

Q. 1. What is it for the moral law to be summarily comprehended in the ten commandments?

A. The moral law is summarily comprehended in the ten commandments, in that the sum and chief heads of the law are therein contained.

Q. 2. Is there, then, any thing included, as commanded or forbidden in the moral law, but what is expressed in the ten commandments?

A. The moral law being spiritual and very large, doth reach both the whole inward man, and all the outward conversation, and therefore the ten general heads in the commandments do include many particular members and branches. 1. Whatever sin is forbidden in any one precept, the contrary duty is commanded, and all sins of the same kind also are forbidden; and not only the outward act, together with the words and gestures tending thereunto, but also all the inward affections to sin, together with all causes, means, occasions, appearances, and whatever may be a provocation unto it, either in ourselves or others. "Ye have heard that it was said by them of old time, Thou shalt not kill; and whosoever shall kill shall be in danger of the judgment: but I say unto you, That whosoever is angry with his brother without a cause shall be in danger of the judgment: and whosoever shall say to his brother, Raca, shall be in danger of the counsel: but whosoever shall say, Thou fool, shall be in danger of hell fire. Ye have heard that it was said by them of old time, Thou shalt not commit adultery: but I say unto you, That whosoever looketh on a woman to lust after her, hath committed adultery with her already in his heart."—Matt. v. 21, 22, 27, 28. 2. Whatever duty is commanded, the contrary is forbidden; and all duties of the same kind are included, together with all suitable affections thereunto, as also the using all means appointed for help, quickening, and furtherance therein, and our endeavours in our places to help and further others in their obedience.

### XLII. Ques. *What is the sum of the ten commandments?*

*Ans.* The sum of the ten commandments is, To love the Lord our God with all our heart, with all our soul, with all our strength, and with all our mind, and our neighbour as ourselves.

Q. 1. In how many tables were the ten commandments at first written?

A. The ten commandments were at first written by God himself in the mount, and given unto Moses in two tables of stone. "At that time the Lord said unto me, Hew thee two tables of stone like unto the first, and come up unto me into the mount. And I will write on the tables the words which were in the first tables, which thou brakest. And he wrote on the tables, according to the first writing, the ten commandments."—Deut. x. 1, 2, 4.

Q. 2. What is the comprehensive duty of the ten commandments written in these tables?

A. The comprehensive duty of the ten commandments, is love.

Q. 3. What is the sum of the first table of the law?

A. The sum of the first table of the law, which hath a more immediate reference unto God, is to love the Lord our God with all our heart, and with all our soul, and with all our strength, and with all our mind. " And thou shalt love the Lord thy God with all thy heart, and with all thy soul, and with all thy mind, and with all thy strength. This is the first commandment."—Mark xii. 30.

Q. 4. What is it to love the Lord with all the heart, and with all the soul, and with all the mind, and with all the strength?

A. To love the Lord with all the heart, and with all the soul, and with all the mind, and with all the strength, doth imply the supremacy, ardency, and activity of our love, whereby we choose the Lord, cleave to him, and delight in him as our chief good, and employ all the faculties and powers of soul and body in obedience, out of love.

Q. 5. What is the sum of the second table of the law?

A. The sum of the second table of the law, which hath a reference unto men, is to love our neighbour as ourselves. " The second is like, namely this, Thou shalt love thy neighbour as thyself."—Mark xii. 31.

Q. 6. Who is our neighbour?

A. Every man is our neighbour; and therefore we are bound to bear a general affection unto all.

Q. 7. What is it to love our neighbour as ourselves?

A. To love our neighbour as ourselves, is to love our neighbour with the same truth and constancy of love as we do ourselves.

XLIII. Ques. *What is the preface to the ten commandments?*

*Ans.* The preface to the ten commandments is in these words, " I am the Lord thy God, which have brought thee out of the land of Egypt, out of the house of bondage."

XLIV. Ques. *What doth the preface to the ten commandments teach us?*

*Ans.* The preface to the ten commandments teacheth us, that because God is the Lord, and our God and Redeemer, therefore we are bound to keep all his commandments.

Q. 1. How many reasons or arguments are there in the preface, to oblige and persuade us to keep all God's commandments?

A. There are in the preface three reasons or arguments to oblige and persuade us to keep all God's commandments. 1. Because God is the Lord: "I am the Lord." 2. Because God is our God: "I am the Lord thy God." 3. Because God is our Redeemer: "Which brought thee out of the land of Egypt, out of the house of bondage."

Q. 2. How can God be said to bring his people out of the land of Egypt, out of the house of bondage now?

A. As God brought his people of old out of the earthly Egypt, and the bondage of men; so he doth now bring his people out of the spiritual Egypt, and the bondage they are in unto the devil and their own lusts.

Q. 3. How are we bound and obliged to keep God's commandments as he is the Lord?

A. We are bound and obliged to keep God's commandments as he is the Lord, because, as he is the Lord, he is our Creator and supreme Sovereign, and we owe to him all obedience, as we are his creatures and subjects. "Serve the Lord with gladness. Know that he made us, and not we ourselves."—Ps. c. 2, 3. "Who would not fear thee, O King of nations? for to thee doth it appertain."—Jer. x. 7.

Q. 4. How are we bound and obliged to keep God's commandments as he is our God?

A. We are bound and obliged to keep God's commandments as he is our God, because, as our God, he hath taken us into covenant, and brought us into a special relation to himself, and hereby laid a greater obligation upon us to do him service. "Thou shalt love the Lord thy God, and keep his charge, and his statutes, and his judgments, and his commandments alway."—Deut. xi. 1.

Q. 5. How are we bound and obliged to keep God's commandments as he is our Redeemer?

A. We are bound and obliged to keep God's commandments as he is our Redeemer, because God hath redeemed us for this end, that, being free from the slavery of sin and Satan, we might be encouraged and enabled to yield obedience unto him. " Ye are not your own, for ye are bought with a price; therefore glorify God in your body, and in your spirit, which are God's."—1 Cor. vi. 19, 20. " That we, being delivered out of the hands of our enemies, might serve him without fear, in holiness and righteousness before him all the days of our life."—Luke i. 74, 75.

XLV. Ques. *Which is the first commandment ?*

*Ans.* The first commandment is, " Thou shalt have no other gods before me."

XLVI. Ques. *What is required in the first commandment ?*

*Ans.* The first commandment requireth us to know and acknowledge God to be the only true God, and our God, and to worship and glorify him accordingly.

Q. 1. How many duties are there chiefly required in the first commandment?

A. There are three duties chiefly required in the first commandment. 1. To know God. " And thou, Solomon my son, know thou the God of thy father."—1 Chron. xxviii. 9. 2. To acknowledge God. " Thou hast avouched the Lord this day to be thy God."—Deut. xxvi. 17. 3. To worship and glorify God. " Thou shalt worship the Lord thy God, and him only shalt thou serve."—Matt. iv. 10.

Q. 2. What are we bound to know concerning God?

A. We are bound to know—1. That God is, or that there is a God. 2. What God is in all those glorious attributes and perfections whereby he hath made himself known.

Q. 3. How ought we to acknowledge God?

A. 1. We ought to acknowledge God to be the only true God. " Unto us there is but one God."—1 Cor. viii. 6. 2. We ought to take and own God for our God. " This God is our God."—Ps. xlviii. 14.

Q. 4. How ought we to worship and glorify God?

A. We ought to worship and glorify God as the only right object of divine worship and honour—1. In our minds, by thinking, meditating, remembering, and highly esteeming of him. "A book of remembrance was written before him, for them that thought on his name."—Mal. iii. 16. "When I remember thee on my bed, and meditate on thee in the night watches."—Ps. lxiii. 6. "O God, who is like unto thee?"—Ps. lxxi. 19. 2. In our wills, by choosing him for our chief good, and devoting ourselves to his service. "Ye have chosen the Lord, to serve him." —Josh. xxiv. 22. 3. In our hearts, by loving him, desiring him, fearing him, believing and trusting in him, grieving for our sins against him, hoping in him, delighting and rejoicing in him. "And now, Israel, what doth the Lord thy God require of thee, but to fear the Lord thy God, and to love him?" &c.—Deut. x. 12. "The desire of our soul is to thy name."—Isa. xxvi. 8. "And the people believed the Lord and his servant Moses."—Exod. xiv. 31. "Trust ye in the Lord for ever."—Isa. xxvi. 4. "I will be sorry for my sin."—Ps. xxxviii. 18. "Let Israel hope in the Lord."—Ps. cxxx. 7. "Delight thyself in the Lord."— Ps. xxxvii. 4. 4. In our lips, by calling upon him, and speaking well of his name. "In everything by prayer and supplication, with thanksgiving, let your requests be made known unto God."—Phil. iv. 6. "My mouth shall speak of the praise of the Lord."—Ps. cxlv. 21. 5. In our lives, by yielding all obedience unto him, being zealous for his glory, careful to please him, fearful of offending him, and by walking humbly before him. "This thing commanded I them, Obey my voice, and walk ye in all the ways that I commanded."—Jer. vii. 23. "The zeal of thine house hath eaten me up."—John ii. 17. "Walk worthy of the Lord, unto all pleasing."—Col. i 10. "How can I do this great wickedness, and sin against God?"—Gen. xxxix. 9. "Walk humbly with thy God."—Micah vi. 8.

XLVII. Ques. *What is forbidden in the first commandment?*

*Ans.* The first commandment forbiddeth the denying, or not worshipping and glorifying the true God as God, and our God, and the giving of that worship and glory to any other which is due to him alone.

Q. 1. What are the chief sins forbidden in the first commandment ?

A. The chief sins forbidden in the first commandment are—1. Atheism. 2. Profaneness. 3. Idolatry.

Q. 2. What is atheism ?

A. Atheism is the denying, or not having a God. "The fool hath said in his heart, There is no God."—Ps. xiv. 1. "At that time ye were without Christ, having no hope, and without God in the world."—Eph. ii. 12.

Q. 3. What is the profaneness forbidden in this commandment ?

A. The profaneness forbidden in this commandment is, the not worshipping and glorifying the true God as God, and our God.

Q. 4. Wherein doth this profaneness in regard of God's worship and honour appear ?

A. Profaneness, in regard of God's worship and honour, doth appear—1. When persons do not know God, or have misapprehensions of him. "My people is foolish, they have not known me."—Jer. iv. 22. "Thou thoughtest I was altogether such an one as thyself."—Ps. l. 21. 2. When persons are forgetful of God. "My people have forgotten me days without number."—Jer. ii. 32. 3. When persons hate God, or love themselves or anything else more than God, desire creatures more than God, trust in arms of flesh more than God, delight in objects of sense more than God, when persons set their affection upon anything in the world more than God, and take off the heart, in whole or in part, from God. "The carnal mind is enmity against God."—Rom. viii. 7. "Love not the world, neither the things that are in the world. If any man love the world, the love of the Father is not in him."—1 John ii. 15. "Set your affections on things above, not on things on the earth."—Col. iii. 2. 4. When persons omit or neglect to give that worship and glory which is due unto God, either with the inward or outward man. "But thou hast not called upon me, O Jacob."—Isa. xliii. 22.

Q. 5. What is that idolatry which is forbidden in the first commandment?

A. The idolatry which is forbidden in the first commandment, is the giving that worship and glory unto any other which is due unto God alone. "Who changed the truth of God into a lie, and worshipped and served the creature more than the Creator, who is blessed for ever."—Rom. i. 25.

Q. 6. How many ways may persons be guilty of the idolatry forbidden in this commandment?

A. Persons may be guilty of the idolatry forbidden in this commandment—1. By having and worshipping other gods besides the true God, with the outward man; as when persons worship the heathenish gods, or angels, or saints. 2. By giving that honour and respect to any thing in the world which is due only unto God, with the inward man, which is heart-idolatry. "And covetousness, which is idolatry."—Col. iii. 5.

XLVIII. Ques. *What are we specially taught by these words,* "Before me," *in the first commandment?*

*Ans.* These words, *"Before me,"* in the first commandment, teach us, that God, who seeth all things, taketh notice of, and is much displeased with, the sin of having any other god.

Q. 1. How doth it appear that God seeth all things?

A. It doth appear that God seeth all things, because God is everywhere present, and is infinite in understanding. "Can any hide himself in secret places, that I shall not see him? saith the Lord: do not I fill heaven and earth?"—Jer. xxiii. 24. "His understanding is infinite."—Ps. cxlvii. 5.

Q. 2. Why doth God take such notice of, and is so displeased with, the sin of having any other god?

A. Because the sin of having any other god is a great affront unto the holy and jealous eye of God, who will not give his glory to another. "If we have stretched out our hands to a strange god, shall not God search this out?"—Ps. xliv. 20, 21. "I am the Lord; that is my name;

and my glory will I not give to another, neither my praise to graven images."—Isa. xlii. 8.

XLIX. *Ques. Which is the second commandment?*

*Ans.* The second commandment is, " Thou shalt not make unto thee any graven image, or any likeness of any thing that is in heaven above, or that is in the earth beneath, or that is in the water under the earth: thou shalt not bow down thyself to them, nor serve them: for I the Lord thy God am a jealous God, visiting the iniquity of the fathers upon the children unto the third and fourth generation of them that hate me; and showing mercy unto thousands of them that love me, and keep my commandments."

L. *Ques. What is required in the second commandment?*

*Ans.* The second commandment requireth the receiving, observing, and keeping pure and entire, all such religious worship and ordinances as God hath appointed in his word.

Q. 1. How doth the worship required in this second commandment differ from the worship required in the first commandment?

A. The worship required in the first commandment hath a respect unto the object of worship, whereby we are bound to worship the true God, and none else: the worship required in the second commandment hath a respect unto the means of worship, whereby we are bound to worship God according to the way and means of his own appointment, and no other.

Q. 2. What is the way and means which God hath appointed for his worship?

A. The only way and means which God hath appointed for his worship, are his ordinances, which he hath prescribed in his Word.

Q. 3. What are the ordinances which God hath appointed in his Word, to be the means of worship, and to be observed by his people?

A. The ordinances which God hath appointed in his Word, to be the means of his worship, and to be observed by his people, are—1. Prayer unto God with thanksgiving, and that publicly in assemblies, privately in families, and secretly in closets. "Be careful for nothing; but in everything by prayer and supplication, with thanksgiving, let your requests be made known unto God."—Phil. iv. 6. "Giving thanks always for all things unto God and the Father, in the name of our Lord Jesus Christ."—Eph. v. 20. "And the whole multitude of people were praying."—Luke i. 10. "Pour out thy fury upon the families which call not upon thy name."—Jer. x. 25. "But thou, when thou prayest, enter into thy closet, and when thou hast shut thy door, pray to thy Father which is in secret, and thy Father, which seeth in secret, shall reward thee openly."—Matt. vi. 6. 2. Reading and searching the Scriptures. "For Moses is read in the synagogues every Sabbath-day."—Acts xv. 21. "Search the Scriptures, for in them ye think ye have eternal life, and they are they which testify of me."—John v. 39. 3. Preaching and hearing of the word. "Preach the word; be instant in season, and out of season; reprove, rebuke, exhort, with all long-suffering and doctrine."—2 Tim. iv. 2. "Hear, and your soul shall live."—Isa. lv. 3. 4. Singing of psalms. "Praise ye the Lord. Sing unto the Lord a new song, and his praise in the congregation of saints."—Ps. cxlix. 1. "Is any merry? let him sing psalms."—James v. 13. 5. Administration and receiving of the sacraments, both of baptism and the Lord's supper. "Go ye therefore, and teach all nations, baptizing them in the name of the Father, and of the Son, and of the Holy Ghost."—Matt. xxviii. 19. "For I have received of the Lord that which also I have delivered unto you, That the Lord Jesus, the same night in which he was betrayed, took bread: and when he had given thanks, he brake it, and said, Take, eat: this is my body, which is broken for you: this do in remembrance of me. After the same manner also he took the cup, when he had supped, saying, This cup is the

New Testament in my blood: this do ye, as oft as ye drink it, in remembrance of me."—1 Cor. xi. 23–25. 6. Fasting. "But the days will come, when the bridegroom shall be taken away from them, and then shall they fast in those days."—Luke v. 35. 7. Instructing of children and household in the laws of the Lord. "For I know him, that he will command his children, and his household after him, and they shall keep the way of the Lord." —Gen. xviii. 19. "And these words which I command thee this day, shall be in thine heart; and thou shalt teach them diligently unto thy children."—Deut. vi. 6, 7. "And ye fathers, provoke not your children to wrath, but bring them up in the nurture and admonition of the Lord."— Eph. vi. 4. 8. Conference and discourse of the things of God. "They that feared the Lord spake often one to another, and the Lord hearkened and heard it."—Mal. iii. 16. "Thou shalt talk of them when thou sittest in thine house, and when thou liest down, and when thou risest up."—Deut. vi. 7. 9. Meditation. "I will meditate of all thy works."—Ps. lxxvii. 12. "Meditate upon these things; give thyself wholly to them, that thy profiting may appear unto all."—1 Tim. iv. 15. 10. Vows to the Lord. "Vow and pay unto the Lord."—Ps. lxxvi. 11. 11. Swearing by the name of the Lord, when lawfully called. "Thou shalt fear the Lord thy God, and serve him, and shalt swear by his name.—Deut. vi. 13. 12. Exercise of Church discipline. "If thy brother shall trespass against thee, go and tell him his fault between thee and him alone. But if he will not hear thee, then take with thee one or two more. And if he shall neglect to hear them, tell it unto the church; but if he neglect to hear the church, let him be unto thee as a heathen man and a publican."—Matt. xviii. 15–17.

Q. 4. What doth God require in the second commandment, in reference to his ordinances and means of worship?

A. God, in the second commandment, doth require, in reference to his ordinances and means of worship—1. The receiving of them. 2. Observing of them. 3. The keeping them pure and entire.

Q. 5. What is it to receive God's ordinances?

A. The receiving God's ordinances implieth an approving of them with the mind, and embracement of them with the will.

Q. 6. What is it to observe God's ordinances?

A. The observing God's ordinances, implieth a doing what is required in them, a making use of them, and attending upon God in them.

Q. 7. What is it to keep pure and entire God's ordinances?

A. The keeping pure and entire God's ordinances implieth a doing what in us lieth to preserve the ordinances from corruption, not suffering any thing to be added to them, or taken away from them. "What thing soever I command you, observe to do it; thou shalt not add thereto, nor diminish from it."—Deut. xii. 32.

Q. 8. How doth it appear that the receiving, observing, and keeping pure and entire all such religious worship and ordinances as God hath appointed, is required in the second commandment, when it doth only forbid: "Thou shalt not make to thyself any graven image," &c.?

A. God's forbidding the making of any graven image, and worshipping it, doth clearly imply—1. That God must be worshipped by some means. 2. That it is a sin to worship God by graven images. 3. That, by consequence, it is a sin to worship God by the means which he hath not appointed. 4. That therefore it is a duty to worship God by the means which he hath appointed, which being his ordinances, they must be received, observed, and kept pure and entire.

LI. Quest. *What is forbidden in the second commandment?*

*Ans.* The second commandment forbiddeth the worshipping of God by images, or any other way not appointed in his word.

Q. 1. What is the first great sin forbidden in the second commandment?

A. The first great sin forbidden in the second commandment, is the sin of idolatry

Q. 2. How doth the idolatry forbidden in the first commandment differ from the idolatry forbidden in the second commandment?

A. The idolatry forbidden in the first commandment hath a respect to the object, when we give that worship and honour, which are due only to God, unto another; the idolatry forbidden in the second commandment hath a respect unto the means, when we worship God by images.

Q. 3. How many ways may persons be guilty of idolatry in their worshipping of God by images?

A. Persons are guilty of idolatry in worshipping of God by images—1. When they worship feigned and false gods (apprehending them to be true) by images and representations. Such was the heathen's idolatry in worshipping Jupiter, Juno, Apollo, Diana, and other feigned gods and goddesses, by their images in their idolatrous temples. 2. When they worship the true God in or by any image or representation of him, whether it be any thing in heaven, or the earth, or the waters, as in the commandment: "Thou shalt not make to thyself any graven image, or the likeness of any thing that is in heaven above, or in the earth beneath, or in the water under the earth. Thou shalt not bow down to them, nor serve them." "Take ye heed, therefore, to yourselves (for ye saw no manner of similitude on the day that the Lord spake unto you in Horeb), lest ye corrupt yourselves, and make you a graven image." —Deut iv. 15, 16. "They have made them a molten calf, and have worshipped it; and have sacrificed thereunto, and said, These be thy gods, O Israel, which have brought thee up out of the land of Egypt."—Exod. xxxii. 8. 3. When they have in their worship carnal imaginations, and representations of God in their minds; as if he were an old man sitting in heaven, or the like.

Q. 4. Why may we not make use of images for a help in our worship of God?

A. 1. Because God has absolutely forbidden it. 2. Because images are not a real help, but a hindrance of devotion, they tending to lessen God in our esteem, who, being the living God, and superlatively excellent, and infinitely removed above all his creatures, cannot, without great reflection of dishonour upon him, be represented by a dead image.

Q. 5. Is it not lawful to have images or pictures of God by us, so we do not worship them, nor God by them?

A. The images or pictures of God are an abomination, and utterly unlawful, because they do debase God, and may be a cause of idolatrous worship.

Q. 6. Is it not lawful to have pictures of Jesus Christ, he being a man as well as God?

A. It is not lawful to have pictures of Jesus Christ, because his divine nature cannot be pictured at all; and because his body, as it is now glorified, cannot be pictured as it is; and because, if it do not stir up devotion, it is in vain—if it do stir up devotion, it is a worshipping by an image or picture, and so a palpable breach of the second commandment.

Q. 7. What is the second great sin against this second commandment?

A. The second great sin against this second commandment is superstition.

Q. 8. What is the superstition forbidden in the second commandment?

A. The superstition forbidden in the second commandment, is the worshipping of God in any other way, or by any other means, than what he hath appointed in his Word, and thus adding human inventions unto God's institutions; which is will-worship, and condemned by the apostle. " Why, as though living in the world, are ye subject to ordinances (touch not, taste not, handle not, which all are to perish with the using), after the commandments and doctrines of men? which things have indeed a show of wisdom in will-worship."—Col. ii. 20–23.

Q. 9. May nothing be added in the worship of God but what is prescribed in the Word of God?

A. Nothing may be added in the worship of God, as parts of worship, but what is prescribed or appointed in the Word of God; because, without divine institution, it is but vain worship, neither pleasing to God nor profitable unto them that worship. " But in vain do they worship me, teaching for doctrines the commandments of men." —Matt. xv. 9.

Q. 10. Are not significant ceremonies allowable, that the dull minds of men may be quickened unto the more devotion?

A. 1. The ceremonies which God himself did appoint under the law are not lawful, much less the ceremonies of men's appointment, which are parts of worship. 2. Significant teaching ceremonies, were they appointed by God, would be the parts of true worship; therefore, such significant teaching ceremonies as are not appointed by God are parts of false worship, or of worship so far corrupted as they are used. 3. The significancy of teaching ceremonies without God's institution, which carrieth with it God's blessing, is insignificant and ineffectual to convey and confer any grace.

Q. 11. May not the Church, by virtue of that command, " Let all things be done decently and in order" (1 Cor. xiv. 40), appoint ceremonies for decency and order's sake?

A. The Church may and ought, by virtue of this command, to see that there is no indecency and disorder in the worship of God; that is, they may order that things appointed by God be done decently and in order, in reference to conveniency of time and place, and the like, which the Word of God doth virtually include in appointing worship itself, which, without such circumstances, cannot be performed; but here is no liberty given unto the Church to introduce and appoint new parts of worship, as significant teaching ceremonies are proved to be; neither may such things be called decent in God's worship which the idolatrous Church of Rome use, without any warrant from the Word of God.

Q. 12. What is the idolatry and superstition of the Church of Rome in the worship of God?

A. The idolatry and superstition of the Church of Rome in the worship of God, is their idolatrous kneeling at the sacrament, asserting that the bread is turned into the real body of Christ; their idolatrous worshipping of Christ by the crucifix; their idolatrous pictures and images of God, which they bow before; their idolatrous bowing at the altars and towards the east; their idolatrous praying to angels and saints, especially to the Virgin Mary; their offering up the unbloody sacrifice of the host; their superstitious fastings and abstaining from flesh in Lent; their superstitious holidays; their superstitious priests' surplice; their adding cream, oil, and spittle to the wafer, and signing with the cross in baptism; their baptizing of bells; their praying upon beads; and many more superstitious customs, for which there is not the least command in the Scripture.

Q. 13. How may we further offend and sin against the second commandment?

A. We offend and sin against the second commandment, not only by idolatry and superstition, but also when we are not zealous for pure worship, according to God's institution, not endeavouring what in us lieth, in our places, the reformation of worship, according to the pattern in the Word; as also, when we disuse and neglect, especially when we contemn and oppose, any of those ordinances which God hath appointed to be the means of worship. "The zeal of thine house hath eaten me up."—John ii. 17. "Not forsaking the assembling of ourselves together, as the manner of some is."—Heb. x. 25. "Woe unto you, scribes and Pharisees, hypocrites! for ye shut up the kingdom of heaven against men: for ye neither go in yourselves, neither suffer ye them that are entering to go in."—Matt. xxiii. 13. "Forbidding us to speak to the Gentiles, that they may be saved, filling up their sins alway."—1 Thess. ii. 16. "And the next Sabbath-day came almost the whole city together, to hear the word of God. But when the Jews saw the multitudes, they were filled with envy, and spake against those things which were spoken by Paul, contradicting and blaspheming. Then Paul and Barnabas waxed bold, and said, It was necessary that the word of God should first have been spoken to you; but seeing ye put it from you, and judge yourselves unworthy of everlasting life, lo, we turn to the Gentiles."—Acts xiii. 44–46.

LII. Ques. *What are the reasons annexed to the second commandment?*

*Ans.* The reasons annexed to the second commandment, are, God's sovereignty over us, his propriety in us, and the zeal he hath to his own worship.

Q. 1. What is the first reason annexed unto the second commandment?

A. The first reason annexed unto the second commandment is, God's sovereignty over us, in these words, " I the Lord."

Q. 2. What is the force of this first reason?

A. The force of this first reason is, because God is the great sovereign King over us, and hath the sole or only authority to make laws for the way of his worship, therefore we ought, by virtue of our allegiance, as we are his subjects, to observe his laws and ordinances, and to worship him no other way than he hath appointed in his Word. " Let us come before his presence with thanksgiving, and make a joyful noise unto him with psalms. For the Lord is a great God, and a great King above all gods."—Ps. xcv. 2, 3.

Q. 3. What is the second reason annexed unto the second commandment?

A. The second reason annexed unto the second commandment is, God's propriety in us, in these words, " Thy God"—" I the Lord, thy God."

Q. 4. What is the force of this second reason?

A. The force of this second reason is, that because we belong unto the Lord, therefore we ought to keep close unto him and his appointments, and take heed especially of idolatry and superstition, which do alienate the heart from him. " O come, let us worship and bow down; let us kneel before the Lord our Maker."—Ps. xcv. 6, 7. " They made a calf in Horeb, and worshipped the molten image. They forgat God their Saviour."—Ps. cvi. 19, 21

Q. 5. What is the third reason annexed unto the second commandment.

A. The zeal which God hath to his own worship, is his jealousy, whereby, out of love to his own worship and institutions, he is highly offended with those that turn aside from them unto their own inventions. " I the Lord thy God am a jealous God." " Thou shalt worship no other God; for the Lord, whose name is Jealous, is a jealous God."—Exod. xxxiv. 14.

Q. 6. Wherein doth this zeal and jealousy of God for his own worship show itself?

A. The zeal or jealousy of God for his own worship doth show itself—1. In his accounting the breakers of this commandment those that hate him, and threatening to punish them unto the third and fourth generation : " I the Lord thy God am a jealous God, visiting the iniquity of the fathers upon the children unto the third and fourth generation of them that hate me." 2. In his esteeming the keepers of this commandment such as love him, and promising mercies unto thousands of them : " Showing mercy unto thousands of them that love me, and keep my commandments."

Q. 7. How can God in justice visit the iniquity of the fathers upon their children?

A. 1. If children do not walk in the steps of the same sins with their parents, God doth not punish them for their sins. " If he beget a son that seeth all his father's sins which he hath done, and considereth, and doeth not such like, he shall not die for the iniquity of his father, he shall surely live."—Ezek. xviii. 14, 17. 2. If God doth visit the iniquity of the fathers upon their children, it is when the children are guilty of the same iniquity, and so fill up the measure, and the punishment of them is most equal and righteous. " Is not my way equal? Are not your ways unequal?"—Ezek. xviii. 25.

LIII. Ques. *Which is the third commandment?*

*Ans.* The third commandment is, " Thou shalt not take the name of the Lord thy God in vain, for the Lord will not hold him guiltless that taketh his name in vain."

LIV. Ques. *What is required in the third commandment?*

*Ans.* The third commandment requireth the holy and reverent use of God's names, titles, attributes, ordinances, word, and works.

Q. 1. What are we to understand by the name of God, which we are forbidden in this commandment to take in vain?

A. The name of God, which we are forbidden in this commandment to take in vain, is to be taken generally and comprehensively for anything whereby God makes himself known.

Q. 2. By what is it that God doth make himself known?

A. God doth make himself known—1. By his names taken particularly, which he hath given unto himself in Scripture, such as GOD, LORD, I AM, JEHOVAH, and the like. "Hear, O Israel, The Lord our God is one Lord."—Deut. vi. 4. "And they shall say unto me, What is his name? What shall I say unto them? And God said unto Moses, I AM THAT I AM: Thou shalt say, I AM hath sent me unto you."—Exod. iii. 13, 14. "I appeared unto Abraham by the name of God Almighty, but by my name JEHOVAH was I not known."—Exod. vi. 3. 2. By his titles; such as, Lord of hosts; Holy One of Israel; the God of Abraham, Isaac, and Jacob; Creator, Preserver of men; the King of kings, and Lord of lords; King of nations; the King of saints; the God and Father of our Lord Jesus Christ; the Father of mercies; the God of salvation; the Hearer of prayer, and the like. "Except the Lord of hosts had left unto us a very small remnant."—Isa. i. 9. "The Zion of the Holy One of Israel."—Isa. lx. 14. "I am the God of Abraham, the God of Isaac, and the God of Jacob."—Exod. iii. 6. "The Lord, the Creator of the ends of the earth."—Isa. xl. 28. "What shall I do unto thee, thou Preserver of men?"—Job vii. 20. "The blessed and only Potentate, the King of kings, and Lord of lords."—1 Tim. vi. 15. "Who would not fear thee, O King of nations."—Jer. x. 7. "Just and true are thy ways, thou King of

saints."—Rev. xv. 3.  "Blessed be God, even the Father
of our Lord Jesus Christ, the Father of mercies."—2 Cor.
i. 3.  "He that is our God is the God of salvation."—
Ps. lxviii. 20.  "O thou that hearest prayer, unto thee shall
all flesh come."—Ps. lxv. 2.  3. By his attributes, which are
his perfections and properties, whereby he distinguisheth
himself from his creatures; such as omnipotency, eternity,
invisibility, infinite wisdom, omnipresence, holiness, un-
changeableness, mercifulness, love, and the like.  "The
Lord God omnipotent reigneth."—Rev. xix. 6.  "Now unto
the King eternal, immortal, invisible, the only wise God,
be honour and glory."—1 Tim. i. 17.  "Great is our Lord,
and of great power; his understanding is infinite."—Ps.
cxlvii. 5.  "Can any hide himself in secret places, that I
shall not see him? saith the Lord: do not I fill heaven and
earth."—Jer. xxiii. 24.  "For the Lord our God is holy."
—Ps. xcix. 9.  "I am the Lord; I change not."—Mal.
iii. 6.  "The Lord is gracious, and full of compassion."—
Ps. cxlv. 8.  "God is love."—1 John iv. 8.  4. By his
ordinances; prayer, hearing, the sacrament.  "Thy way,
O God, is in the sanctuary."—Ps. lxxvii. 13.  5. By his
Word, law and gospel.  "Thou hast magnified thy Word
above all thy name."—Ps. cxxxviii. 2.  6. By his works
of creation and providence.  "The heavens declare the
glory of God, and the firmament showeth his handywork."
—Ps. xix. 1.  "The Lord is known by the judgment
which he executeth."—Ps. ix. 16.  "He left not himself
without a witness, in that he did good, and gave us rain,
and fruitful seasons."—Acts xiv. 17.

Q. 3. What doth the third commandment require, in reference unto those things whereby God doth make himself
known?

A. The third commandment doth require, in reference
unto the things whereby God doth make himself known—
1. The use of them.  2. The holy and reverent use of them;
that we should use them with holy ends, designing the
glory of God, and in a reverent manner, as is suitable unto
the majesty of God, who maketh himself known by them.
"Give unto the Lord the glory due unto his name."—
Ps. xcvi. 8.  "Great and marvellous are thy works, Lord

God Almighty. Who shall not fear thee, and glorify thy name?"—Rev. xv. 3, 4.

Q. 4. How should our holiness and reverence show itself towards these things?

A. Our holiness and reverence should show itself—1. In reference unto God's names, titles, and attributes; in our holy and reverent thoughts, and meditating on them, so as to admire, fear, love, desire, and delight in God; and in our holy and reverent mention of them with our tongues. 2. In reference unto God's ordinances; in our holy and reverent making use of them, waiting upon, and seeking after God in them. 3. In reference unto God's Word; in our holy and reverent minding the majesty and authority of God therein, so as to yield ready obedience thereunto. 4. In reference unto God's works of creation; in our holy and reverent contemplation of God's infinite power, and wisdom, and greatness, therein manifested: and in reference unto God's works of providence; in our holy and reverent eyeing, following, and complying with God's designs in all his providential dispensations, blessing and praising him for all his mercies, submitting unto, and patiently bearing his corrections, and any sort of afflictions.

Q. 5. When should we especially, holily, and reverently make use of those things whereby God maketh himself known?

A. At all times; but especially when we are called to the duties of his immediate worship, we should be holy and reverent in the use of these things, sanctifying the name of God in them.

Q. 6. What is the difference between the worship of God required in this third commandment, and that which is required in the first and second commandments?

A. The first commandment hath a respect unto the object of God's worship; the second commandment hath a respect unto the means of worship; but this third commandment hath a respect unto the manner of worship, requiring that it be performed with humility and holy fear, with sincerity, fervency, and all kind of holy affections.

LV. Quest. *What is forbidden in the third commandment?*

*Ans.* The third commandment forbiddeth all profaning or abusing of any thing whereby God maketh himself known.

Q. 1. How are God's names, titles, and attributes profaned and abused?

A. God's names, titles, and attributes are profaned and abused—1. When persons do think slightly and irreverently of them, without any suitable affections to them; especially when their hearts are filled with despising, hatred, and aversion towards the name of God. "If I then be a father, where is mine honour? and if I be a master, where is my fear? saith the Lord of hosts unto you that despise my name."—Mal. i. 6. 2. When persons speak irreverently concerning God, making mention of any of his names, titles, or attributes, in ordinary discourse, crying, O Lord, O God, God forgive me, God save me, and the like, without minding what they say, or having any awe of God upon them, whilst they are speaking of him. "Thine enemies take thy name in vain."—Ps. cxxxix. 20. 3. When persons do swear by the name of God, and that either vainly and wickedly mingling their ordinary speech with hideous oaths, priding themselves in their invention of new oaths, and emphatically pronouncing of them; or when persons being called to swear lawfully before a magistrate, or the like, they do swear falsely. "But I say unto you, Swear not at all. But let your communication be, Yea, yea; Nay, nay: for whatsoever is more than these cometh of evil."—Matt. v. 34, 37. "It shall enter into the house of him that sweareth falsely by my name."—Zech. v. 4. 4. When persons do curse either themselves or others in the name of the Lord, either jestingly, rashly, or maliciously. "And the Philistine cursed David by his gods."—1 Sam. xvii. 43. "Then began he to curse and to swear, saying, I know not the man."—Matt. xxvi. 74. 5. When persons blaspheme the name of the Lord, by speaking against any of those names, titles, or attributes, whereby he hath made himself known, or by ascribing any thing unto him which is unworthy of him. "Whom hast thou reproached and blasphemed? and against whom hast thou exalted thy voice, and lifted up thine eyes on high? even against the Holy One of Israel."—2 Kings xix. 22. "Let no man say when he is tempted, I am tempted of God; for God cannot be tempted with evil, neither tempteth he any man."—James i. 13. 6. When persons use the name of the Lord in any charms. "Then certain of the vagabond Jews, exorcists, took upon them to call over them which had evil spirits the name of the Lord Jesus," &c. "And the man in whom the evil spirit was, leapt upon them, and overcame them, so that they fled out of the house naked and wounded."—Acts xix. 13, 16.

Q. 2. How are God's ordinances profaned and abused?

A. God's ordinances are profaned and abused—1. When persons are irreverent in their attendance upon them, in regard of the outward gesture of their bodies, laughing, talking, sleeping, or any other way indecently behaving themselves in the time of prayer, preaching, singing, receiving the sacrament, or any other part of God's worship. "Keep thy foot when thou goest to the house of God."—Eccles. v. 1. "Let all things be done decently and in order."—1 Cor. xiv. 40. 2. When persons, under ordinances, are slight and formal, as to the inward frame of their minds; when their minds are roving and wandering, and their hearts are dead and dull, very unbeseeming the majesty of God, whom in his ordinances they wait upon, who, being a Spirit, doth chiefly look to the spiritual part of his service. "God is a Spirit; and they that worship him, must worship him in spirit and in truth."—John iv. 24. 3. And chiefly, persons profane and abuse God's ordinances, when they make a profession of religion, and attend upon ordinances, that they may be accounted religious by men, without any sincere endeavours to approve the heart unto God; making use of religion only as a cloak for covetousness, or maliciousness, or voluptuousness. "Having a form of godliness, but denying the power thereof."—2 Tim. iii. 5. "Woe unto you, scribes and Pharisees, hypocrites! for ye devour widows' houses, and for a pretence make long prayers; therefore ye shall receive the greater damnation."—Matt. xxiii. 14.

Q. 3. How is God's Word profaned and abused?

A. God's Word is profaned and abused—1. When persons think or speak slightingly, especially when they pervert the Word of God, or any part thereof, into profane jests. "And when this people, or prophet, shall ask thee, saying, What is the burden of the Lord? thou shalt say, What burden? I will even forsake you, saith the Lord. And the burden of the Lord shall ye mention no more; for ye have perverted the words of the living God."—Jer. xxiii. 33, 36. 2. When persons wrest the Word of God into false doctrine, perversely disputing against the sound and wholesome doctrine therein contained. "In which are some things hard to be understood, which they that are unlearned and unstable wrest, as they do also the other Scriptures, unto their own destruction."—2 Pet. iii. 16. "If any man teach otherwise, and consent not to wholesome words, the words of our Lord Jesus Christ, and the doctrine which is according to godliness, he is proud, knowing nothing, but doting about questions and strifes of words, whereof cometh envy, strife, railings, evil surmisings, perverse disputings of men of corrupt minds, and destitute of the truth."—1 Tim. vi. 3–5. 3. When persons misapply the Word of God—the threatenings unto the righteous, to make them sad; the promises to the wicked, to encourage them in their wicked ways. "With lies ye have made the heart of the righteous sad, whom I have not made sad; and strengthened the hands of the wicked, that he should not return from his wicked way, by promising him life."—Ezek. xiii. 22.

Q. 4. How are God's works profaned and abused?

A. God's works are profaned and abused—1. When persons pamper their flesh, gratify their lusts, and are intemperate in their use of God's creatures. "Let us walk honestly as in the day; not in rioting and drunkenness, not in chambering and wantonness, not in strife and envying; but put ye on the Lord Jesus Christ, and make not provision for the flesh, to fulfil the lusts thereof."—Rom. xiii. 13, 14. 2. When, in prosperity, persons are forgetful of God, unthankful for mercies, and indulge themselves the more in sin, because of God's patience and bounty. "They were filled, and their heart was exalted; therefore have they forgotten me."—Hos. xiii. 6. "Or despisest thou the riches of his goodness and forbearance? But, after thy hardness and impenitent heart, treasurest up unto thyself wrath," &c.—Rom. ii. 4, 5. 3. When, in adversity, persons murmur, are impatient; when they are incorrigible, and grow more hardened in their sins. "Neither murmur ye, as some of them murmured, and were destroyed of the destroyer."—1 Cor. x. 10. "Thou hast stricken them, but they have not grieved; thou consumed them, but they have refused to receive correction; they have made their faces harder than a rock; they have refused to return."—Jer. v. 3.

LVI. Ques. *What is the reason annexed to the third commandment?*

*Ans.* The reason annexed to the third commandment is, That however the breakers of this commandment may escape punishment from men, yet the Lord our God will not suffer them to escape his righteous judgment.

Q. 1. Whence is it that such as profane God's name do escape punishment from men?

A. Such as profane God's name, for the most part, do escape punishment from men—1. Because no laws of men do, or can, reach all profanations of God's name. 2. Because such laws as do reach blasphemy, perjury, swearing, and the like grosser profanations of God's name, are not executed by many in authority, who oftentimes, being profane and wicked persons themselves, are more ready to punish them that hallow God's name than those that profane it.

Q. 2. How doth it appear that such as profane God's name shall not escape God's righteous judgment?

A. Such as profane God's name shall not escape God's righteous judgment, because God is righteous, and he will not hold them guiltless.

Q. 3. When doth the Lord punish them that profane his name?

A. 1. Sometimes God doth punish them in this life,

and that with dreadful temporal plagues. "If thou wilt not observe tŏ do all these words, that thou mayest fear this glorious and fearful name, THE LORD THY GOD; then the Lord will make thy plagues wonderful."—Deut. xxviii. 58, 59. 2. Be sure if such escape here, they shall not escape eternal wrath and vengeance hereafter. "Thou treasurest up to thyself wrath against the day of wrath, and revelation of the righteous judgment of God."—Rom. ii. 5.

LVII. Ques. *Which is the fourth commandment?*

*Ans.* The fourth commandment is, " Remember the Sabbath-day, to keep it holy. Six days shalt thou labour, and do all thy work; but the seventh day is the Sabbath of the Lord thy God; in it thou shalt not do any work, thou, nor thy son, nor thy daughter, thy man-servant nor thy maid-servant, nor thy cattle, nor thy stranger that is within thy gates. For in six days the Lord made heaven and earth, the sea, and all that in them is, and rested the seventh day: wherefore the Lord blessed the Sabbath-day, and hallowed it."

LVIII. Ques. *What is required in the fourth commandment?*

*Ans.* The fourth commandment requireth the keeping holy to God such set times as he hath appointed in his Word, expressly one whole day in seven, to be a holy Sabbath to himself.

Q. 1. What is the difference between the worship required in this fourth commandment, and the worship required in the first, second, and third?

A. The first commandment hath a respect unto the object of worship; the second commandment hath a respect unto the means of worship; the third commandment hath a respect unto the manner of worship; but this fourth commandment hath a respect unto the time of worship.

Q. 2. What time for worship doth the fourth commandment require?

A. The fourth commandment doth require such set times for worship to be kept holy unto God as he hath appointed in his Word.

Q. 3. May not the Popish holidays be observed?

A. The Popish holidays ought not to be observed, because they are not appointed in the Word : and, by the same reason, no other holidays may be kept, whatsoever pretence there be of devotion towards God, when there is no precept or example for such practice in the Holy Scripture.

Q. 4. What set time hath God appointed in his Word to be kept holy to himself?

A. God hath appointed in his Word one whole day in seven to be kept a holy Sabbath to himself. " Keep the Sabbath-day to sanctify it, as the Lord thy God hath commanded thee."—Deut. v. 12.

Q. 5. What are we to understand by one whole day in seven, which is to be kept holy to the Lord?

A. By one whole day in seven we are not to understand only the whole artificial day, from sun rising to sun setting, or from day-break in the morning until the evening or night, but the whole natural day, consisting of twenty-four hours.

Q. 6. When doth this holy day or Sabbath begin, in the evening before, or that morning from midnight?

A. In the evening before, by virtue of that word, " Remember to keep holy the seventh day," we ought to begin to prepare for the Sabbath; but the Sabbath itself doth not begin until the evening is spent, and midnight thereof over, and the morning after twelve of the clock beginneth.

Q. 7. Doth not the Scriptures require us to begin the Sabbath in the evening, when it is said, " The evening and the morning were the first day" (Gen. i. 5); and, " From even unto even shall ye celebrate your Sabbath?" —Lev. xxxiii. 32.

A. 1. It doth not follow that the evening of the first day was before the morning, though it be first spoken of ; no more than that Shem and Ham were elder than

Japheth, because they are reckoned up in order before him. "The sons of Noah, Shem, Ham, and Japheth" (Gen. x. 1); and yet Japheth is called the elder brother. —Verse 21. But Moses, reckoning up the works of God on the first day, retires back from the evening to the morning, and saith, they both make up the first day. Surely in the account of all nations, and in Scripture account too, the morning is before the evening. "The same day at evening, being the first day of the week, came Jesus," &c. (John xx. 10), where the evening following this day, and on the evening before the day, is called the evening of the same day. 2. That place in Leviticus, concerning the celebration of the Sabbath from evening to evening, hath a reference only unto a ceremonial Sabbath, or day of atonement, on the tenth day of the seventh month, wherein the Israelites were to afflict their souls; but it hath not a reference unto the weekly Sabbath.

Q. 8. How do you prove by the Scripture that the weekly Sabbath doth begin in the morning?

A. That the weekly Sabbath is to begin in the morning, is evident—1. by Exod. xvi. 23 : " This is that which the Lord hath said, To-morrow is the rest of the holy Sabbath unto the Lord." If the Sabbath had begun in the evening, Moses would have said, This evening doth begin the rest of the Sabbath; but he saith, To-morrow is the rest of the Sabbath. 2. Most evidently it doth appear that the Sabbath doth begin in the morning, and not in the evening, by Matt. xxviii. 1 : " In the end of the Sabbath, as it began to dawn towards the first day of the week, came Mary Magdalene, and the other Mary, to see the sepulchre." If the end of the Jewish Sabbath were not in the evening, when it began to grow dark towards the night, but when it began to dawn towards the first day of the week, which must needs be towards the morning, and in no rational sense can be interpreted of the evening, then the Sabbath did also begin in the morning, and not in the evening, for the beginning and ending must needs be about the same time. But the former is evident from this place, concerning the Jewish Sabbath's ending; and therefore, consequently concerning its beginning. 3. Further, it is also said in this place, that the first day, which is the Christian Sabbath, did begin towards the dawning, as it grew on towards light, and not as it grew on towards darkness; therefore the Christian Sabbath doth begin in the morning. 4. Moreover, the resurrection of Christ, in commemoration of which the Christian Sabbath is observed, was not in the evening, but early in the morning (" Now when Jesus was risen early, the first day of the week "—Mark xvi. 9); therefore the Sabbath is to begin in the morning. 5. If the Sabbath did begin in the evening before, it would end in the evening after; and it would be lawful for men to work in their callings, or to go to their recreations, on the evening of the Sabbath, which surely would be very unsuitable after the holy employments of that day.

Q. 9. Is this fourth commandment, concerning the keeping of the Sabbath, ceremonial or moral ?

A. Though the commandment which the Lord laid upon the Israelites, for the observation of other Sabbaths, was ceremonial, and abrogated, and not to be observed by Christians, yet this fourth commandment, concerning the weekly Sabbath, was moral, and binding upon all nations, and that throughout all generations.

Q. 10. How doth it appear that the fourth commandment was moral, and not ceremonial ?

A. The morality of the fourth commandment doth appear—1. From the time of the Sabbath's first institution, which was in paradise, in the state of innocency, before there was any ceremony. 2. From all the arguments made use of to back it, which are perpetual, and not ceremonial. 3. Because it is placed in the midst of the decalogue, or ten commandments, and all the other nine are moral, and therefore this too; and, with the rest, it was written by God on tables of stone—which showeth the perpetuity of it. 4. Because the Gentiles were required to observe this, the stranger as well as others; but they were not under the ceremonial law. 5. From the testimony of Christ: " Pray ye that your flight be not in the winter, neither on the Sabbath-day."—Matt. xxiv. 20. This flight was to be at the destruction of Jerusalem, in

Vespasian's time, when all ceremonies were abolished; and yet then our Saviour speaks of the Sabbath in force, which would aggravate their grief, if they should be forced to break it.

LIX. Ques. *Which day of the seven hath God appointed to be the weekly Sabbath?*

*Ans.* From the beginning of the world to the resurrection of Christ, God appointed the seventh day of the week to be the weekly Sabbath; and the first day of the week, ever since, to continue to the end of the world, which is the Christian Sabbath.

Q. 1. Is the seventh day of the week always to be kept as holy, and the weekly Sabbath unto the Lord?

A. The seventh day in *number* is always to be kept as holy, and the weekly Sabbath; the seventh part of our time being God's due, and, by virtue of this commandment, to be separated from common use, and employed in his worship, and more immediate service every week; but the seventh day in order from the creation is not necessary always to be observed as a Sabbath, it being in the power of God, who appointed the seventh in order, to alter that order at his pleasure.

Q. 2. Which day of the seven did God at first appoint to be the weekly Sabbath?

A. God did at first appoint the seventh day in order to be the weekly Sabbath: " Six days shalt thou labour and do all which thou hast to do, but the seventh is the Sabbath of the Lord thy God; in it thou shalt not do any work," &c.

Q. 3. Wherefore did God appoint the seventh day at first to be the weekly Sabbath?

A. God did at first appoint the seventh day to be the weekly Sabbath, because it was the day of his rest from his works of creation, that thereon men might rest from their works, and remember his: " For in six days God made heaven and earth, the sea, and all that in them is, and rested the seventh day," &c.

Q. 4. When did God first appoint the seventh day to be the Sabbath ?

A. God did appoint the seventh day to be the Sabbath immediately after the first creation : " And God blessed the seventh day, and sanctified it."—Gen. ii. 3.

Q. 5. Was the seventh day observed as the weekly Sabbath before God wrote the commandment for its observation on tables of stone in the mount, which he delivered unto Moses ?

A. It is more than probable that this seventh day was observed all along by the true worshippers of God, as the other precepts of the law were observed, though no mention be made thereof in the short history of the affairs of some thousand years. For Adam, who lived until the days of Methuselah, no doubt did teach his children this precept, which he had from God in paradise; and Methuselah, who lived till the days of Shem, surely did deliver it down to posterity all the days of the old world; and Shem, who lived till Abraham's time, and is supposed to be Melchizedek, in all probability, did deliver this precept successively unto him in the new world; and as Abraham with ease might, so without question he did, teach it with other precepts to his children, and they teach it one to another, until the time of Moses; and Moses speaketh to the Israelites of the Sabbath to be kept holy to the Lord on the morrow (Exod. xvi. 23), as a thing well known unto them, and of practice among them, which was some time before the Lord gave the law upon Mount Sinai.

Q. 6. How long was the seventh day to be observed as the weekly Sabbath ?

A. The seventh day was to be observed as the weekly Sabbath, from the beginning of the world to the resurrection of Christ.

Q. 7. What day is to be observed for the weekly Sabbath, from the resurrection of Christ ?

A. The first day of the week, from the resurrection of Christ, is to be observed by Christians unto the end of the world for their weekly Sabbath.

Q. 8. How could the seventh day Sabbath be changed from the last of seven to the first of seven, when we do not read expressly of any repeal in the Scripture of the last of seven?

A. 1. It is one day of seven which God hath appointed to be the Sabbath; and in the commandment, the Lord doth bless and hallow, not the seventh day, but the Sabbath-day, which might be on another seventh day in order, if God should so please. 2. It is but one day in seven which God hath appointed to be the weekly Sabbath, God having both allowed and appointed the other six days of the week for our labour. 3. God having substituted or appointed another day for to be a holy Sabbath to himself, this substitution of another doth virtually include in it a repeal of the old Sabbath; that is, in reference unto the time of its observation.

Q. 9. How doth it appear that the first day of the week is appointed by God to be the weekly Sabbath?

A. 1. There is a like reason for the appointment of the first day as there was for the seventh. The reason of God's appointing the seventh was, his resting from his works of creation; and there is a like reason for appointing the first day, which was the day of Christ's resurrection, namely, the Son of God's resting from his suffering works about man's redemption, into which rest he is said to enter, and which we are more nearly concerned to remember. " For he that is entered into his rest, hath ceased from his own works, as God did from his."—Heb. iv. 10. 2. The Lord Jesus hath put his name upon the first day of the week. " I was in the Spirit on the Lord's-day."—Rev. i. 10. There is reason to believe that the Lord's-day here spoken of was the first day of the week, because it is a certain determinate day, and it is spoken of as a day which was well known among Christians by that name; and the first day of the week being the day of the Lord's resurrection, and wherein Christians did use to assemble themselves together upon, had the only reason for such denomination. There is also reason to believe that the Lord did put his own name upon this day, because none had authority to put his name upon any day but himself; and the apostle calling it the Lord's-day, by the inspiration of the Spirit no doubt but it was the Lord's will it should be so called, and by consequence it was his will that this day should be used and observed as an holy day unto himself. As the second sacrament is called the Lord's supper, because it was appointed by the Lord; so the first day of the week is called the Lord's day, because it was appointed by the Lord; and this day being appointed, no other is to be observed now as the Christian Sabbath. 3. The appointment of the first day of the week to be the Sabbath may be inferred from 1 Cor. xvi. 1, 2: "Now, concerning the collection for the saints, as I have given order to the Churches of Galatia, even so do ye. Upon the first day of the week, let every one of you lay by him in store, as God hath prospered him." The apostle having given order from the Lord to the Churches of Galatia and Corinth, and by consequence to the other Churches of the Gentiles, for collections on the first day of the week, as God had prospered them on other days, we may infer, this being a Sabbath-day's work, that he had also, from the Lord, given order for the observation of this first day, as the weekly Sabbath. 4. We read of the disciples being assembled together on the first day of the week, and that Jesus then came among them (John xx. 19); and that eight days after, they met again, which was another first day, and Jesus came to them.—Verse 26. Moreover, that it was the practice of Christ's disciples to meet together to worship the Lord, to hear the word, and break bread, or receive the sacrament of the Lord's supper, on the first day of the week. "And upon the first day of the week, when the disciples were come together to break bread, Paul preached unto them," &c.—Acts xx. 7. Paul had been with them seven days (verse 6), and yet we read of no solemn meeting but on the first day of the week, the last of the seven wherein he abode with them. It was not on the old Sabbath, the last day of the week, that the solemn assembly for worship was held, but on the first day; which, had it not been the Sabbath of new appointment, and of necessary observation to Christians, would have been most inconvenient for Paul to have spent in religious exercises until midnight, when the next morning he was to take his journey. All which being considered, together with the practice of Christians from the apostles' days, it may be evident unto them that desire not to cavil, that the first day of the week is appointed by the Lord to be the Christian Sabbath.

### LX. Ques. *How is the Sabbath to be sanctified?*

*Ans.* The Sabbath is to be sanctified by a holy resting all that day, even from such worldly employments and recreations as are lawful on other days; and spending the whole time in the public and private exercises of God's worship, except so much as is to be taken up in the works of necessity and mercy.

Q. 1. What is it to sanctify the Sabbath?

A. The Sabbath is sanctified by God, in his appointing it to be holy; and the Sabbath is sanctified by man, in his observing and keeping it as holy: " Remember the Sabbath-day, to keep it holy."

Q. 2. How are we to observe and keep the Sabbath as holy?

A. We are to observe and keep the Sabbath as holy, partly by a holy resting, partly in holy exercises on that day.

Q. 3. What are we to rest from on the Sabbath-day?

A. We are on the Sabbath-day to rest, not only from those things which are in themselves sinful, which we are bound to rest from on every day of the week; but also we are to rest from those worldly employments and recreations which on the other six days of the week are lawful, and our duty: " Six days shalt thou labour, and do all thy work. But the seventh day is the Sabbath of the Lord thy God; in it thou shalt not do any work," &c.

Q. 4. May not such works be done in our particular callings on the Sabbath-day as cannot so seasonably and advantageously be done on the other days of the week?

A. There are some works in our particular callings which may seem to be most seasonable and advantageous on the Sabbath-day, and yet it is our duty to rest from them, and wholly to forbear them; such as—1. Killing of beasts on the Sabbath, to prepare for the Monday market. 2. Ploughing, sowing, gathering in of corn, making hay while the sun shines and the weather best serveth, on the Sabbath-day. 3. Selling of fruit, or any other wares, on the Sabbath-day, when there may be most custom for them. 4. Selling or buying of fish on the Sabbath, which in hot weather might stink if kept until the Monday. These, and the like worldly employments, we are to forbear, by virtue of this commandment, they being our own works; and whatever loss we may seem to sustain by such forbearance, be sure it is not comparable to the loss of God's favour, and the wounding of our conscience, and the loss of our souls for ever, which will be the fruit of living in the breach of God's law. And if such works as these must be forborne on the Sabbath, much more such works of our calling as may be done on the week-day, as well as on the Sabbath. " In those days saw I in Judah some treading wine-presses on the Sabbath, and bringing in sheaves, and lading asses; as also wine, grapes, and figs, and all manner of burdens, which they brought into Jerusalem on the Sabbath-day: and I testified against them in the day wherein they sold victuals. There dwelt men of Tyre also therein, which brought fish, and all manner of ware, and sold on the Sabbath unto the children of Judah, and in Jerusalem. Then I contended with the nobles of Judah, and said unto them, What evil thing is this that ye do, and profane the Sabbath-day? Did not your fathers thus, and did not our God bring all this evil upon us, and upon this city? yet ye' bring more wrath upon Israel by profaning the Sabbath."—Neh. xiii. 15–18.

Q. 5. May we not lawfully recreate ourselves upon the Sabbath-day, especially since the day is appointed to be a day of rest from our toiling labour in the week?

A. We may and ought to recreate our minds on the Sabbath-day in the worship of God, we being bound to call and make in this respect the Sabbath our delight. But we ought to forbear recreating our minds with carnal delight, either by words or deeds, which we may do on other days; and much more we ought to forbear recreating our bodies by sports and pastimes, though after the public exercise of God's worship be over. "If thou turn away thy foot from the Sabbath, from doing thy pleasure on my holy day; and call the Sabbath a delight, the holy of the Lord, honourable; and shalt honour him, not doing thine own ways, nor finding thine own pleasure, nor speaking thine own words: then shalt thou delight thyself in the Lord; and I will cause thee to ride upon the high places of the earth, and feed thee with the heritage of Jacob thy father: for the mouth of the Lord hath spoken it."—Isa. lviii. 13, 14.

Q. 6. Though masters and governors of families are bound themselves to rest upon the Sabbath-day, yet may they not command their children and servants to work, or permit them to play and take their recreation?

A. Indeed the commandment is principally directed to masters and governors of families, but withal so as it doth enjoin them to do what in them lieth to hinder their children and servants from the profanation of the day by servile working, or bodily recreations, and to put them upon the observation of this day of rest: "In it thou shalt not do any work, thou, nor thy son, nor thy daughter, thy man-servant, nor thy maid-servant," &c.

Q. 7. May not children or servants lawfully work or play upon the Sabbath-day, if they be commanded hereunto by their parents or masters?

A. Though it be the sin of the parents or masters to command their children or servants to work, or any other way to break the Sabbath, yet it is the duty of children and servants to disobey them, whatever temporal loss they sustain by it; they being bound to obey the God of heaven rather than any man upon earth.

Q. 8. Is it lawful to dress meat on the Sabbath-day?

A. Although it was the will of the Lord that the children of Israel should neither gather nor dress the manna that fell from heaven on the Sabbath-day, there being so much servile work to be done about it before it was fit to be eaten, namely, the grinding of it in mills, or beating it in mortars, and then breaking it, which servile work is still unlawful, unless in cases of necessity; and although fires were forbidden to be kindled in all their habitations,

(Exod. xxxv. 3), that is, to forbear worldly employments, (as the works forbidden in the former verse were, and this instance is a special of the general); yet the Scripture doth nowhere forbid the dressing meat at all, for ordinary food, nor the kindling of fires for such use; but the lawfulness of meat may be collected from the Scripture, inasmuch as our Saviour himself was present at a feast on the Sabbath-day (Luke xiv. 1), where no doubt meat was dressed for so many guests as were there bidden. And when we are allowed to provide food for our cattle on the Sabbath, surely we may lawfully dress meat for ourselves.

Q. 9. What works doth God allow us to do on the Sabbath-day, besides those which he doth principally command us?

A. The works which God doth allow us to do on the Sabbath-day, besides what he doth principally command us, are works of necessity and mercy; such as eating, drinking, defending ourselves from enemies, quenching the fire of houses, visiting the sick, relieving the poor, feeding cattle, and the like; in all which employments we ought not to have a reference chiefly to ourselves, or any temporal advantage, but to be as spiritual as may be in them. " At that time Jesus went on the Sabbath-day through the corn, and his disciples were an hungered, and began to pluck the ears of corn, and to eat. But when the Pharisees saw it, they said unto him, Behold, thy disciples do that which is not lawful to do upon the Sabbath-day. But he said unto them, Have ye not read what David did?" &c. —Matt. xii. 1–3. And, verse 8: " If you had known what this meaneth, I will have mercy, and not sacrifice, ye would not have condemned the guiltless." And verses 10–12: " They said unto him, Is it lawful to heal on the Sabbath-day? and he said unto them, What man shall there be among you, that shall have one sheep, and if it fall into a pit on the Sabbath-day, will he not lay hold on it and lift it out? How much then is a man better than a sheep? wherefore it is lawful to do well on the Sabbath-days." " And the ruler of the synagogue answered with indignation, because that Jesus had healed on the Sabbath-day. The Lord then answered him, and said, Thou hypocrite, doth not each one of you on the Sabbath loose his ox or his ass from the stall, and lead him away to watering? And ought not this woman, being a daughter of Abraham, whom Satan hath bound, lo, these eighteen years, be loosed from this bond on the Sabbath-day?"— Luke xiii. 14–16.

Q. 10. What are the holy exercises, or the works which we are principally commanded to do on the Sabbath-day?

A. The holy exercises which we are to be employed in, or the works which we are principally commanded to do on the Sabbath-day, are the public and private exercises, especially the public exercises of God's worship, such as hearing the word, prayer, receiving the sacrament, singing of psalms, in the public assemblies of God's people. " And it shall come to pass that, from one Sabbath to another, shall all flesh come to worship before me, saith the Lord." —Isa. lxvi. 23. " And he came to Nazareth, where he had been brought up; and, as his custom was, he went into the synagogue on the Sabbath-day, and stood up for to read."—Luke iv. 16. " And upon the first day of the week, when the disciples came together to break bread, Paul preached unto them."—Acts xx. 7. " A psalm or song for the Sabbath-day."—Ps. xcii. (title).

Q. 11. How are we to perform these public exercises of God's worship on the Sabbath-day?

A. We are to perform these public exercises of God's worship on the Sabbath-day—1. With sincerity, having a single respect unto the honour and glory of God, whose day the Sabbath is. " If thou call the Sabbath the holy of the Lord, honourable, and shalt honour him."—Isa. lviii. 13. 2. With reverence, and that both of body and mind. " Keep thy foot when thou goest to the house of God."—Eccles. v. 1. " To this man will I look, even to him that is poor, and of a contrite spirit, and trembleth at my word."—Isa. lxvi. 2. 3. With diligence and attention. " And on the Sabbath we went out of the city by a river side, where prayer was wont to be made. And Lydia, which worshipped God, heard us, whose heart the Lord opened, that she attended unto the things which were spoken of Paul."—Acts xvi. 13, 14. 4. With love and

fervour of spirit. " Fervent in spirit, serving the Lord."
—Rom. xii. 11.   5. With delight and joy.   " If thou call
the Sabbath a delight."—Isa. lviii. 13.

Q. 12. What are we to do by way of preparation for the
public exercises of God's worship on the Sabbath-day?

A. By way of preparation for the public exercises of
God's worship on the Sabbath-day, we are—1. To remember,
before the day come, to keep it holy, so as to finish our
worldly business and employments on the week-days, and
timely to break off from them on the Saturday evening,
and to take pains to get our hearts in a readiness for the
holy duties of the Sabbath.   2. In the morning of the Sabbath, we must begin the day with God, in holy meditation
upon the works of God's creation, and especially upon the
works of redemption, which were completed by Christ's resurrection upon this day; we must read the Scripture, and
some other good books, as we have time, for the better
fitting us for our more public and solemn worship; especially we must pray in secret, and in our families, for God's
presence in his ordinances, and that God would assist his
ministers, who are his mouth to us, and ours to him; and
that he would assist us in a sincere and hearty performance of public duties, that we may attain more knowledge, experience, and mortification, further degrees of
grace, and more communion with God.

Q. 13. What are we to do on the Sabbath-day, after the
public exercises of God's worship are over?

A. After the public exercises of God's worship are over
the work of the Sabbath is not over; but we must retire to
our families (not seek our pleasure in the fields, or in vain
company), and there repeat over what we have heard;
catechise and instruct children and servants, sing psalms,
pray with our families, and whilst we moderately make
use of any creature refreshment, we must discourse of the
things of God.  We ought also to take time in the evening to retire into secret, and there examine ourselves as
to the carriage of our hearts before God in the day; labour
in meditation to get the word wrought more thoroughly
upon our hearts; we must also endeavour to pour out our
hearts before God in secret prayer, humbly confessing sin,

earnestly and believingly requesting pardon and further supplies of grace, and thankfully praising God for all his mercies, especially for his Son Jesus Christ, and the Gospel privileges which we have in and by him. In such variety of holy exercises we may spend the whole Sabbath, which we should make as long as we can; and when the day is at an end, we should long for the Sabbath in heaven, which will never have an end.

LXI. Ques. *What is forbidden in the fourth commandment ?*

*Ans.* The fourth commandment forbiddeth the omission, or careless performance of the duties required, and the profaning the day by idleness, or doing that which is in itself sinful; or by unnecessary thoughts, words, or works, about our worldly employments or recreations.

Q. 1. What sort of sins are forbidden in the fourth commandment?

A. The sins forbidden in the fourth commandment are either sins of omission or sins of commission.

Q. 2. What sins of omission are forbidden?

A. The sins of omission forbidden in the fourth commandment are—1. The omission of the duties of the Sabbath themselves, such as neglecting works of necessity and mercy, when called to them; but especially neglecting the public or private exercise of God's worship, and that either in whole or in part; when we forsake the assemblies of God's people, or omit worshipping God in our families, or praying and seeking God in secret upon this day. 2. The omission of the careful performance of the duties of the Sabbath, when we are hypocritical, dull, dead, full of distractions, weariness, unwatchful, sleepy, and attend upon ordinances without any heart and life, and the Sabbath-day is the most burdensome of all other days of the week unto us. " Ye hypocrites, well did Esaias prophesy of you, saying, This people draweth nigh unto me with their mouth, and honoureth me with their lips; but their heart is far from me."—Matt. xv. 7, 8. " Saying, When will the new moon be gone, that we may sell corn? and the Sabbath, that we may set forth wheat?" —Amos viii. 5. " Ye said also, Behold, what a weariness is it! and ye have snuffed at it, saith the Lord of hosts; and ye brought that which was torn, and the lame, and the sick; thus ye brought an offering: should I accept this of your hand? saith the Lord."—Mal. i. 13.

Q. 3. What sins of commission are forbidden in this fourth commandment?

A. The sins of commission forbidden in this fourth commandment are, the profaning the Sabbath-day—1. By idleness, when we spend the day either in whole or in part idly, neither working in our callings, nor employing ourselves in the duties of God's worship, but loiter away that precious time in our houses or the fields, either in vain and idle thoughts, or in vain and idle discourse, or the like. 2. By doing that which is in itself more grossly sinful; as if, instead of going to the house of God to worship, we should go to the tavern or ale-house, on the Sabbath-day, and be drunk, or go to a base house, or in any house to be wanton and unclean; or if, on the Sabbath-day, instead of hallowing and praising God's name, and praying to him, we should swear by his name in our ordinary discourse, or take his name in vain; if, instead of worshipping God with his people, we should persecute God's people for worshipping him, or rail at them or scoff and deride them, because of the holiness which is in them. 3. By unnecessary thoughts and contrivances about worldly affairs, unnecessary words and discourses about earthly employments, unnecessary works in our particular callings, or by carnal pleasures and recreations, which are lawful on other days; thus thinking our own thoughts, speaking our own words, doing our own works, and finding our own pleasure, are forbidden, Isa. lviii. 13: " Not doing thine own ways, nor finding thine own pleasure, nor speaking thine own words."

LXII. Ques. *What are the reasons annexed to the fourth commandment?*

*Ans.* The reasons annexed to the fourth commandment are, God's allowing us six days of the week for our own employments, his challenging a special propriety in the seventh, his own example, and his blessing the Sabbath-day.

Q. 1. How many reasons are there annexed to the fourth commandment?

A. There are four reasons annexed to the fourth commandment, the more effectually to induce and persuade us unto the strict observation of the Sabbath-day.

Q. 2. What is the first reason?

A. The first reason annexed to the fourth commandment is, God's allowing us six days for our own employment. When he might have taken more time for himself, he hath taken but one day in seven, and alloweth us other six, which are sufficient for the works of our particular callings, and any kind of needful recreations. " Six days shalt thou labour, and do all which thou hast to do."

Q. 3. What is the second reason?

A. The second reason annexed to the fourth commandment is, God's challenging a special property in the seventh day. The seventh day, or Sabbath, being the Lord's, which he hath sanctified and set apart from common use, to be employed in his worship, it is theft and sacrilege to alienate this day in whole or in part to our own use, any further than he hath given us allowance. " But the seventh day is the Sabbath of the Lord thy God."

Q. 4. What is the third reason?

A. The third reason annexed to the fourth commandment is, God's own example, in resting himself from his works of creation on the seventh day, and therefore he would have us also to rest from the works of our particular calling, and sanctify a Sabbath in imitation of him. " For in six days the Lord made heaven and earth, the sea, and all that in them is, and rested the seventh day."

Q. 5. What is the fourth reason?

A. The fourth reason annexed to the fourth commandment is, God's blessing of the Sabbath, by virtue whereof we may hope for his presence with us in the duties of the day, and to receive blessings from him upon ourselves.

" Wherefore the Lord blessed the Sabbath-day, and hallowed it."

LXIII. Ques. *Which is the fifth commandment?*
*Ans.* The fifth commandment is, " Honour thy father and thy mother, that thy days may be long upon the land which the Lord thy God giveth thee."

LXIV. Ques. *What is required in the fifth commandment?*

*Ans.* The fifth commandment requireth the preserving the honour and performing the duties belonging to every one, in their several places and relations, as superiors, inferiors, or equals.

Q. 1. What is the subject of this fifth commandment, or who are the persons of whom the duties of this commandment are required?

A. The subject of the fifth commandment, or the persons of whom the duties of this commandment are required, are relations, especially children and all inferiors, in reference to their parents and superiors, and inclusively superiors in reference to their inferiors, and equals also in reference one to another.

Q. 2. Whom are we to understand by inferiors?

A. By inferiors we are to understand, not only children, but also wives, servants, people, subjects, the younger, and the weaker in gifts or graces.

Q. 3. Whom are we to understand by superiors?

A. By superiors, under the name of father and mother, we are to understand, not only parents, but also husbands, masters, ministers, magistrates, the aged, and stronger in gifts or graces.

Q. 4. Whom are we to understand by equals?

A. By equals we may understand brethren, sisters, kindred, friends, and any acquaintance between whom there is no great distance or difference in regard of age, estate, place, or dignity.

Q. 5. What are the duties of children to their parents?

A. The duties of children to their parents, comprehended in the general precept, "Honour thy father and thy mother," are—1. Inward honour, reverence, and estimation. "A son honoureth his father."—Mal. i. 6. "Ye shall fear every man his mother, and his father; I am the Lord your God."—Lev. xix. 3. 2. Outward reverent carriage and behaviour. "Her children rise up, and call her blessed."—Prov. xxxi. 28. "The king rose up to meet her, and bowed himself unto her, and caused a seat to be set for the king's mother; and she sat on his right hand."—1 Kings ii. 19. 3. Diligent hearkening to their instructions. "Hear, ye children, the instruction of a father, and attend to know understanding."—Prov. iv. 1. "My son, attend unto my wisdom, and bow thine ear to my understanding."—Prov. v. 1. 4. Willing obedience unto all their lawful commands. "Children, obey your parents in the Lord; for this is right."— Eph. vi. 1. "Children, obey your parents in all things; for this is well pleasing to the Lord."—Col. iii. 20. 5. Meek and patient, bearing their reproofs and corrections, with amendment of the faults they are reproved and corrected for. "We have had fathers of our flesh, which corrected us, and we gave them reverence."—Heb. xii. 9. "He that heareth reproof getteth understanding."—Prov. xv. 32. 6. Ready following their reasonable counsel, in reference to their calling, station, marriage, and any great affairs of their lives. "So Moses hearkened unto the voice of his father-in-law, and did all that he had said."—Exod. xviii. 24. "And he came to his father and mother, and said, I have seen a woman in Timnath; get her for me to wife." —Judg. xiv. 2. 7. Grateful kindness to them, in nourishing them, providing for them, and bearing with their infirmities, when aged, and fallen into want and poverty. "He shall be unto thee a restorer of thy life, and a nourisher of thine old age."—Ruth iv. 15. "And Joseph nourished his father with bread."—Gen. xlvii. 12. "Despise not thy mother when she is old."—Prov. xxiii. 22.

Q. 6. What are the duties of parents to their children?

A. The duties of parents to their children, are—1. Tender love and care of them, especially when infants and helpless; particularly, mothers ought to give suck to their children, if they are able. " Can a woman forget her sucking child, that she should not have compassion on the son of her womb ?"—Isa. xlix. 15. 2. Training them up in the knowledge of the Scriptures, and principles of religion, and giving them good instructions in the laws and ways of the Lord, so soon as they are capable of receiving them. " And ye fathers, bring up your children in the nurture and admonition of the Lord."—Eph. vi. 4. " Train up a child in the way he should go; and when he is old, he will not depart from it."—Prov. xxii. 6. " From a child thou hast known the Holy Scriptures."—2 Tim. iii. 15. 3. Prayer for them, and giving good examples of holiness, temperance, and righteousness unto them. " Job sent and sanctified them, and rose up early in the morning, and offered burnt-offerings, according to the number of them all."—Job i. 5. " I will walk within my house with a perfect heart. I will set no wicked thing before mine eyes."—Ps. ci. 2, 3. 4. Keeping them under subjection whilst young, yet requiring nothing of them but what is agreeable to the law of the Lord. " And he went down with them, and was subject unto them."—Luke ii. 51. As children must obey, so parents must command in the Lord.—Eph. vi. 1, 4. 5. Encouragement of them by kind looks and speeches, and rewards in well-doing, together with discountenance, reproof, and loving and seasonable correction of them for evil-doing. " And David said to Solomon his son, Be strong, and of good courage," &c. —1 Chron. xxviii. 20. " Chasten thy son whilst there is hope, and let not thy soul spare for his crying."—Prov. xix. 18. " The rod and reproof give wisdom; but a child left to himself bringeth his mother to shame. Correct thy son, and he shall give thee rest; yea, he shall give delight to thy soul." — Prov. xxix. 15, 17. 6. Provision for them of what is needful for the present; as also laying up for them, according to the proportion of what they have, for the future. "If any provide not for his own, and especially for those of his own house, he hath denied the faith, and is worse than an infidel."—1 Tim. v. 8. " For the children ought not to lay up for the parents, but the parents for the children."—2 Cor. xii. 14. 7. Disposal

of them to trades, callings, and in marriage, when grown
up, as may be most for their good; therein using no force,
but consulting and considering their capacity and inclination. "And Adam knew Eve his wife; and she conceived
and bare Cain. And she again bare his brother Abel.
And Abel was a keeper of sheep, but Cain was a tiller of
the ground."—Gen. iv. 1, 2. "But if any man think that
he behaveth himself uncomely towards his virgin, if she
pass the flower of her age, and need so require, let him do
what he will, he sinneth not; let them marry.—So then,
he that giveth her in marriage doth well."—1 Cor. vii.
36, 38.

Q. 7. What are the duties of wives to their husbands ?

A. The duties of wives to their husbands are—1. Love
of them above all other persons in the world. "That they
teach the young women to be sober, to love their husbands, to love their children."—Tit. ii. 4. 2. Loyalty and
faithfulness, in reference unto the bed and estate, and any
secrets intrusted with them. "Marriage is honourable in
all, and the bed undefiled."—Heb. xiii. 4. "Even so must
their wives be grave, not slanderers, sober, faithful in all
things."— 1 Tim. iii. 11. 3. Reverence and fear of
offending them. "Let the wife see that she reverence her
husband."—Eph. v. 33. 4. Subjection unto them in all
things lawful under Christ. "Wives, submit yourselves
unto your own husbands, as unto the Lord. As the Church
is subject unto Christ, so let the wives be to their own
husbands in everything."—Eph. v. 22, 24. 5. Care to
please them, suiting themselves to their disposition, and
all things to their liking. "She that is married careth for
the things of the world, how she may please her husband."
—1 Cor. vii. 34. 6. Helping them to bear their burdens,
and in making provision for their families. "And the
Lord said, It is not good that the man should be alone;
I will make him an help meet for him."—Gen. ii. 18.
"She looketh well to the ways of her household, and
eateth not the bread of idleness."—Prov. xxxi. 27. 7.
Giving ear to, and complying with, the counsels of their
husbands, if good, for their souls' welfare; and endeavouring, with meekness and wisdom, with kindness and loving

admonitions, and a chaste, sweet conversation, to win their husbands over to the ways of God, when they are wicked. " Ye wives, be in subjection to your own husbands; that, if any obey not the word, they also may, without the word, be won by the conversation of the wives, while they behold your chaste conversation, coupled with fear."—1 Pet. iii. 1, 2.

Q. 8. What are the duties of husbands to their wives?

A. The duties of husbands to their wives, are—1. Most endeared love to them, like unto the love of Christ to his Church. " Husbands, love your wives, even as Christ loved the Church, and gave himself for it."—Eph. v. 25. 2. Dwelling with them, and, according to knowledge, honouring them, and delighting in their company. " For this cause shall a man leave his father and mother, and shall be joined unto his wife."—Eph. v. 31. " Husbands, dwell with them according to knowledge, giving honour unto the wife as unto the weaker vessel."—1 Pet. iii. 7. " Rejoice with the wife of thy youth. Let her be as the loving hind and pleasant roe: let her breasts satisfy thee at all times, and be thou ravished always with her love." — Prov. v. 18, 19. 3. Tenderness towards them, and careful provision of food and raiment, and all things necessary for them, as for their own bodies. " So ought men to love their wives as their own bodies: he that loveth his wife loveth himself. For no man ever yet hated his own flesh; but nourisheth and cherisheth it."—Eph. v. 28, 29. 4. Fidelity to them in keeping the marriage-covenant, so as to forbear the use of any other besides themselves. " Thou shalt not be for another man; so will I also be for thee."—Hos. iii. 3. 5. Protection of them from injuries, and covering of their infirmities with the wings of love. " And David rescued his two wives."— 1 Sam. xxx. 18. " For charity [or *love*] shall cover a multitude of sins."—1 Pet. iv. 8. 6. Care to please them in all things lawful and fit, and praise of them when they do well. " He that is married, careth for the things that are of the world, how he may please his wife."—1 Cor. vii. 33. 7. Prayer with them and for them, counsel and admonition of them, and every way helping them, especially in reference to their souls, walking with them in the ways and ordinances of the Lord. "Ye husbands, dwell with them according to knowledge, as being heirs together of the grace of life, that your prayers be not hindered."—1 Pet. iii. 7. "And they were both righteous before God, walking in all the commandments and ordinances of the Lord blameless."—Luke i. 6.

Q. 9. What are the duties of servants to their masters?

A. The duties of servants to their masters are — 1. Honour of their masters in their heart, speech, and behaviour. "A servant honoureth his master."—Mal. i. 6. "Let as many servants as are under the yoke count their own masters worthy of all honour."—1 Tim. vi. 1. 2. Service of them with diligence, willingness, fear, and out of obedience unto Christ. "Servants, be obedient to them that are your masters according to the flesh, with fear and trembling, in singleness of your heart, as unto Christ; not with eye-service, as men-pleasers, but as the servants of Christ, doing the will of God from the heart; with good will doing service as to the Lord, and not to men."—Eph. vi. 5–7. 3. Faithfulness to them in their estate, and any trust committed to them, with endeavours to please them well in all things. "Exhort servants to please their own masters well in all things; showing all good fidelity, that they may adorn the doctrine of God our Saviour in all things." — Tit. ii. 9, 10. 4. Meekness and patience under reproof and strokes, and that not only when they do deserve them, but also when they are innocent. "Servants, be subject to your masters with all fear, not only to the good and gentle, but also to the froward. For this is thankworthy, if a man for conscience toward God endure grief, suffering wrongfully. For what glory is it, if, when ye be buffeted for your faults, ye shall take it patiently? but if, when ye do well, and suffer for it, ye take it patiently, this is acceptable with God."—1 Pet ii. 18–20.

Q. 10. What are the duties of masters to their servants?

A. The duties of masters to their servants are—1. Wisdom and gentleness in their guidance and government of their servants, and acceptance of their diligence and willingness in their service, not threatening for every fault, remembering that they also are servants to Christ, and have many faults to be covered. "And ye masters, do the same things unto them, forbearing [or *moderating*] threatening; knowing that your Master also is in heaven; and there is no respect of persons with him."—Eph. vi. 9. 2. Provision of convenient and sufficient food for them. "Thou shalt have enough for thy food, for the food of thy household, and for the maintenance of thy maidens."—Prov. xxvii. 27. 3. Payment of their wages in full, and at the promised time. "Masters, give unto your servants that which is just and equal."—Col. iv. 1. "Thou shalt not oppress an hired servant. At his day thou shalt give him his hire; for he is poor, and setteth his heart upon it; lest he cry against thee unto the Lord, and it be sin unto thee."—Deut. xxiv. 14, 15. 4. Reproof of them for sin, and correction of them with more than words for some faults. "A servant will not be corrected with words; for though he understand, he will not answer."—Prov. xxix. 19. 5. Instruction of them in the ways of God; worshipping God with them; allowance of time every day for worshipping God by themselves; restraining them as much as they can from every sin, especially from external breach of the Sabbath; exhortation and persuasion of them unto the obedience and service of the Lord, and therein to be both examples unto, and companions with them. "I know him, that he will command his household, and they shall keep the ways of God."—Gen. xviii. 19. "As for me and my house, we will serve the Lord."—Josh. xxiv. 15. "A devout man, and one that feared God, with all his house."—Acts x. 2.

Q. 11. What are the duties of the people to their ministers?

A. The duties of people to their ministers are—1. High estimation of them, and endeared love to them, for their work's sake. "And we beseech you, brethren, to know them which labour among you, and are over you in the Lord; and to esteem them very highly, in love for their work's sake."—1 Thess. v. 12, 13. "Ye received me as an angel of God, even as Christ Jesus. For I bear you record, that if it had been possible, ye would have plucked out your own eyes, and have given them to me."—Gal. iv. 14, 15. 2. Diligent attendance upon the word preached, and other ordinances administered by them. "He that heareth you, heareth me."—Luke x. 16. 3. Meek and patient suffering the word of reproof, and ready obedience unto the word of command, which ministers shall, from the Scriptures, make known unto them, together with submission unto the discipline intrusted with them by the Lord. "Receive with meekness the ingrafted word," &c. James i. 21. "Obey them that have the rule over you, and submit yourselves; for they watch for your souls."—Heb. xiii. 17. 4. Communicating to them of their temporals. "The Lord hath ordained that they which preach the gospel should live of the gospel."—1 Cor. ix. 14. "Let him that is taught in the word, communicate unto him that teacheth in all good things."—Gal. vi. 6. 5. Prayer for them. "Now I beseech you, brethren, for the Lord Jesus Christ's sake, and for the love of the Spirit, that ye strive together with me in your prayers to God for me."—Rom. xv. 30. "Brethren, pray for us."—1 Thess. v. 25. 6. Shutting their ear against reproaches and slanders, believing nothing without proof; and standing up in their defence against an ungodly world, and many false brethren, and rotten-hearted hypocrites, who are made use of by the devil to cast dirt upon them, that thereby people receiving prejudices against them, might be kept either from hearing them, or receiving benefit by their doctrine, and so be either drawn to ways of error, or hardened in ways of profaneness. "Against an elder receive not an accusation, but before two or three witnesses."—1 Tim. v. 19.

Q. 12. What are the duties of ministers to their people?

A. The duties of ministers to their people are—1. Dear and tender love to their souls. "We were gentle among you, as a nurse cherisheth her children : being so affectionately desirous of you, we were willing to have imparted to you, not the gospel only, but also our own souls, because ye were dear unto us."—1 Thess. ii. 7, 8. 2. Diligent, sincere, and frequent preaching of the word unto them, with administration of all ordinances. "For our exhortation was not of deceit, nor in guile; but as we were allowed of God to be put in trust with the gospel, even so we speak, not as pleasing men, but God, which trieth our hearts."—1 Thess. ii. 3, 4. "Preach the word; be instant in season, out of season; reprove, rebuke, exhort, with all long-suffering and doctrine."—2 Tim. iv. 2. 3. Watchfulness over them, with willingness and cheerfulness. "Feed the flock of God which is among you, taking the oversight thereof, not by constraint, but willingly; not for filthy lucre, but of a ready mind."—1 Pet. v. 2. 4. Prayer for them, and praise for the grace of God which is in them. "Wherefore, I also, after I heard of your faith in the Lord Jesus, and love unto all the saints, cease not to give thanks for you, making mention of you in my prayers."—Eph. i. 15, 16. 5. Showing themselves an example of holiness and good works unto them. "In all things showing thyself a pattern of good works."—Tit. ii. 7. "Be thou an example of the believers, in word, in conversation, in charity, in spirit, in faith, in purity."—1 Tim. iv. 12.

Q. 13. What are the duties of subjects to their magistrates?

A. The duties of subjects to their magistrates, are—1. High estimation and honour of them. "Fear God; honour the king."—1 Pet. ii. 17. 2. Subjection to them, and obedience unto their laws, so far as they are not contrary to the laws of Christ. "Let every soul be subject unto the higher powers."—Rom. xiii. 1. 3. Ready payment of their dues. "Render unto all their dues: tribute to whom tribute is due, custom to whom custom."—Rom. xiii. 7. 4. Defence of them in danger. "Wherefore hast thou not kept thy lord the king? for there came in one to destroy the king thy lord."—1 Sam. xxvi. 15. 5. Prayer and thanksgiving for them. "I exhort that prayers and giving of thanks be made for all men; for kings, and for all that are in authority, that we may lead a quiet and peaceable life in all godliness and honesty."—1 Tim. ii. 1, 2.

Q. 14. What are the duties of magistrates to their subjects? ·

A. The duties of magistrates to their subject are—1. Government of their subjects under Christ, with wisdom, justice, and clemency, endeavouring above all things to promote the interest of religion among them. " Give me wisdom and knowledge, that I may go out and come in before this people."—2 Chron. i. 10. " And Solomon determined to build an house for the name of the Lord, and an house for his kingdom."—2 Chron. ii. 1. 2. Making good laws for the benefit of their subjects, and appointing faithful officers, with charge of due execution of them. " And he set judges in the land, and said, Take heed what ye do; for ye judge not for man, but for the Lord; for there is no iniquity with the Lord our God, nor respect of persons, nor taking of gifts."—2 Chron. xix. 5–7. 3. Care of the common safety of their subjects. " And Jehoshaphat reigned in his stead; and he placed forces in all the fenced cities of Judah, and set garrisons in the land of Judah."—2 Chron. xvii. 1, 2. 4. Encouragement of them that do well, by their example, countenance, and reward, together with discouragement and punishment of evil-doers. " Governors are for the punishment of evildoers, and for the praise of them that do well."—1 Pet. ii. 14.

Q. 15. What are the duties of the younger and inferior in gifts and graces, to the aged and superior?

A. The duties of the younger and inferior in gifts and graces, to the elder and superior, are—1. To rise up before them, and give place to them, with reverence and respect. " Thou shalt rise up before the hoary head, and honour the face of the old man, and fear thy God."—Lev. xix. 32. 2. Humble submission to them, so as to follow their wise counsels. " Likewise, ye younger, submit yourselves unto the elder."—1 Pet. v. 5. 3. Imitation of them in their graces and holy conversation. " Be ye followers of me, even as I also am of Christ."—1 Cor. xi. 1.

Q. 16. What are the duties of the aged and superior in gifts and graces, unto the younger and inferior?

A. The duties of the aged and superior in gifts and graces, unto the younger and inferior, are—To adorn their old age, and show forth the power of their grace in a holy and exemplary conversation. " That the aged men be sober, grave, temperate, sound in faith, in charity, in patience: the aged women likewise, that they be in behaviour as becometh holiness, teachers of good things."—Tit. ii. 2, 3.

Q. 17. What are the duties of equals one to another?

A. The duties of equals one to another, are—1. To live in peace with, and sincere love to one another, preferring each other in honour. " Be at peace among yourselves." —1 Thess. v. 13. " Let love be without dissimulation. Be kindly-affectioned one to another with brotherly love, in honour preferring one another."—Rom. xii. 9, 10. 2. To be pitiful, courteous and affable, and ready to promote one another's good, and to rejoice therein. "Love as brethren, be pitiful, be courteous."—1 Pet. iii. 8. " Let no man seek his own, but every man another's wealth."—1 Cor. x. 24. " Rejoice with them that do rejoice."—Rom. xii. 15.

LXV. Ques. *What is forbidden in the fifth commandment?*

*Ans.* The fifth commandment forbiddeth the neglecting of, or doing any thing against, the honour and duty which belongeth to every one in their several places and relations.

Q. 1. How many ways may we sin against the fifth commandment?

A. We may sin against the fifth commandment two ways—1. By neglecting of the duties therein prescribed. 2. By doing any thing against the honour which belongeth unto every one in their several places and relations.

Q. 2. What are the sins of children against their parents?

A. The sins of children against their parents are—1. Irreverence towards them, and anywise dishonouring of them, either in speech or behaviour. " Cursed be he that setteth light by his father or his mother: and all the people shall say, Amen."—Deut. xxvii. 16. " Whoso curseth his father or his mother, his lamp shall be put out in obscure darkness."—Prov. xx. 20. 2. Disobedience to their commands. " The eye that mocketh at his father, and despiseth to obey his mother, the ravens of the valley shall pick it out, and the young eagles shall eat it."—Prov. xxx. 17. 3. Unteachableness and refusal of their instruction.

" Hear instruction, and be wise, and refuse it not."—Prov. viii. 23. " And thou mourn at last, and say, How have I hated instruction, and have not obeyed the voice of my teachers?"—Prov. v. 11–13. 4. Stubbornness and incorrigibleness under their reproofs and corrections. " And he said, Why do ye such things? for I hear of your evil dealings. Notwithstanding, they hearkened not unto the voice of their father."—1 Sam. ii. 23–25. 5. Wastefulness of their substance, unthankfulness for their care and favours, or anywise unkindness to them, especially when they are aged and in distress. " He that wasteth his father, and chaseth away his mother, is a son that causeth shame, and bringeth reproach."—Prov. xix. 26. " Despise not thy mother when she is old."—Prov. xxiii. 22. 6. Disposal of themselves unto callings or in marriages, without their consent or advice. " And Esau was forty years old when he took to wife Judith, the daughter of Beeri the Hittite and Bashemath the daughter of Elon the Hittite; which were a grief of mind unto Isaac and to Rebekah."—Gen. xxvi. 34, 35.

Q. 3. What are the sins of parents against their children?

A. The sins of parents against their children are—1. Want of natural affection and tenderness towards them, especially when infants, or sick and helpless. " Without natural affection."—Rom. i. 31. " She is hardened against her young ones, as though they were not hers."—Job xxxix. 16. 2. Too fond love, giving them their will, and subjecting themselves thereunto; together with partial love, and that expressing itself more to the less deserving, and less to the more deserving. 3. Neglect of their souls, to give them instruction, and seasonable and needful correction; as also neglect of their bodies to make convenient provision for them. " He that spareth his rod, hateth his son."—Prov. xiii. 24. " If any provide not for his own, he is worse than an infidel."—1 Tim. v. 8. 4. Cruelty towards them, and unreasonable provoking of them unto anger. " Ye fathers, provoke not your children to wrath."—Eph. vi. 4. " Fathers, provoke not your children to wrath, lest they be discouraged."—Col. iii. 21. 5. Encouragement of them, either by their command or example, in ill-doing; or discouragement of them, either by their prohibition or frowns and displeasure, in well-doing.  6. Opposition of that which is really for their good, either in reference unto their calling or marriage.

Q. 4. What are the sins of wives against their husbands?

A. The sins of wives against their husbands are—1. Want of that due reverence, and honour, and endeared love, which they should have for their husbands above all others.  " And Michal saw David dancing before the Lord, and she despised him in her heart."—2 Sam. vi. 16. 2. Infidelity in breaking the marriage covenant, or revealing any secrets committed by their husbands unto them. " To deliver thee from the strange woman, who forsaketh the guide of her youth, and forgetteth the covenant of her God."—Prov. ii. 16, 17.   3. Pride and profusive spending and wasting their estates in costly clothes, beyond their degree, or any other ways.  " Whose adorning, let it not be that outward adorning, of plaiting the hair, and of wearing of gold, or of putting on of apparel."—1 Pet. iii. 3. 4. Unsubjection unto, and imperiousness over their husbands, as if they were their foot, to be commanded by them, and not their head, to rule over them; and this accompanied with frowardness and a contentious spirit, disturbing their husbands with their evil speeches and clamours.  " The contentions of a wife are a continual dropping."—Prov. xix. 13.   5. Evil surmises, and suspicions of their husbands without reason; unkind behaviour towards them whatsoever kindnesses they receive from them, foolish speaking of their faults before others, to their provocation, instead of love and meek admonitions, when they are alone, to their amendment.  6. Deafening their ear unto the loving counsels and faithful reproof of their husbands, for their souls' good, growing the worse, and not the better thereby.

Q. 5. What are the sins of husbands against their wives?

A. The sins of husbands against their wives are—1. Want of that endeared love and kindness which is due to their wives, bitter speeches, unkind and unreasonable

jealousies, revilings, and rage at their advice, especially
when it is loving and meek, and for the real good of their
body, or estate, or name, or soul. "Husbands, love your
wives, and be not bitter against them."—Col. iii. 19. 2.
Unfaithfulness unto their wives, and that either in reference unto their bodies by adultery, or in reference unto
their souls, by neglect of such advice, reproof, or instruction, as may be for their souls' good, especially by drawing
them unto sin, to their souls' ruin. "The Lord hath been
witness between thee and the wife of thy youth, against
whom thou hast dealt treacherously; yet is she thy companion, and the wife of thy covenant."—Mal. ii. 14.
"Then the men which knew that their wives had burnt
incense unto other gods, answered, As for the word which
thou hast spoken unto us in the name of the Lord, we will
not hearken unto thee."—Jer. xliv. 15, 16.

Q. 6. What are the sins of servants against their masters?

A. The sins of servants against their masters are—1.
Disobedience unto their lawful and fit commands, or unwilling obedience; or eye-service of them only, neglecting
their business when their backs are turned. "Servants,
obey in all things your masters; not with eye-service as
men-pleasers, but in singleness of heart, fearing God; and
whatsoever ye do, do it heartily, as to the Lord."—Col.
iii. 22, 23. 2. Dishonouring them, by reviling speeches to
them, or reproachful speeches of them, or by any kind of
rude and saucy behaviour before them. 3. Lying, or anywise dissembling with them; wronging or anywise defrauding of them in their estates. "He that worketh deceit
shall not dwell within my house; he that telleth lies shall
not tarry in my sight."—Ps. ci. 7. 4. Repining at their
provisions without cause, impatience, anger, discontent,
surliness, and answering again when reproved for their
faults. "Not answering again."—Tit. ii. 9. 5. Receiving no instruction from them; withdrawment from, or
negligent and sleepy attendance upon, family worship.

Q. 7. What are the sins of masters against their servants?

A. The sins of masters against their servants are—1.

Requiring and commanding them to do anything which is in itself sinful; or encouraging of them by their example so to do. "It may be the Lord will hear the words of Rabshakeh, whom his master hath sent to reproach the living God."—Isa. xxxvii. 4. 2. Requiring their whole time for themselves, and not allowing them sufficient for the refreshment of nature, and daily secret worship of God. 3. Proud, imperious carriage towards them, and ruling over them with severity, and continual chiding and threatenings, discontent, and dissatisfaction with all their willing endeavours to do them service, too eager insisting upon, and too frequent upbraiding them with their faults. "Forbearing threatening."—Eph. vi. 9. 4. Niggardly pinching, and withholding from them their convenient food, or things needful for them when they are sick, as also keeping back from them their due wages. "Behold, the hire of the labourers which have reaped down your fields, which is of you kept back by fraud, crieth."—James v. 4. 5. Neglect of their souls, and of family worship with them. "Pour out thy fury upon the families that call not upon thy name."—Jer. x. 15.

Q. 8. What are the sins of people against their ministers?

A. The sins of people against their ministers are—1. Hatred and persecution of them, either with the hand or tongue, making slanders, or taking them up without proof, and nowise esteeming and honouring of them as ministers of Christ, and ambassadors sent from heaven unto them. "I will remember his deeds which he doeth, prating against us with malicious words."—3 John 10. "His letters (say they) are weighty and powerful, but his bodily presence is weak, and his speech contemptible."—2 Cor. x. 10. "He that despiseth you, despiseth me."—Luke x. 16. 2. Forbearing to hear them through an itching ear, slightness of spirit in hearing, and anywise grieving of them by their unbelief, hardness of heart, unfruitfulness, divisions among themselves, unstedfastness, and unsuitable conversation unto the gospel which their ministers do preach amongst them. "For the time will come, when they will not endure sound doctrine; but after their own lusts, shall they heap to themselves teachers, having itching ears: and they shall turn away their ears from the truth, and shall be turned unto fables."—2 Tim. iv. 3, 4. "He looked about with anger, being grieved for the hardness of their hearts."—Mark iii. 5. "Out of much affliction, and anguish of heart, I wrote unto you with many tears."—2 Cor. ii. 4. 3. Restraining prayer for them, denial of required submission and obedience unto them, withholding due maintenance from them, or anywise neglecting the duties required of people to their ministers.

Q. 9. What are the sins of ministers against their people?

A. The sins of ministers against their people are—1. Want of sincere and tender love to their souls, seeking more to receive earthly gain from them, than to do any good unto them. "I seek not yours, but you."—2 Cor. xii. 14. "His watchmen are blind; they are greedy dogs which can never have enough; they look every one for his gain from his quarter."—Isa. lvi. 10. 2. Negligence in their prayers and studies for them, and in their preaching the word to them. "Give attendance to reading, to exhortation, to doctrine : neglect not the gift that is in thee, which was given thee by prophecy, with the laying on of the hands of the presbytery."—1 Tim. iv. 13, 14. 3. Unwatchfulness over them, unprofitableness in their discourse among them, unsuitableness of conversation unto their doctrine and profession, unteaching that by their lives which they teach in their pulpits. 4. Corrupting the word they preach, and infecting the minds of their people with erroneous opinions. "We are not as many, which corrupt the word of God."—2 Cor. ii. 17.

Q. 10. What are the sins of subjects against their magistrates?

A. The sins of subjects against their magistrates are—1. Rebellion against them, and any treasonable seeking their overthrow and ruin. "An evil man seeketh only rebellion, therefore a cruel messenger shall be sent against him."—Prov. xvii. 11. 2. Unsubjection and disobedience unto their good and righteous laws. "Wherefore ye must needs be subject, not only for wrath, but also for conscience' sake."—Rom. xiii. 5. 3. Neglecting of prayer for them, and, instead thereof, speaking evil of them. "Presumptuous are they, self-willed, they are not afraid to speak evil of dignities."—2 Pet. ii. 10. 4. Reviling speeches unto them, and irreverent behaviour before them. "Thou shalt not revile the gods, nor curse the ruler of thy people."—Exod. xxii. 28. "And Araunah went out, and bowed himself before the king."—2 Sam. xxiv. 20. 5. Denial of their just dues, and anywise defrauding of them. "Owe no man any thing."—Rom. xii. 8.

Q. 11. What are the sins of magistrates against their subjects?

A. The sins of magistrates against their subjects are—1. Making laws which are contrary to the laws of God. "Hast thou not signed a decree, that every man that shall ask a petition of any god or man within thirty days, save of thee, O king, shall be cast into the den of lions?"—Dan. vi. 12. 2. Oppression, tyranny, and cruelty in their government. "As a roaring lion and a raging bear, so is a wicked ruler over the poor people. The prince that wanteth understanding is also a great oppressor; but he that hateth covetousness shall prolong his days."—Prov. xxviii. 15, 16. 3. Seeking their own interest, rather than the interest of the commonwealth. 4. Discountenance and discouragement of the good and righteous, together with encouragement and preferment of the wicked and unrighteous. 5. Unsubjection to the laws of God themselves, and, by their evil example, encouraging others to do the like. "The wicked walk on every side when the vilest men are exalted."—Ps. xii. 8.

Q. 12. What are the sins of the younger and weaker in gifts and graces against them that are aged and stronger?

A. The sins of the younger and weaker in gifts and graces, against them which are aged and stronger, are—1. A proud conceitedness of wisdom and worth in themselves, beyond their elders and betters, together with a despising of them in their hearts, and judging of them for making use of their known liberty. "Not a novice, lest, being lifted up with pride, he fall into the condemnation of the devil."—1 Tim. iii. 6. "Let not him that eateth not, judge him that eateth."—Rom. xiv. 3. 2. A rude and indecent taking place of them, or anywise irreverent carriage towards them. "Sit not down in the highest room, lest a more honourable man than thou be bidden, and he say, Give this man place."—Luke xiv. 8, 9. 3. A masterly spirit and stiff will, which will not yield to their wise counsels, and advice for their good.

Q. 13. What are the sins of the aged and stronger in gifts and graces against the younger and weaker?

A. The sins of the aged and stronger in gifts and graces, against the younger and weaker, are—1. Giving them evil examples of unholiness, covetousness, unrighteousness, intemperance, or any wickedness. 2. Contemptuous carriage towards them, or not giving due encouragement unto good beginnings. 3. Not bearing with their weakness, and despising of them because of their infirmities. "We, then, that are strong, ought to bear the infirmities of the weak, and not to please ourselves."—Rom. xv. 1. "Let not him that eateth, despise him that eateth not."—Rom. xiv. 3.

Q. 14. What are the sins of equals against one another?

A. The sins of equals, one against another, are—1. Hatred, envy, malice, inordinate anger towards, and evil speaking either to or of, one another, and any way injuring, defaming, and dishonouring each other. "Let all bitterness, and wrath, and anger, and clamour, and evilspeaking, be put away from you, with all malice; and be ye kind one to another, tender-hearted, forgiving one another."—Eph. iv. 31, 32. 2. Instead of provoking one another unto love and good works, enticing one another, or yielding unto one another's enticements unto sin. "Let us consider one another, to provoke unto love and good works."—Heb. x. 24. "My son, if sinners entice thee, consent thou not."—Prov. i. 10. 3. A private, contracted, selfish spirit, which keepeth them from any cordial and diligent seeking of one another's good, unless their own private carnal interest be promoted thereby. "Let no man seek his own, but every man another's wealth."—1 Cor. x. 24.

LXVI. Ques. *What is the reason annexed to the fifth commandment?*

*Ans.* The reason annexed to the fifth commandment, is a promise of long life and prosperity, (as far as it shall serve for God's glory and their own good,) to all such as keep this commandment.

Q. 1. What is the promise itself, which is annexed for the encouragement of those that keep this fifth commandment?

A. The promise itself which is annexed for the encouragement of them that keep this fifth commandment, is the promise of long life; and this is the first particular commandment with promise. " Honour thy father and thy mother, that thy days may be long in the land which the Lord thy God giveth thee."—Exod. xx. 12. " Honour thy father and thy mother; which is the first commandment with promise."—Eph. vi. 2.

Q. 2. How is the fifth commandment the first commandment with promise, when there is a promise of God's showing mercy unto thousands, annexed unto the second commandment?

A. The promise of God's showing mercy unto thousands, annexed unto the second commandment, hath not respect unto that commandment only, but is made to those that love God, and, with that, keep all his other commandments; whereas this promise of long life is particularly applied unto the keepers of this fifth commandment.

Q. 3. What is included in this promise of long life?

A. This promise of long life doth include, not only the continuance of life for a long time, which may be so accompanied with miseries that death may be more desirable; but also, it includeth the blessing and prosperity of life. " Honour thy father and thy mother, that it may be well with thee, and thou mayest live long upon the earth." —Eph. vi. 2, 3.

Q. 4. Do all those, then, that honour their parents live long and prosper upon the earth?

A. 1. Many that honour their parents, and are faithful in all relative duties, do now attain long life and prosperity in the world, and that by virtue of this promise; and those that do otherwise, are many of them cut off in their youth, or in the midst of their days, and bring the curse of poverty and want upon themselves whilst they live: yet withal, we may observe that temporal promises and judgments were fulfilled more in the letter formerly in the Old Testament times, than in the latter gospel-days, wherein they are often exchanged into spiritual. 2. This promise is to be understood with this exception—so far as it may serve for God's glory and the real good of all those that keep this commandment; and oftentimes God is glorified, and they are benefited, when they are exercised with affliction, and God sees it best to take some of them home in their youth, or strength of their years, to himself, to hide them from the miseries that befall them that survive, and, instead of long life on the earth, he giveth them eternal life in heaven. " It is good for me that I have been afflicted, that I might learn thy statutes."—Ps. cxix. 71. " The righteous perisheth, and merciful men are taken away from the evil to come."—Isa. lvii. 1. " This is the promise he hath promised us, even eternal life."— 1 John ii. 25.

LXVII. Ques. *Which is the sixth commandment?*
*Ans.* The sixth commandment is, " Thou shalt not kill."

LXVIII. Ques. *What is required in the sixth commandment?*
*Ans.* The sixth commandment requireth all lawful endeavours to preserve our own life, and the life of others.

Q. 1. What doth the sixth commandment respect?
A. The sixth commandment doth respect our own and others' life.

Q. 2. What doth the sixth commandment require, in reference to our own life?
A. The sixth commandment doth require, in reference unto our own life, all lawful endeavours for the preservation of it.

Q. 3. May we not deny Christ and his truths for the

preservation of our life, if we should certainly lose our life for owning and acknowledging them?

A. The denial of Christ and his truths is an unlawful mean for the preservation of our life, and therefore not to be used; and saving our life this way, is the way to lose our life and our souls for ever. " Whosoever shall deny me before men, him will I also deny before my Father which is in heaven."—Matt. x. 33. " Whosoever will save his life, shall lose it. What is a man profited, if he shall gain the whole world, and lose his own soul?"—Matt. xvi. 25, 26.

Q. 4. May we not in any case endeavour the saving of our life by a lie, as Isaac did at Gerar, when he said his wife was his sister, lest the men of the place should kill him for his wife's sake?—Gen. xxvi. 7.

A. The apostle doth answer this case. " We be slanderously reported, that we say, Let us do evil, that good may come; whose damnation is just."—Rom. iii. 8. Therefore the lie of Isaac, for preservation of his life, was his sin, and offensive to God; and no more to be approved than the adultery of David, which the Scripture doth record, not for imitation, but for caution.

Q. 5. May we not defend our life against an enemy that doth assault us on the Sabbath-day, though we intermit the duties of God's worship thereby?

A. Though sins ought never to be committed, whatever good might come thereby, negative precepts binding to all times; yet positive precepts binding always, but not at all times, duties may be intermitted at some time without sin; and God doth dispense with his worship on his day, when it is necessary we should be employed otherwise in the defence of our life against a public enemy.

Q. 6. What are the lawful endeavours which we ought to use for the preservation of our life?

A. The lawful endeavours which we ought to use for the preservation of our life are—1. Defence of ourselves with arms and weapons, against the violence of thieves and cutthroats that seek to murder us. " He that hath no sword, let him sell his garment, and buy one."—Luke xxii. 36. 2. Defence of ourselves with clothes, and in houses, against the violence of the weather and cold. " She is not afraid of the snow for her household; for all her household are clothed with scarlet."—Prov. xxxi. 21. 3. The nourishing and refreshing our bodies in a sober and moderate use of meat, drink, and sleep. " For no man hateth his own flesh, but nourisheth and cherisheth it."—Eph. v. 29. " Drink no longer water, but use a little wine for thy stomach's sake, and thine often infirmities."—1 Tim. v. 23. " If he sleep he shall do well."—John xi. 12. 4. The exercising of our bodies with labour and moderate recreations. " The sleep of a labouring man is sweet."—Eccles. v. 12. " To every thing there is a season, and a time to every purpose under the heaven; a time to weep, and a time to laugh; a time to mourn, and a time to dance."—Eccles. iii. 14. 5. The use of physic for the removal of sickness and the recovery of health. " They that be whole need not a physician, but they that are sick."—Matt. ix. 12. 6. Patience, peaceableness, contentment, cheerfulness, and the moderate exhilarating our spirits with God's gifts, especially rejoicing in the Giver, and using all good means to get and keep our mind and heart in a good temper, which doth much tend to the preservation of our health, and a good temper also in our body. " A merry heart doth good like a medicine; but a broken spirit drieth the bones."—Prov. xvii. 22.

Q. 7. What doth the sixth commandment require, in reference unto the life of others?

A. The sixth commandment doth require, in reference unto the life of others, all lawful endeavours to preserve others' life.

Q. 8. May no lie be made use of to preserve the life of others, especially if they be God's people, and their life be unjustly sought by God's enemies; as Rahab by a lie, saved the lives of the Israelites in her house, for which she is recorded with commendation, and herself and house were saved, when all the city beside were destroyed?

A. 1. No lie must be used upon this or any account, the loss of the lives of the most righteous not being so evil as the least evil of sin. 2. Rahab was commended and spared for her faith, and because of the promise which the

Israelites had made unto her, not because of her lie, which was her sin; which sin, without pardon, would have been punished in hell. "By faith the harlot Rahab perished not with them that believed not, when she had received the spies with peace."—Heb. xi. 31.

Q. 9. How may and ought we to endeavour the preservation of others' lives?

A. 1. Such as are magistrates, judges, and have power in their hand, ought to defend the innocent when oppressed, wronged, and in danger of losing their livelihood, especially when in danger of death. "Defend the poor and fatherless. Deliver the poor and needy; rid them out of the hand of the wicked."—Ps. lxxxii. 3, 4. "If thou forbear to deliver them that are drawn unto death, and those that are ready to be slain : if thou sayest, Behold, we knew it not; doth not He that pondereth the heart consider it? and shall not He render to every man according to his works?"—Prov. xxiv. 11, 12. 2. All ought to distribute necessaries of life according to their ability, unto such as are poor and in want. "If a brother or sister be naked, and destitute of daily food, and one of you say unto them, Depart in peace, be ye warmed and filled, notwithstanding ye give them not those things which are needful to the body, what doth it profit?"—James ii. 15, 16. 3. All ought to forbear all wrongs, and doing any injury unto any person, and to forgive such injuries as are done unto us, returning good for evil. "Be blameless and harmless, the children of God, without rebuke."—Phil. ii. 15. "Forgive one another, if any man have a quarrel against any." —Col. iii. 13. "Be not overcome of evil, but overcome evil with good."—Rom. xii. 21.

LXIX. Ques. *What is forbidden in the sixth commandment?*

*Ans.* The sixth commandment forbiddeth the taking away of our own life, or the life of our neighbour unjustly, or whatsoever tendeth thereunto.

Q. 1. Whom doth the sixth commandent forbid us to kill?

A. The sixth commandment forbiddeth us to kill either ourselves or others.

Q. 2. How are we forbidden to kill ourselves or others?

A. We are forbidden to kill ourselves or others, either directly, by taking away our own or others' life; or indirectly, by doing anything that tendeth thereunto.

Q. 3. Is it lawful upon any account to kill ourselves, as when thereby we shall prevent others from putting us to death with torture and disgrace; as Cato and other heathens, who slew themselves, and Saul, who fell upon his own sword, that he might not be slain and abused by the uncircumcised Philistines?

A. 1. It is unlawful in any case to kill ourselves. " And the keeper of the prison drew out his sword, and would have killed himself; but Paul cried with a loud voice, Do thyself no harm."—Acts xvi. 27, 28. 2. Although the heathens counted it a virtue, and the part of a brave heroic spirit, in some cases to kill themselves, yet the law of God alloweth no such thing, but accounteth such persons self-murderers. 3. It was Saul's sin to die in that act of self-murder; and we ought rather to submit ourselves to any abuses and tortures of others, which is their sin, than to lay violent hands on ourselves, and so die in a sin which there is no time nor place for repenting of afterwards.

Q. 4. Is it possible for them that kill themselves to be saved, when there can be no repenting afterwards for this sin?

A. 1. It is possible for some to give themselves their death wound, and yet repent before they die, and be saved, although this be very rare. 2. It is possible that some, who are children of God, may in a frenzy (Satan taking advantage to inject temptations hereunto) kill themselves, and yet, through habitual faith and repentance, attain to salvation.

Q. 5. Is it lawful in any case to kill others?

A. It is lawful to kill others—1. In the execution of the just sentence of the public laws, especially on such as have been murderers. " Whoso killeth any person, the murderer shall be put to death."—Numb. xxxv. 30. 2. In lawful war. " Cursed be he that keepeth back his sword from blood."—Jer. xlviii. 18.    3. In necessary self-defence.   "If a thief be found breaking up, and be smitten that he die, there shall be no blood shed for him." —Exod. xxii. 2.

Q. 6. Is it lawful to fight and kill one another in a duel?

A. 1. It is unlawful to fight a private duel, except a man be set upon by another, and he cannot avoid it; then it is lawful for a man, in his own defence, to fight and slay his enemy that assaulteth him.    2. It is lawful to fight a public duel, if a single enemy, at the head of an army, do make a challenge, and it may be the means to prevent the effusion of more blood; as David did well to fight with, and kill Goliath.

Q. 7. May we not be guilty of the murder of ourselves or others any other way than by directly taking our own or others' lives?

A. We may be guilty of the murder of ourselves or others indirectly, by doing any thing that tendeth to take away our own or others' lives.   As—1. By neglecting or withholding the lawful and necessary means for the preservation of life; such as meat, drink, sleep, clothes, physic, needful recreations, and the like: when we forbear to make use of the necessary preservatives of life ourselves, either through a pinching humour, or Satan's temptations, that we have no right to them, and thereby hasten our end, we are guilty of self-murder: when we deny the necessaries of life to others in extreme want, through covetousness and want of pity, we are guilty of their murder.   2. By excess in eating, drinking, carking care, envy, immoderate sorrow, or doing any thing which may break and debilitate, or take off the vigour of our minds, and which may breed distempers in our bodies; this tendeth to self-murder.   "Take heed lest your hearts be overcharged with surfeiting, and drunkenness, and cares of this life."—Luke xxi. 34.   "Envy is the rottenness of the bones."—Prov. xiv. 30.   "A broken spirit drieth the bones."—Prov. xvii. 22.   3. By hatred, sinful anger, malice, bitter speeches, oppression; especially by striking, wounding, and anywise hurting the bodies of others; this tendeth to the taking away the lives of others, and is murder in God's account.' 'Whosoever hateth his brother is a murderer."—1 John iii. 15. "Ye have heard that it was said by them of old time, Thou shalt not kill; and whosoever shall kill shall be in danger of the judgment. But I say unto you, That whosoever is angry with his brother without a cause shall be in danger of the judgment; and whosoever shall say, Thou fool, shall be in danger of hell-fire."—Matt. v. 21, 22. "If ye bite and devour one another, take heed that ye be not consumed one of another."—Gal. v. 15. "There is that speaketh like the piercings of a sword."—Prov. xii. 18. "In the midst of thee have they dwelt by oppression: in thee have they vexed the fatherless and the widow."—Ezek. xxii. 7.

LXX. Ques. *Which is the seventh commandment?*
*Ans.* The seventh commandment is, " Thou shalt not commit adultery."

LXXI. Ques. *What is required in the seventh commandment?*
*Ans.* The seventh commandment requireth the preservation of our own and our neighbour's chastity, in heart, speech, and behaviour.

Q. 1. What doth the seventh commandment respect?
A. The seventh commandment doth respect our own and others' chastity.
Q. 2. What doth the seventh commandment require, in reference unto our own and others' chastity?
A. The seventh commandment doth require, in reference unto our own and others' chastity, the preservation thereof, in keeping of ourselves unpolluted, and doing what in us lieth to prevent the defilement of others. " For this is the will of God, even your sanctification, that ye should abstain from fornication: that every one of you should know how to possess his vessel in sanctification and honour."—1 Thess. iv. 3, 4.
Q. 3. Wherein are we bound by this commandment to preserve our own and our neighbour's chastity?

A. We are bound by this commandment to preserve our own and our neighbour's chastity—1. In heart, by such love unto, and desire after, and delight in one another's company, as is pure and chaste; and that whether we be men, as to the company of women; or women, as to the company of men. "See that ye love one another with a pure heart fervently."—1 Pet. i. 22. 2. In speech, by such discourse one with another, as is uncorrupt, and may tend to one another's edification and sanctification. "Let no corrupt communication proceed out of your mouth, but that which is good to the use of edifying, that it may minister grace unto the hearers."—Eph. iv. 29. 3. In behaviour, by such a conversation and actions as are modest and chaste. "That if any obey not the word, they also may without the word be won by the conversation of the wives, while they behold your chaste conversation coupled with fear."—1 Pet. iii. 1, 2.

Q. 4. Whereby may we preserve our chastity?

A. We may preserve our chastity—1. By watchfulness; and that, (1.) Over our hearts and spirits, to oppose uncleanness in the first desires of it, and inclinations of heart to it, and risings of it in the thoughts. "Keep thy heart with all diligence."—Prov. iv. 23. "Therefore take heed to your spirit."—Mal. ii. 16. (2.) Over our senses; our eyes, to turn them away from such objects as may provoke lust. "I made a covenant with mine eyes, why then should I think upon a maid?"—Job xxxi. 1. Our ears, to shut them against all lascivious discourse; we must watch also against such touches and wanton dalliances as may be an incentive to unchaste desires, and take heed of all light and lewd company, and watch to avoid all occasions, and resist temptations to the sin of uncleanness. "Remove thy way far from her, and come not nigh the door of her house."—Prov. v. 8. "His master's wife cast her eyes upon Joseph; and she said, Lie with me. But he refused; and said, How can I do this great wickedness, and sin against God?"—Gen. xxxix. 7–9. 2. By diligence in our callings, wherein, when our bodies and minds are busily employed, both may be preserved from those unclean practices and desires which idle persons are more prone unto. " She eateth not the bread of idleness. Many daughters have done virtuously, but thou excellest them all."—Prov. xxxi. 27, 29. " And Dinah went out to see the daughters of the land. And Shechem took her and lay with her, and defiled her."— Gen. xxxiv. 1, 2. 3. By temperance in eating and drinking, excess in either of which doth pamper the body, and excite unto lust. " They were as fed horses in the morning: every one neighed after his neighbour's wife."—Jer. v. 8. " Look not thou upon the wine when it is red, when it giveth his colour in the cup," &c. " Thine eyes shall behold strange women."—Prov. xxiii. 31, 33. 4. By abstinence, and keeping under the body, when there is need, with frequent fastings. " But I keep under my body, and bring it into subjection, lest that by any means, when I have preached to others, I myself should be a cast-away." —1 Cor. ix. 27. 5. By the fear of God, and awful apprehension of his presence and all-seeing eye. " And why wilt thou, my son, be ravished with a strange woman, and embrace the bosom of a stranger? For the ways of man are before the eyes of the Lord, and he pondereth all his goings."—Prov. v. 20, 21. 6. By faith in Jesus Christ, and thereby drawing virtue from him for the purifying of the heart and the crucifying of the fleshly lusts. " Purifying their hearts by faith."—Acts xv. 9. " And they that are Christ's have crucified the flesh, with the affections and lusts."—Gal. v. 24. 7. By application of the promises of cleansing the heart, and subduing iniquity. " Then will I sprinkle clean water upon you, and ye shall be clean; from all your filthiness will I cleanse you."— Ezek. xxxvi. 25. " He will subdue our iniquities."— Micah vii. 19. " Having therefore these promises, dearly beloved, let us cleanse ourselves from all filthiness of the flesh and spirit, perfecting holiness in the fear of God."— 2 Cor. vii. 1. 8. By the help of the Spirit. " For if ye live after the flesh, ye shall die; but if ye, through the Spirit, do mortify the deeds of the body, ye shall live."— Rom. viii. 13. 9. By frequent and fervent prayer. " Wash me throughly from mine iniquity, and cleanse me from my sin. Purge me with hyssop, and I shall be clean;

wash me, and I shall be whiter than the snow."—Ps. li. 2, 7. "Turn away mine eyes from beholding vanity."— Ps. cxix. 37. "And lead us not into temptation, but deliver us from evil."—Matt. vi. 13. 10. When no other means will avail to quench burning desires, marriage is to be made use of; and that must be in the Lord. "But if they cannot contain, let them marry; for it is better to marry than to burn. If her husband be dead, she is at liberty to be married to whom she will; only in the Lord." —1 Cor. vii. 9, 39.

Q. 5. Why must we preserve our chastity?

A. We must preserve our chastity—1. Because we are men and women, and not beasts, who are under no law; it is suitable to the principles of reason, and law of God written upon the heart, as well as the express command of the word, to keep ourselves chaste and clean. 2. Because we are Christians and not heathens, who have no knowlege or fear of God. "Not in the lust of concupiscence, even as the Gentiles who know not God."—1 Thess. iv. 5. "This I say, therefore, and testify in the Lord, that ye henceforth walk not as other Gentiles walk, who, being past feeling, have given themselves over to lasciviousness, to work all uncleanness with greediness."—Eph. iv. 17, 19. 3. Because we are true believers, our bodies are members of Christ, and temples of the Holy Ghost, and not our own, and therefore ought to be kept clean and holy. "Know ye not that your bodies are the members of Christ? Shall I then take the members of Christ, and make them the members of an harlot? God forbid. What! know ye not that he which is joined to an harlot is one body? What! know ye not that your body is the temple of the Holy Ghost which is in you, which ye have of God, and ye are not your own?"—1 Cor. vi. 15, 16, 19. "If any man defile the temple of God, him shall God destroy: for the temple of God is holy, which temple ye are." —1 Cor. iii. 17.

LXXII. Ques. *What is forbidden in the seventh commandment?*

*Ans.* The seventh commandment forbiddeth all unchaste thoughts, words, and actions.

Q. 1. What is the sin forbidden in the seventh commandment?

A. The sin forbidden in the seventh commandment is, all unchastity and uncleanness. " Fornication, and all uncleanness, let it not be once named amongst you."— Eph. v. 3.

Q. 2. Wherein is all unchastity and uncleanness forbidden?

A. All unchastity and uncleanness is forbidden—1. In the thoughts and desires of the heart, such as wanton thoughts and lustful desires. " Whosoever looketh upon a woman, to lust after her, hath committed adultery with her already in his heart."—Matt. v. 28. " Every man is tempted, when he is drawn away of his own lust, and enticed. Then, when lust hath conceived, it bringeth forth sin."—James i. 14, 15. 2. In words and speeches, such as all obscene words, lascivious songs, and enticing speeches unto any, to draw them to this sin. " Neither filthiness, nor foolish talking."—Eph. v. 4. " Come, let us take our fill of love until the morning, and solace ourselves with loves. With her much fair speech she caused him to yield, with the flattering of her lips she forced him."—Prov. vii. 18, 21. 3. In the actions, and that both the acts of unchastity and uncleanness itself, and whatever actions do tend thereunto.

Q. 3. What are the acts of unchastity and uncleanness which are forbidden?

A. The acts of unchastity and uncleanness which are forbidden, are either such as are without marriage, or in those that are married.

Q. 4. What are the acts of unchastity and uncleanness without marriage forbidden?

A. The acts of unchastity and uncleanness without marriage forbidden are—1. Self-pollution. 2. Fornication and adultery. " Now the works of the flesh are manifest, which are these, adultery, fornication, uncleanness, lasciviousness." —Gal. v. 19. " Thou shalt not lie carnally with thy neighbour's wife, to defile thyself with her."—Lev. xviii. 20. 3. Incest. " None of you shall approach unto any that is near of kin to him, to uncover their nakedness: I am the

Lord."—Lev. xviii. 6.   4. Rape, and all forcing of any into the sin of uncleanness.  " If a man find a betrothed damsel in the field, and the man force her, and lie with her, the man shall die."—Deut. xxii. 25.   5. Sodomy.

Q. 5. What are the acts of unchastity and uncleanness forbidden between those that are married?

A. The acts of unchastity and uncleanness forbidden between those that are married, are, all unseasonable and immoderate use of the marriage-bed. "Thou shalt not approach unto a woman, to uncover her nakedness, as long as she is put apart for her uncleanness." Lev. xviii. 19. "Defraud ye not one another, except it be with consent for a time, that ye may give yourselves to fasting and prayer."—1 Cor. vii. 5.

Q. 6. What are those actions forbidden which do tend to unchastity and uncleanness?

A. The actions forbidden which do tend to unchastity and uncleanness, are—1. Drunkenness. "And they made their father drunk with wine that night; and the first-born went in, and lay with her father."—Gen. xix. 33.  2. Gluttony and idleness. "Behold, this was the iniquity of thy sister, Sodom; pride, fulness of bread, and abundance of idleness was in her; and she committed abomination before me."—Ezek. xvi. 49, 50.  3. Wanton gestures and attires. "The daughters of Zion walk with stretched forth necks, and wanton eyes, walking, and mincing as they go."—Isa. iii. 16.  "There met him a woman, with the attire of an harlot; and she caught him, and kissed him."—Prov. vii. 10, 13.  4. Frequenting light and lewd company, reading lascivious books, beholding unchaste pictures, or doing anything which may provoke lust.

Q. 7. Wherefore ought all to forbear all unchastity and uncleanness, especially the grosser acts of fornication and adultery?

A. All ought to forbear unchastity and uncleanness, especially the grosser acts of fornication and adultery—1. Because fornication and adultery is a sin very offensive and dishonourable unto God. "And David sent messengers, and took her: and she came in unto him, and he lay with her. But the thing that David had done displeased the Lord."—2 Sam. xi. 4, 27.  2. Because fornication and adultery is very pernicious and hurtful unto themselves that are guilty of it.  (1.) It is a sin against their body, which defileth it, and oftentimes wasteth and consumeth it.  "Flee fornication.  Every sin that a man doeth is without the body; but he that committeth fornication, sinneth against his own body."—1 Cor. vi. 18.  "Remove thy way far from her, lest thou mourn at last, when thy flesh and thy body are consumed."—Prov. v. 8, 11.  (2.) It is a sin against their soul, which doth blind the mind, waste the conscience, and, in the issue, doth bring destruction upon the soul.  "Whoredom and wine take away the heart;" that is, the understanding.—Hos. iv. 11. "Whoso committeth adultery with a woman, lacketh understanding; he that doeth it, destroyeth his own soul." —Prov. vi. 32.  (3.) It woundeth and blotteth the name. "Whoso committeth adultery, a wound and dishonour shall he get, and his reproach shall not be wiped away."— Prov. vi. 32, 33.  (4.) It wasteth the estate and substance. "Lest strangers be filled with thy wealth, and thy labours be in the house of a stranger."—Prov. v. 10.  "For by means of a whorish woman, a man is brought to a piece of bread."—Prov. vi. 26.  (5.) It bringeth many to an untimely end.  "The adulteress will hunt for the precious life."—Prov. vi. 26.  "She hath cast down many wounded; yea, many strong men have been slain by her."—Prov. vii. 26.  3. Because fornication and adultery is injurious to others; the party with whom uncleanness is committed, is involved in the same guilt; and if the party be married, it is an injury to the other married relation.

LXXIII. Ques. *Which is the eighth commandment?*

*Ans.* The eighth commandment is, "Thou shalt not steal."

LXXIV. Ques. *What is required in the eighth commandment?*

*Ans.* The eighth commandment requireth the lawful procuring and furthering the wealth and outward estate of ourselves and others.

Q. 1. What doth the eighth commandment respect?

A. The eighth commandment doth respect the wealth and outward estate of ourselves and others.

Q. 2. What doth the eighth commandment require, in reference unto our own and others' wealth and outward estate?

A. The eighth commandment doth require, in reference unto our own and others' wealth and outward estate, the procuring and preservation thereof.

Q. 3. May we use any means for the procuring and preserving of our own and others' wealth and outward estate?

A. We must use none but lawful means for the procuring or preserving of our own or others' wealth and outward estate?

Q. 4. How may and ought we to endeavour the procurement and preservation of our own wealth and outward estate?

A. We may and ought to endeavour the procurement and preservation of our own wealth and outward estate— 1. By making choice of a lawful and fit calling for us; and therein to abide with God. " And the Lord God took the man, and put him into the garden of Eden, to dress it, and to keep it."—Gen. ii. 15. " And Abel was a keeper of sheep, but Cain was a tiller of the ground."—Gen. iv. 2. " Let every man abide in the same calling wherein he was called. Brethren, let every man wherein he is called therein abide with God."—1 Cor. vii. 20–24. 2. By a moderate care in our callings, to provide such things of this world's good things for ourselves, as are honest and decent, and useful for us. " She considereth a field, and buyeth it; with the fruit of her hands she planteth a vineyard."—Prov. xxxi. 16. " Provide things honest in the sight of all men."—Rom. xii. 17. 3. By prudence and discretion in the managing of the affairs of our callings to the best advantage. " A good man showeth favour, and lendeth; he will guide his affairs with discretion."— Ps. cxii. 5. " Discretion shall preserve thee, and understanding shall keep thee."—Prov. ii. 11. 4. By frugality, in decent sparing unnecessary expenses, wasting nothing, and denying ourselves the extravagant and costly cravings of our carnal desires and appetites. " There is a treasure to be desired, and oil in the dwelling of the wise; but a foolish man spendeth it up."—Prov. xxi. 20. " When they were filled, he said unto his disciples, Gather up the fragments that remain, that nothing be lost."—John vi. 12. " Teaching us, that denying ungodliness and worldly lusts, we should live soberly," &c.—Tit. ii. 12. 5. By diligence and laboriousness in our callings. " The hand of the diligent maketh rich."—Prov. x. 4. " Wealth gotten by vanity shall be diminished; but he that gathereth by labour shall increase."—Prov. xiii. 11. " Let him that stole steal no more; but rather let him labour, working with his hands the thing which is good, that he may have to give to him that needeth."—Eph. vi. 28. 6. By seeking unto the Lord for his blessing upon our endeavours, and dependence upon him in the use of means for temporal provisions. " The blessing of the Lord it maketh rich, and he addeth no sorrow with it."—Prov. x. 22. " Be careful for nothing; but in everything by prayer and supplication let your requests be made known unto God."—Phil. iv. 6. " Casting all your care upon him; for he careth for you." —1 Pet. v. 7. 7. By a cheerful use of the good things which God giveth us ourselves, so far as we have need, and a ready distribution to the necessity of others. " There is that scattereth, and yet increaseth; and there is that withholdeth more than is meet, but it tendeth to poverty. The liberal soul shall be made fat; and he that watereth shall be watered also himself."—Prov. xi. 24, 25. 8. By seeking our due, in a moderate endeavour to keep or recover that which doth of right belong unto us, when wrongfully sought or detained from us.

Q. 5. Is it lawful, in the sight of God, to make use of the laws of men to recover or defend that which is our own, when it is said by our Saviour (Matt. v. 40), " If any man will sue thee at the law, and take away thy coat, let him have thy cloak also ?" and by the apostle (1 Cor. vi. 7), " Now therefore there is utterly a fault among you, because ye go to law one with another; why do ye not rather take wrong ? why do ye not rather suffer yourselves to be defrauded ?"

A. 1. Neither of these places of Scripture does absolutely forbid the making use of the law at all, or at any time, for the defence or recovery of our right. 2. That of our Saviour doth forbid contention; and rather than to uphold it, to part with some of our right, such as a coat or a cloak, or any such smaller goods, which, without much prejudice, we might spare; but it doth not hence follow, if another should wrong us in a greater matter, and seek to undo us, that we ought to let him take all which we have in the world, without seeking our right by the laws under which we live; for if this were so, all sincere Christians would quickly be robbed and spoiled by the wicked, amongst whom they live, of all their livelihood. 3. That of the apostle doth forbid Christians going to law one with another before the heathen and infidel magistrates, which was a scandal to the Christian religion which they did profess; and he telleth them, they ought rather to make up their differences about wrong and right amongst themselves, and to suffer wrong rather than do anything to the prejudice of the gospel; but this doth not prohibit Christians, in a Christian commonwealth, to defend or recover their own by law; yet, so much is forbidden in these places, namely, the contending at law about small matters, especially in case of scandal, and the using the law at all, if there be not necessity. 4. That it is lawful in the sight of God to make use of the laws of men for defence or recovery of our right, is evident, from God's appointment of a magistracy to execute those laws, who would be of no use might we not have the benefit of the laws; and because those laws are suitable to the judicial laws of God's own appointment, which the children of Israel might make use of for the defence and recovery of their right; and by the same reason Christians may do so too.

Q. 6. How ought we to endeavour the procurement and furtherance of the wealth and outward estate of others?

A. We ought to endeavour the procurement and preservation of the wealth and outward estate of others, in general, by a public spirit, in seeking the good of the commonwealth above our own, and seeking others' private wealth and advantage, as well as our own. "Let no man seek his own (that is, only), but every man another's wealth."—1 Cor. x. 24.

Q. 7. What is our duty in reference unto such as are poor and in want?

A. Our duty unto such as are poor and in want, is to relieve them, according to our ability and their necessity, by lending and giving freely unto them for their supply and help, especially if they be of the household of faith. " If thy brother be waxen poor, and fallen in decay with thee, then thou shalt relieve him; yea, though he be a stranger or sojourner, that he may live with thee."—Lev. xxv. 35. " As we have opportunity, let us do good unto all men, especially unto them that are of the household of faith."—Gal. vi. 10. " Distributing to the necessities of the saints."—Rom. xii. 13. " Give to him that asketh thee; and from him that would borrow of thee, turn not thou away."—Matt. v. 42. " If a brother or sister be naked, and destitute of daily food, and one of you say, Depart in peace, be ye warmed and filled, notwithstanding ye give them not those things which are needful to the body; what doth it profit ?"—James ii. 15, 16. " Whoso hath this world's good, and seeth his brother have need, and shutteth up his bowels of compassion from him, how dwelleth the love of God in him ?"—1 John iii. 17.

Q. 8. What is our duty towards all, in reference unto their wealth and outward estate?

A. Our duty towards all, in reference unto their wealth and outward estate, is kindness and justice.

Q. 9. Wherein should our kindness show itself in reference unto the wealth and outward estate of others?

A. Our kindness in reference unto the wealth and outward estate of others, should show itself in our readiness unto any offices of love, which may promote and further it. " Let us do good unto all men."—Gal. vi. 10. " I commend unto you Phebe our sister, that ye receive her in the Lord, as becometh saints; and that ye assist her in whatsoever business she hath need of you."—Rom. xvi. 1, 2.

Q. 10. What is the rule of justice to be observed in reference unto the wealth and outward estate of others ?

A. The rule of justice to be observed, in reference unto

the wealth and outward estate of others, is, to do unto others as it is fit, and as we would that others should do unto us. " Therefore all things whatsoever ye would that men should do unto you, do ye even so unto them; for this is the law and the prophets."—Matt. vii. 12.

Q. 11. Wherein must we show our justice in our dealings with others?

A. We must show our justice in our dealings with others—1. In our truth and sincerity in all our concerns with others. " He that walketh uprightly, and worketh righteousness, and speaketh truth in his heart."—Ps. xv. 2. " For our rejoicing is this, that in simplicity and godly sincerity, not with fleshly wisdom, but by the grace of God, we had our conversation in the world."—2 Cor. i. 12. 2. In our faithfulness to fulfil all our lawful covenants and promises, and to discharge whatever trust is committed unto us. " He that sweareth to his own hurt, and changeth not."—Ps. xv. 4. " It is required in stewards, that a man be found faithful."—1 Cor. iv. 2. 3. In our buying and selling, giving a just price for those things that we buy, and taking a reasonable rate for such things as we sell. " If thou sell ought unto thy neighbour, or buyest ought of thy neighbour's hand, ye shall not oppress one another."—Lev. xxv. 14. 4. In paying every one his dues. " Render, therefore, to all their dues; tribute to whom tribute is due; custom to whom custom. Owe no man anything, but to love one another."—Rom. xiii. 7, 8. " Withhold not good from them to whom it is due, when it is in the power of thine hand to do it. Say not to thy neighbour, Go, and come again, and to-morrow I will give, when thou hast it by thee."—Prov. iii. 27, 28. 5. In restoring the pledge which is left with us, or goods of others which are found by us, or anything that is gotten by stealth or fraud. " He shall restore that which he took violently away, or the thing which he hath deceitfully gotten, or that which was delivered him to keep, or the lost thing which he found."—Lev. vi. 4. " Hath not oppressed any, but hath restored to the debtor his pledge, " &c.—Ezek. xviii. 6. " If I have taken anything from any man by false accusation, I restore him fourfold."—Luke xix. 8.

**LXXV. Ques.** *What is forbidden in the eighth commandment ?*

*Ans.* The eighth commandment forbiddeth whatsoever doth or may unjustly hinder our own or our neighbour's wealth or outward estate.

Q. 1. What doth the eighth commandment forbid, as a hindrance of our own wealth and outward estate?

A. The eighth commandment forbiddeth, as a hindrance of our own wealth and outward estate—1. Prodigality and lavish spending of our substance, in gluttony, drunkenness, lewd company, gaming, and the like. " And not many days after, the younger son gathered all together, and took his journey into a far country, and there wasted his substance with riotous living."—Luke xvi. 13. " The drunkard and the glutton shall come to poverty."—Prov. xxiii. 21. " He that loveth pleasure shall be a poor man; he that loveth wine and oil shall not be rich."—Prov. xx. 17. " He that followeth after vain persons shall have poverty enough."—Prov. xxviii. 19. 2. Imprudence in venturing out *all* upon great uncertainties, rash engaging in suretiship, or anywise indiscreet management of our callings, to our detriment. " He that hasteth to be rich hath an evil eye, and considereth not that poverty shall come upon him."—Prov. xxviii. 22. " Be not thou one of them that strike hands, or of them that are sureties for debts. If thou hast nothing to pay, why should he take away thy bed from under thee?"—Prov. xxii. 26, 27. 3. Idleness and slothful neglect of the duties of our particular callings. " Drowsiness shall clothe a man with rags."—Prov. xxiii. 21. " I went by the field of the slothful, and by the vineyard of the man void of understanding; and, lo, it was all grown over with thorns, and nettles had covered the face thereof, and the stone wall thereof was broken down. Yet a little sleep, a little slumber, a little folding of the hands to sleep: so shall thy poverty come as one that travelleth, and thy want as an armed man."—Prov. xxiv. 30–34.

Q. 2. What doth the eighth commandment forbid in

the excess, in reference unto our own wealth and outward estate?

A. The eighth commandment forbiddeth in the excess, in reference unto our own wealth and outward estate— 1. Covetousness, in getting an estate with carking cares, inordinate desires to be rich, or with immoderate labour, so as to waste the body, and to exclude time for religious duty. " Let your conversation be without covetousness, and be content with such things as ye have."—Heb. xiii. 5. " I would have ye without carefulness."—1 Cor. vii. 32. " Take heed, lest at any time your hearts be overcharged with surfeiting and drunkenness, and cares of this life."—Luke xxi. 34. " They that will be rich, fall into temptation and a snare, and into many foolish and hurtful lusts, which drown men in destruction and perdition; for the love of money is the root of all evil, which while some coveted after, they have erred from the faith, and pierced themselves through with many sorrows."—1 Tim. vi. 9, 10. " There is one alone, and not a second; yea, he hath neither child nor brother; yet is there no end of all his labour, neither is his eye satisfied with riches, neither saith he, For whom do I labour and bereave myself of good?"—Eccles. iv. 8. 2. Covetousness, in keeping what we have gotten of the good things of the world, without an heart to make use of them. " There is an evil under the sun, and it is common among men; a man to whom God hath given riches and wealth, so that he wanteth nothing for his soul, of all that he desireth, yet God giveth him not power to eat thereof, but a stranger eateth it : this is vanity, and an evil disease."—Eccles. vi. 1, 2. 3. Unlawful contracts, such as simony in the sale of holy things, the gifts of the Holy Ghost, pardons of sin, and dispensations unto it, church-livings, and the charge of souls. " Thy money perish with thee, because that thou hast thought that the gift of God may be purchased with money."—Acts viii. 20. 4. Bribery in the sale of public justice. " And thou shalt take no gift; for the gift blindeth the wise, and perverteth the words of the righteous."—Exod. xxiii. 8. " Thy princes are rebellious, and companions of thieves; every one loveth gifts, and followeth after rewards; they judge not the fatherless, neither doth the cause of the widow come unto them."—Isa. i. 23. 5. Unlawful arts, fortune telling, figure casting, and making use of any unwarrantable ways for the getting of money. "Thou hast trusted in thy wickedness. Let now the astrologers, the star-gazers, the monthly prognosticators, stand up and save thee."—Isa. xlvii. 10, 13. "Many also of them which used curious arts, brought their books together, and burnt them before all men. A certain man named Demetrius, a silver-smith, which made silver shrines for Diana, brought no small gain unto the craftsmen."—Acts xix. 19, 24.

Q. 3. What doth the eighth commandment forbid in reference unto others which are in want?

A. The eighth commandment forbiddeth, in reference unto others which are in want, a withholding relief from them, and stopping the ear against their cry. "Whoso stoppeth his ears at the cry of the poor, he shall cry himself, but shall not be heard."—Prov. xxi. 13. "If there be a poor man of thy brethren, thou shalt not harden thine heart, nor shut thine hand from thy poor brother."—Deut. xv. 7.

Q. 4. What doth the eighth commandment forbid in reference unto all men?

A. The eighth commandment forbiddeth, in reference unto all men, any kind of injustice and unrighteousness, in any of our dealings with them; such as—1. Defrauding others in our buying, when we discommend that which we know to be good, or take an advantage of others' ignorance of the worth of their commodities, or their necessity of selling them, so as to give a great under-rate for them. "It is naught, it is naught, saith the buyer; but when he is gone his way, then he boasteth."—Prov. xx. 14. "If thou buyest ought of thy neighbour, ye shall not oppress."—Lev. xxv. 14. 2. Defrauding others in selling, when we praise that which we sell, and against our consciences say, It is excellent good, though we know it to be stark naught; and when we take an unreasonable price for our commodities; or when we cozen them, in the sale of goods, by false weights and measures. "That no man go beyond and defraud his brother in any matter; because the Lord is the avenger of all such."—1 Thess. iv. 6. "Thou shalt not have in thy bag divers weights, a great and a small. But thou shalt have a perfect and a just weight, a perfect and just measure shalt thou have."—Deut. xxv. 13, 15. "A false balance is an abomination to the Lord; but a just weight is his delight."—Prov. xi. 1. "Are there yet the treasures of wickedness in the house of the wicked, and the scant measure that is abominable? Shall I count them pure with the wicked balances, and with the bag of deceitful weights?"—Micah vi. 10, 11. 3. Especially, the eighth commandment doth directly forbid stealing one from another—"Thou shalt not steal." "Ye shall not steal, neither deal falsely, neither lie one to another."—Lev. xix. 11.

Q. 5. What stealing doth the eighth commandment forbid?

A. The eighth commandment forbiddeth all stealing, either within the family or without the family.

Q. 6. What stealing within the family doth the eighth commandment forbid?

A. The eighth commandment doth forbid within the family—1. Servants stealing and purloining, as also anywise wasting and wronging their masters, in their goods or estates. "Exhort servants to be obedient to their own masters; not purloining, but showing all good fidelity."—Titus ii. 9, 10. "A certain rich man had a steward; and the same was accused unto him that he had wasted his goods."—Luke xvi. 1. 2. Children stealing and robbing their parents. "Whoso robbeth his father or his mother, and saith, It is no transgression, the same is the companion of a destroyer."—Prov. xxviii. 24. "He that wasteth his father, is a son that causeth shame."—Prov. xix. 26.

Q. 7. What stealing without the family doth the eighth commandment forbid?

A. The eighth commandment doth forbid without the family, all theft, both public and private.

Q. 8. What is the public theft which the eighth commandment doth forbid?

A. The public theft which the eighth commandment

doth forbid, is—1. Sacrilege, which is, when any do either violently or fraudulently take away or alienate any thing that hath been dedicated to sacred uses ; or when sacred persons, without just cause, are taken off from their employment. " Thou that abhorrest idols, dost thou commit sacrilege ?"—Rom. ii. 22. " It is a snare to a man to devour that which is holy."—Prov. xx. 25. " Will a man rob God? yet ye have robbed me : but ye say, Wherein have we robbed thee ? In tithes and offerings. Ye are cursed with a curse ; for ye have robbed me, even this whole nation."—Mal. iii. 8, 9. 2. Robbing public treasuries, or any way wronging and defrauding the commonwealth, by taking away its just liberties and privileges, or by doing a public detriment for private advantage's sake; amongst which public robberies may be numbered inclosures, engrossings, forestallings, monopolies, and the like.

Q. 9. What is the private theft which the eighth commandment doth forbid without the family ?

A. The private theft which the eighth commandment doth forbid without the family, is—1. Man-stealing, or woman-stealing, or stealing of children, that they may be sent or sold for slaves. " The law is not made for a righteous man, but for the lawless and disobedient, for murderers, for man-slayers, for whoremongers, for menstealers, for liars, for perjured persons."—1 Tim. i. 9, 10. " He that stealeth a man, and selleth him, shall surely be put to death."—Exod. xxi. 16. 2. Robbery, either by land or sea, either of money, cattle, or any goods. " And the men of Shechem set liers in wait in the tops of the mountains, and they robbed all that came along that way by them."—Judg. ix. 25. " Now, Barabbas was a robber."—John xviii. 40. " The robber swalloweth up their substance."—Job v. 5.

Q. 10. What further is inclusively forbidden in the eighth commandment ?

A. There is further inclusively forbidden in the eighth commandment—1. All partaking with thieves in receiving stolen goods, or otherwise. " Cast in thy lot among us, let us all have one purse."—Prov. i. 14. " Whoso is partner with a thief, hateth his own soul."—Prov. xxix. 24.

" When thou sawest a thief, thou consentedst with him."
—Ps. l. 18. 2. Detaining that which is strayed or lost.
" Thou shalt not see thy brother's ox or his sheep go
astray, and hide thyself from them; thou shalt in any
case bring them again to thy brother. In like manner
shalt thou do with his raiment, and with all lost things of
thy brother's which thou hast found."—Deut. xxii. 1, 3.
3. Falsehood and unfaithfulness in our promises, and in
regard of any thing committed to our trust. " This he
said, not that he cared for the poor; but because he was
a thief, and had the bag, and bare what was put therein."
—John xii. 6. 4. Rigorous requiring what is owed to us,
without compassion or forbearance. " But the same servant went out, and found one of his fellow-servants, which
owed him an hundred pence; and he laid hands on him,
and took him by the throat, saying, Pay me that thou
owest. And his fellow-servant fell down at his feet, and
besought him, saying, Have patience with me, and I will
pay thee all. And he would not; but went and cast him
into prison, till he should pay the debt."—Matt. xviii.
28–30. 5. Cruel keeping the pledge when it is the means
of our neighbour's living. " If thou at all take thy neighbour's raiment to pledge, thou shalt deliver it unto him by
that the sun goeth down : for that is his covering only, it
is his raiment for his skin: wherein shall he sleep ? And
it shall come to pass, when he crieth unto me, that I will
hear; for I am gracious."—Exod. xxii. 26, 27. 6. All
withholding that which is due, especially the wages and
hire of servants and labourers. " The wicked borroweth,
and payeth not again."—Ps. xxxvii. 21. " The wages of
him that is hired shall not abide with thee all night until
the morning."—Lev. xix. 13. 7. Removing the ancient
land-marks, or any otherwise seeking to defraud others of
the just title which they have to their estates. " Remove
not the ancient land-mark which thy fathers have set."—
Prov. xxii. 28. 8. Extortion and all oppression, especially
of the poor and afflicted. " Rob not the poor, because he
is poor; neither oppress the afflicted in the gate; for the
Lord will plead their cause, and spoil the soul of those
that spoiled them."—Prov. xxii. 22, 23. " Hear this, O ye

that swallow up the needy, even to make the poor of the land to fail; falsifying the balances by deceit, to buy the poor for silver, and the needy for a pair of shoes, and sell the refuse of the wheat, The Lord hath sworn by the excellency of Jacob, Surely I will never forget any of their works."—Amos viii. 4–7.   9. Usury and taking increase merely for loan.  "If thou lend money to any of my people that is poor by thee, thou shalt not be to him as an usurer, neither shalt thou lay upon him usury."—Exod. xxii. 25.  "He that hath not given forth upon usury, neither hath taken any increase."—Ezek. xviii. 8.

Q. 11.  Why should we forbear all manner of theft, and endeavours to enrich ourselves by the wronging of others?

A. We ought to forbear all manner of theft, and endeavours to enrich ourselves by the wronging of others, because it is the express prohibition of God written in the Word, and most agreeable to the law of nature written upon the heart; as also, because that riches got by theft and wrong are accompanied with God's curse; and if not here, be sure God's vengeance will overtake such persons as are guilty of theft and unrighteousness, in the other world.  "This is the curse that goeth forth over the face of the whole earth; for every one that stealeth, shall be cut off on this side: and it shall enter into the house of the thief, and shall consume it, with the timber thereof, and the stones thereof."—Zech. v. 3, 4.  "As the partridge sitteth on eggs, and hatcheth them not; so he that getteth riches, and not by right, shall leave them in the midst of his days, and at his end shall be a fool."—Jer. xvii. 11. "Go to now, ye rich men, weep and howl for your miseries that shall come upon you! ye have heaped treasure together for the last days."—James v. 1, 3.

Q. 12.  How may we be kept from the sins forbidden in this eighth commandment?

A. We may be kept from the sins forbidden in this eighth commandment, by mortified affections to the world through Christ's death and Spirit, by raised affections to the things above, by a love of justice, by prayer, by faith in God's promises and special providence, in making all needful provision without this sin for his.

LXXVI. Ques. *Which is the ninth commandment?*

*Ans.* The ninth commandment is, "Thou shalt not bear false witness against thy neighbour."

LXXVII. Ques. *What is required in the ninth commandment?*

*Ans.* The ninth commandment requireth the maintaining and promoting of truth between man and man, and of our own and our neighbour's good name, especially in witness-bearing.

Q. 1. Wherein doth this ninth commandment differ from the sixth, seventh, and eighth commandments?

A. This ninth commandment doth differ from the sixth, seventh, and eighth commandments, in that the sixth commandment doth respect our own and our neighbour's life; the seventh commandment doth respect our own and our neighbour's chastity; the eighth commandment doth respect our own and our neighbour's wealth and outward estate: but this ninth commandment doth respect our own and our neighbour's good name.

Q. 2. What is more generally required in the ninth commandment?

A. The ninth commandment doth more generally require the maintaining and promoting truth between man and man.

Q. 3. How ought we to maintain and promote truth between man and man?

A. We ought to maintain and promote truth between man and man, by speaking the very truth to and of one another, and that from the heart. "These are the things that ye shall do, Speak ye every man the truth to his neighbour; execute the judgment of truth and peace in your gates."—Zech. viii. 16. "Wherefore putting away all lying, speak every man truth with his neighbour, for we are members one of another."—Eph. iv. 25. "Lord, who shall abide in thy tabernacle? who shall dwell in thy holy hill? He that walketh uprightly, and worketh righteousness, and speaketh the truth in his heart."—Ps. xv. 1, 2.

Q. 4. What doth the ninth commandment more particularly require, in reference unto our own and others' good name?

A. The ninth commandment doth more particularly require, in reference unto our own and others' good name, the maintaining and promoting thereof, especially in witness-bearing.

Q. 5. How ought we to maintain and promote our own good name?

A. We ought to maintain and promote our own good name by deserving it, and defending it.

Q. 6. How may we deserve a good name?

A. Although we can deserve nothing in the sight of God, yet we may deserve a good name in the sight of men, by being good, and by doing good.

Q. 7. What is that which we may be and do that we may deserve a good name amongst men?

A. That we may deserve a good name amongst men, we must be holy, humble, harmless, wise, loving, patient, meek, just, righteous, sober, chaste, true, honest, and every way gracious and virtuous, as to our inward dispositions and affections; our conversations also, and actions, must be correspondent, doing always those things which be praise-worthy and of good report. "Sanctify the Lord God in your hearts; having a good conscience: that whereas they speak evil of you, as of evil-doers, they may be ashamed that falsely accuse your good conversation in Christ."—1 Pet. iii. 15, 16. "That ye may be blameless and harmless, the sons of God, without rebuke, in the midst of a crooked and perverse nation, among whom ye shine as lights in the world."—Phil. ii. 15. "A man's wisdom maketh his face to shine."—Eccles. viii. 1. " Put on therefore (as the elect of God, holy and beloved), bowels of mercies, kindness, humbleness of mind, meekness, long-suffering."—Col. iii. 12. "Finally, brethren, whatsoever things are true, whatsoever things are honest, whatsoever things are just, whatsoever things are pure, whatsoever things are lovely, whatsoever things are of good report; if there be any virtue, if there be any praise, think on these things. Those things which ye have both learned and received, and heard and seen in me, do; and the God of peace shall be with you."—Phil. iv. 8, 9.

Q. 8. How may we defend our good name?

A. We may defend our good name—1. By clearing ourselves from the false aspersions, and vindicating our innocency against the false accusations, of our adversaries. " I do the more cheerfully answer for myself; that thou mayest understand that there are yet but twelve days since I went up to Jerusalem, and they neither found me in the temple disputing with any man, neither raising up the people, neither in the synagogue, nor in the city; neither can they prove the things whereof they now accuse me."—Acts xxiv. 10–13. 2. By speaking sometimes in commendation of ourselves, when there is need only, and that very sparingly, modestly, humbly, and unwillingly, always abasing ourselves, giving God all the glory for anything in ourselves which is praiseworthy. " I am become a fool in glorying; ye have compelled me: for I ought to have been commended of you, for in nothing am I behind the very chiefest apostles, though I be nothing." —2 Cor. xii. 11. " By the grace of God I am what I am: and his grace which was bestowed on me was not in vain; but I laboured more abundantly than they all: yet not I, but the grace of God which was with me."—1 Cor. xv. 10.

Q. 9. Who ought especially to maintain and promote their good name?

A. All ought to maintain and promote their good name, especially all believers and professors of religion; chiefly magistrates, and such unto whom public trust is committed; and ministers, unto whom is committed the charge of souls. " In all things showing thyself a pattern of good works; that he that is of the contrary part may be ashamed, having no evil thing to speak of you. Exhort servants to be obedient unto their own masters, that they may adorn the doctrine of God our Saviour in all things." —Tit. ii. 7–10.

Q. 10. Why ought all to maintain and promote their own good name?

A. All ought to maintain and promote their own good name—1. Because it is for the glory of God, which is the duty of all principally to aim at, and to design their own honour only in subordination hereunto. " Let your light so shine before men, that they may see your good works, and glorify your Father which is in heaven."—Matt. v. 16. " Having your conversation honest among the Gentiles ; that, whereas they speak against you as evil-doers, they may, by your good works which they shall behold, glorify God in the day of visitation."—1 Pet. ii. 12. 2. Because a good name is precious, and rendereth men the more useful one to another, causing mutual love unto, and confidence in one another, whereby their mutual concernments and advantage, both civil and spiritual, are exceedingly promoted. " A good name is better than precious ointment."—Eccles. vii. 1. " A good name is rather to be chosen than great riches, and loving favour rather than silver and gold."—Prov. xxii. 1.

Q. 11. What doth the ninth commandment require of us, in reference to the good name of our neighbour ?

A. The ninth commandment requireth of us, in reference unto the good name of our neighbour, the maintaining and promoting thereof as our own, and that both in regard of ourselves and in regard of others.

Q. 12. How ought we to maintain and promote our neighbour's good name, in regard of ourselves ?

A. We ought to maintain and promote our neighbour's good name, in regard of ourselves—1. By looking unto, and having a due esteem of, the worth and the good things which are in them. " Look not every man on his own things, but every man also on the things of others."— Phil. ii. 4. " Esteem them very highly in love for their work's sake."—1 Thess. v. 13. 2. By liking, and loving, and desiring, and giving thanks to God for their good name and fame. " I thank my God through Jesus Christ for you all, that your faith is spoken of throughout the whole world."—Rom. i. 8. 3. By a ready receiving a good report concerning them, and rejoicing therein. " I rejoiced greatly when the brethren came, and testified of the truth that is in thee, even as thou walkest in the truth."—3 John 3. " Rejoiceth not in iniquity, but rejoiceth in the truth."—1 Cor. xiii. 6. 4. By deafening the ear against and discouraging tale-bearers, backbiters, slanderers, who speak evil of their neighbours. " That taketh not up a reproach against his neighbour."—Ps. xv. 3. " The north wind driveth away rain; so doth an angry countenance a backbiting tongue."—Prov. xxv. 23. 5. By grieving at their faults, which expose them unto disgrace, with desires and endeavours to promote their amendment and the recovery of their reputation. " For, out of much affliction and anguish of heart, I wrote unto you with many tears; not that ye should be grieved, but that ye might know the love which I have more abundantly unto you."—2 Cor. ii. 4.

Q. 13. How ought we to maintain and promote our neighbour's good name, in reference unto others?

A. We ought to maintain and promote our neighbour's good name, in reference unto others—1. By giving that honour unto them which is their due, speaking well of them behind their backs, freely acknowledging their gifts and graces, and good things, and preferring them in honour before ourselves. " Honour all men. Love the brotherhood. Fear God. Honour the king."—1 Pet. ii. 17. " Demetrius hath good report of all men, and of the truth itself: yea, and we also bear record, and ye know that our record is true."—3 John 12. " I thank my God always on your behalf, for the grace of God which is given you by Jesus Christ; that in every thing ye are enriched by him, in all utterance, and in all knowledge; so that ye come behind in no gift; waiting for the coming of our Lord Jesus Christ."—1 Cor. i. 4, 5, 7. " Be kindly affectioned one to another, with brotherly love; in honour preferring one another."—Rom. xii. 10. " Let nothing be done through strife or vain-glory, but, in lowliness of mind, let each esteem other better than themselves."—Phil. ii. 3. 2. By defending their reputation and good name, in endeavours to prevent or stop any evil or false report concerning them, and to vindicate them so far as we can; especially when we are called before a magistrate to bear witness to their innocency, so far as it is consistent with truth. " Then Ahimelech answered the king, and said, And who is so faithful among all thy servants as David, who is the king's son-in-law, and goeth at thy bidding, and is honourable in thine house?"—1 Sam. xxii. 14. 3. By concealing and covering their faults and infirmities when we may, with unwillingness to expose them unto disgrace; and, in the spirit of meekness, endeavouring to restore them when they are overtaken and fallen into sin. "Charity shall cover the multitude of sins."—1 Pet. iv. 8. "Joseph, being a just man, and not willing to make her a public example, was minded to put her away privately."—Matt. i. 19. "Brethren, if a man be overtaken in a fault, ye which are spiritual, restore such an one in the spirit of meekness; considering thyself, lest thou also be tempted." —Gal. vi. 1. 4. By reproving them before others only when there is need, and that with a respect unto their condition, and remembrance of what is praise-worthy in them. "If thy brother shall trespass against thee, go and tell him his fault between thee and him alone. But if he will not hear thee, then take with thee one or two more," &c.—Matt. xviii. 15, 16. "I know thy works, and thy labour, and thy patience," &c. "Nevertheless, I have somewhat against thee," &c.—Rev. ii. 2. 4.

### LXXVIII. Ques. *What is forbidden in the ninth commandment?*

*Ans.* The ninth commandment forbiddeth whatsoever is prejudicial to truth, or injurious to our own or our neighbour's good name.

Q. 1. What is more generally forbidden in this ninth commandment?

A. In this ninth commandment is more generally forbidden two things—1. Whatsoever is prejudicial to truth. 2. Whatsoever is injurious to our own or our neighbour's good name.

Q. 2. What is forbidden in the ninth commandment, as prejudicial to truth?

A. The ninth commandment forbiddeth, as prejudicial to truth, all falsehood and lying whatsoever, whether it be lies to make mischief, as false accusation of others; or lies to make gain, as falsifying of our word, over-reaching our neighbours for advantage to ourselves; or lies to make wonder, as in the inventing of strange or false news; or lies to make sports, as in lying jests; or lies to make excuse, as in all lies for the covering of our own or others' faults. " Lie not one to another, seeing that ye have put off the old man with his deeds."—Col. iii. 9. " All liars shall have their part in the lake which burneth with fire and brimstone."—Rev. xxi. 8.

Q. 3. What doth the ninth commandment forbid, as injurious to our own good name?

A. The ninth commandment forbiddeth, as injurious unto our own good name—1. The doing any thing which is justly of evil report, and may prejudice our reputation among men, such as committing adultery, theft, fraud, and any kind of baseness and wickedness, which is not only dishonourable unto God, but dishonourable unto ourselves. " Whoso committeth adultery with a woman, lacketh understanding; a wound and dishonour shall he get, and his reproach shall not be wiped away."—Prov. vi. 32, 33. " Nay, my sons; for it is no good report that I hear.—Now the Lord saith, Be it far from me; for them that honour me I will honour, and they that despise me shall be lightly esteemed."—1 Sam. ii. 24, 30. 2. All boasting and vainglory, and that whether we boast of a false gift, or those gifts which we really have, whereby we really debase and render ourselves contemptible in the eyes of God, and of the more judicious Christians. " Charity vaunteth not itself, is not puffed up, behaveth not itself unseemly."—1 Cor. xiii. 4, 5. " Whoso boasteth himself of a false gift, is like clouds and wind without rain."—Prov. xxv. 14. " Whosoever shall exalt himself shall be abased; and he that shall humble himself shall be exalted."—Matt. xxiii. 12. 3. Bearing false witness against ourselves, in accusing ourselves in that wherein we are not guilty, and, by denying the gifts and graces which God hath given us, endeavouring to lessen our esteem, that thereby we might be numbered amongst those from whom we are through grace redeemed. " Let no man beguile you of your reward, in a voluntary humility."—Col. ii. 18. 4. Unnecessary and imprudent discovery of all real infirmities, unto the scorn of the wicked and ungodly.

Q. 4. What doth the ninth commandment forbid, as injurious unto the good name of our neighbour?

A. The ninth commandment doth forbid, as injurious unto the good name of our neighbour—1. Perjury, or false swearing and false accusations, or anywise bearing false witness ourselves, or suborning others to bear false witness against our neighbour. " Let none of you imagine evil in your hearts against your neighbour, and love no false oath; for all these are things that I hate, saith the Lord."— Zech. viii. 17. " This know also, that in the last days perilous times shall come; for men shall be lovers of their ownselves, covetous, boasters, proud, blasphemers, disobedient to parents, unthankful, unholy, without natural affection, truce-breakers, false accusers, incontinent, fierce, despisers of those that are good."—2 Tim. iii. 1-3. " False witnesses did rise up; they laid to my charge things that I knew not."—Ps. xxxv. 11. " A false witness shall not be unpunished; and he that speaketh lies shall not escape." —Prov. xix. 5. " And they brought him to the council, and set up false witnesses, which said, This man ceaseth not to speak blasphemous words against this holy place," &c.—Acts vi. 12, 13. 2. Judging, evil-speaking, and rash censuring of our neighbours for doubtful or smaller matters, especially when we are guilty of the same or greater faults ourselves. " And they said, No doubt this man is a murderer, whom, though he hath escaped the sea, yet vengeance suffereth not to live."—Acts xxviii. 4. " Judge not, that ye be not judged. And why beholdest thou the mote that is in thy brother's eye, but considerest not the beam that is in thine own eye?"—Matt. vii. 1, 3. " Therefore thou art inexcusable, O man, whosoever thou art that judgest; for wherein thou judgest another, thou condemnest thyself; for thou that judgest doest the same things."—Rom. ii. 1. " Speak not evil one of another, brethren. He that speaketh evil of his brother, and judgeth his brother, speaketh evil of the law, and judgeth the law; but if thou judge the law, thou art not a doer of the law, but a judge."—James iv. 11. 3. Scoffing, deriding, reviling, and reproachful speeches unto the face of our neighbours, and all backbiting of them, which may wound or detract from their due reputation. " Thou givest thy mouth to evil, and thy tongue frameth deceit. Thou sittest and speakest against thy brother: thou slanderest thine own mother's son."—Ps. l. 19, 20. " Who shall dwell in thy holy hill? He that backbiteth not with his tongue, nor doeth evil to his neighbour."—Ps. xv. 1, 3. " Thou shalt not go up and down as a tale-bearer among thy people."—Lev. xix. 16. " And withal they learn to be idle, wandering about from house to house; and not only idle, but tattlers also, speaking things which they ought not."—1 Tim. v. 13. " Lest there be debates, envyings, backbitings, whisperings, swellings, tumults."—2 Cor. xii. 20. 4. Raising or taking up evil reports against our neighbours, without good proof. " Thou shalt not raise a false report."—Exod. xxiii. 1. " Nor take up a reproach against his neighbour."—Ps. xv. 3. " If a ruler hearken to lies, all his servants are wicked."—Prov. xxix. 12.

LXXIX. Ques. *Which is the tenth commandment?*

*Ans.* The tenth commandment is, " Thou shalt not covet thy neighbour's house, thou shalt not covet thy neighbour's wife, nor his man-servant, nor his maid-servant, nor his ox, nor his ass, nor any thing that is thy neighbour's."

LXXX. Ques. *What is required in the tenth commandment?*

*Ans.* The tenth commandment requireth, full contentment with our own condition, with a right and charitable frame of spirit towards our neighbour, and all that is his.

Q. 1. What doth the tenth commandment require, in reference to ourselves?

A. The tenth commandment doth require, in reference to ourselves, full contentment with our own condition. "Let your conversation be without covetousness; and be content with such things as ye have."—Heb. xiii. 5.

Q. 2. Wherein doth contentment with our own condition consist?

A. Contentment with our own condition doth consist in our free acquiescence and complacency with God's disposal of us, whereby we like our present condition, as best, and most fit for us.

Q. 3. How may we attain contentment in a prosperous condition, when we abound in wealth and the good things of this life?

A. We may attain contentment in a prosperous condition, and when we abound in wealth and the good things of this life—1. By not setting our hearts too much on, nor expecting too much from, any of these things. " If riches increase, set not your heart upon them."—Ps. lxii. 10. " Take heed, and beware of covetousness; for a man's life consisteth not in the abundance of the things which he possesseth."—Luke xii. 15. 2. By placing our chief happiness in God and things above; and chiefly seeking to enjoy God in the good things which we have. "The Lord is the portion of mine inheritance, and of my cup: thou maintainest my lot. The lines are fallen unto me in pleasant places; I have a goodly heritage."—Ps. xvi. 5, 6. 3. By readiness to distribute to the necessities of others, which is accompanied with God's love and blessing, who giveth the greatest comfort in these things unto such. " God loveth a cheerful giver. And God is able to make all grace abound towards you, that ye always, having all sufficiency in all things, may abound unto every good work."—2 Cor. ix. 7, 8. 4. By prayer, and seeking to God through Christ for this grace of contentment, without which the more we have in the world, the more our desires after increase will be enlarged, and the less we shall be satisfied.

Q. 4. How may we attain contentment in a low, necessitous, and afflicted condition?

A. We may attain contentment in a low, necessitous, and afflicted condition—1. By attaining true godliness, unto which alone true contentment is annexed. " Godliness with contentment is great gain."—1 Tim. vi. 6. 2. By being fully persuaded of, and seriously and understandingly eyeing the wise and good hand of God's providence in his disposal of us, and bringing any affliction upon us. " The Lord gave, and the Lord hath taken away; blessed be the name of the Lord."—Job i. 21. " I was dumb, and I opened not my mouth, because thou didst it." —Ps. xxxix. 9. " I know, O Lord, that thy judgments are right, and that thou in faithfulness hast afflicted me." —Ps. cxix. 75. 3. By getting an interest, and trusting in God's promise, to cause all things, even the worst things that can befall us, to work together for our good. " And we know that all things work together for good to them that love God, to them who are the called according to his purpose."—Rom. viii. 28. 4. By humility, and a deep sense of our undeservings and ill-deserving at God's hands for our sins. " I am not worthy of the least of all thy mercies, and of all the truth which thou hast showed unto thy servant."—Gen. xxxii. 10. " O Lord, to us belongeth confusion of face, because we have sinned against thee." —Dan. ix. 8. 5. By looking to others better than ourselves, who have been lower in the world, and more afflicted than we have been. Our Saviour had not where to lay his head; and those of whom the world was not worthy had no certain dwelling-place in the world, and many of them destitute, afflicted, and tormented. 6. By labouring so much the more to abound in spiritual riches, the less we have of temporal; and if we have no earthly inheritance to secure our right unto, living by faith upon our heavenly inheritance; hereby the poorest sometimes become the richest, and those that have most outward trouble have most inward joy. " Hath not God chosen the poor of this world, rich in faith, and heirs of the kingdom which he hath promised to them that love him ?"—James ii. 5. " Having received the word in much affliction, with joy of the Holy Ghost."—1 Thess. i. 6. 7. By considering how we brought nothing into the world, and that we can carry nothing with us out of it. " Naked came I out of my mother's womb, and naked 'shall I return thither."—Job i. 21. " For we brought nothing into this world, and it is certain we can carry nothing out. And having food and raiment, let us be therewith content."—1 Tim. vi. 7, 8. 8. By going to Christ to teach us the lesson of universal contentment, and fetching

strength from him to exercise this grace in every condition. "Not that I speak in respect of want; for I have
learned in whatsoever state I am, therewith to be content.
I know both how to be abased, and I know how to abound;
everywhere, and in all things, I am instructed both to be
full and to be hungry, both to abound and to suffer need.
I can do all things through Christ which strengtheneth
me."—Phil. iv. 11–13.

Q. 5. What doth the tenth commandment require, in
reference unto our neighbour?

A. The tenth commandment doth require, in reference
unto our neighbour, a right and charitable frame of spirit
towards him, and all that is his.

Q. 6. Wherein doth this right and charitable frame of
spirit toward our neighbour, and all that is his, consist?

A. This right and charitable frame of spirit towards
our neighbour, and all that is his, doth consist—1. In our
affections of love, desire, and delight, towards and in our
neighbour, and his welfare; together with grief and sorrow
with and for our neighbour's evil and sufferings. "Be
kindly affectioned one to another with brotherly love.
Rejoice with them that rejoice, and weep with them that
weep."—Rom. xii. 10, 15. "Remember them that are in
bonds, as bound with them, and them which suffer adversity, as being yourselves also in the body."—Heb. xiii. 3.
2. In a ready disposition and habitual inclination unto
these affections towards our neighbour.

Q. 7. How may we attain such affections and dispositions
towards our neighbour?

A. We may attain such affections and dispositions
towards our neighbour—1. By getting the law of God written in our hearts, whereby we are wrought into a love of
the law, and to an inclination to do it. "I will put my
laws into their mind, and write them in their hearts."—
Heb. viii. 10. 2. By getting our affections chiefly set
upon God, which will incline unto any right affections one
towards another. "Every one that loveth him that begat,
loveth him also that is begotten of him."—1 John v. 1.
3. By faith in Jesus Christ, which worketh the heart both
to a true love to God and towards one another. "But

faith which worketh by love."—Gal. v. 6. 4. By looking unto, and following the example of, Jesus Christ. "And walk in love, as Christ also hath loved us, and hath given himself for us."—Eph. v. 2.

LXXXI. Ques. *What is forbidden in the tenth commandment?*

*Ans.* The tenth commandment forbiddeth all discontentment with our own estate, envying or grieving at the good of our neighbour, and all inordinate motions and affections to any thing that is his.

Q. 1. What are the sins forbidden in the tenth commandment?

A. The sins forbidden in the tenth commandment are—1. All discontentment with our own estate. 2. All envying the good of our neighbour. 3. All inordinate motions and affections towards any thing that is his.

Q. 2. Wherein doth discontentment with our own estate show itself?

A. Discontentment with our own estate doth show itself in our not liking, or not being well pleased with our own present condition, in our murmuring and repining, in our vexing and fretting, in our quarrelling and complaining of our condition, and taking no rest nor quiet therein. "And Naboth said to Ahab, The Lord forbid that I should give the inheritance of my fathers unto thee. And Ahab came into his house, heavy and displeased; and he laid him down upon his bed, and turned away his face, and would eat no bread."—1 Kings xxi. 3, 4. "And Haman told them of the glory of his riches, and the multitude of his children, and all the things wherein the king had promoted him. Yet all this availeth me nothing, so long as I see Mordecai the Jew sitting at the king's gate."—Esth. v. 11, 13. "Neither murmur ye, as some of them also murmured, and were destroyed of the destroyer."—1 Cor. x. 10.

Q. 3. Whence doth discontentment with our own estate arise?

A. Discontentment with our own estate doth arise—1.

From our not believing or not trusting the providence of God, who orders every particular circumstance of our estate and condition, and hath promised to order it for the best. "Are not two sparrows sold for a farthing? and one of them shall not fall on the ground without your Father. But the very hairs of your head are all numbered. Fear ye not, therefore, ye are of more value than many sparrows."— Matt. x. 29–31.  2. From pride and overvaluing ourselves, as if we had some desert of our own, and such high thoughts, as if it were fit that such worthy persons as we are should be in a better condition than that wherein God hath placed us.  3. From a carnal heart, filled with inordinate self-love; which, if God's providence doth not gratify with full provisions for the flesh, it doth vex and grieve, and is disquieted.  4. From inordinate affections unto, and expectations of and from, these outward things, which causeth inordinate grief and trouble in the loss of these things, and great discontent in the disappointment of what we expected of them, and from them.

Q. 4. How may we be cured of discontentment with our own estate?

A. We may be cured of discontentment with our own estate, by mourning for it, and application of ourselves unto the Lord Jesus Christ for pardon and healing; and by the diligent use of the means before directed, for the attainment of the grace of true contentment.

Q. 5. What is the second sin forbidden in the tenth commandment?

A. The second sin forbidden in the tenth commandment is envy.  "Let us not be desirous of vain-glory, provoking one another, envying one another."—Gal. v. 26.

Q. 6. What is envy?

A. Envy is a grief at another's good, when the parts and gifts of the mind, or strength and beauty of the body, or the wealth and outward prosperity, or the esteem and honour, or any good thing which another hath, more than ourselves, is a grief or trouble unto us.  "His horn shall be exalted with honour.  The wicked shall see it, and be grieved: he shall gnash with his teeth, and melt away." —Ps. cxii. 9, 10.  "When Sanballat and Tobiah heard it, it grieved them exceedingly, that there was come a man to seek the welfare of the children of Israel."—Neh. ii. 10.

Q. 7. Why ought we to forbear envying one another?

A. We ought to forbear envying one another—1. Because this sin is very offensive unto God, reflecting great dishonour upon his goodness. "Is thine eye evil, because I am good?"—Matt. xx. 15. 2. Because this sin is promoted by, and makes us like the devil, that envious spirit. "Ye are of your father the devil, and the lusts of your father ye will do."—John viii. 44. 3. Because this sin of envy is heart-murder, and the spring of much strife and contention, and of much evil and mischief, which we shall be ready to do unto those whom we envy. "Where envy and strife is, there is confusion and every evil work." —James iii. 16. 4. Because this sin of envy is very injurious unto ourselves—(1.) To our bodies: it causeth a wasting and decay, and is the foundation of many distempers and diseases, where it doth prevail. "Envy is the rottenness of the bones."—Prov. xvi. 30. (2.) To our souls: it puts our souls out of frame, and unfits us for the duties of God's worship. "Wherefore, laying aside all malice, and all guile, and hypocrisies, and envies, and all evil speakings, as new-born babes, desire the sincere milk of the word, that ye may grow thereby."—1 Pet. ii. 1, 2. (3.) To both body and soul: being such a sin as, without repentance, and the mortification of it, will destroy both body and soul in hell.

Q. 8. How may we be delivered from the sin of envy?

A. We may be delivered from the sin of envy—1. By conviction of its evil, and hearty grief for it. 2. By application of the blood of Christ through faith, for the cleansing of our hearts from it." "The blood of Christ cleanseth us from all sin."—1 John i. 7. 3. By cordial love and charity towards our neighbour. "Charity suffereth long, and is kind; charity envieth not."—1 Cor. xiii. 4. 4. By the indwelling of the Spirit, through whom alone this sin can be mortified and subdued. "If ye through the Spirit do mortify the deeds of the body, ye shall live."—Rom. viii. 13.

Q. 9. What is the third sin which the tenth commandment doth forbid?

A. The third sin which the tenth commandment doth forbid, is all inordinate motions and affections towards any thing that is our neighbour's. "Mortify, therefore, your members which are upon the earth; fornication, uncleanness, inordinate affections, evil concupiscence, and covetousness, which is idolatry."—Col. iii. 5.

Q. 10. What special inordinate motion and affection is forbidden in this commandment ?

A. The special inordinate motion and affection which is forbidden in this commandment, is coveting that which is our neighbour's, either his house, or wife, or man-servant, or maid-servant, or ox, or ass, or any thing that is his.

Q. 11. Why ought we not to covet any thing which is our neighbour's ?

A. We ought not to covet any thing which is our neighbour's— 1. Because God hath directly forbidden it. 2. Because it is both uncharitableness and injustice towards our neighbour, to covet any thing that is his. 3. Because we lose the comfort of that which is our own, by coveting and inordinately desiring that which is another's.

Q. 12. Doth this tenth commandment forbid only the actual coveting that which is another's ?

A. The tenth commandment doth not only forbid the actual coveting that which is another's, but also all habitual inclinations hereunto, and all those inordinate motions of the spirit this way which do precede the consent of the will, which is part of original sin, with which human nature is universally polluted and depraved.

LXXXII. Ques. *Is any man able perfectly to keep the commandments of God?*

*Ans.* No mere man since the fall is able, in this life, perfectly to keep the commandments of God, but doth daily break them, in thought, word, and deed.

Q. 1. What is it perfectly to keep the commandments of God ?

A. To keep perfectly the commandments of God, is to keep all the commandments of God, and at all times, without the least breach of them, in regard of disposition, inclination, thought, affection, word, or conversation.

Q. 2. Was ever any man able perfectly to keep the commandments of God?

A. Before the fall, the first man, Adam, was able perfectly to keep God's commandments, he having power given unto him in the first creation, to fulfil the condition of the first covenant of works, which required perfect obedience; but since the fall no mere man is able to do this.

Q. 3. Was not the Lord Jesus Christ able perfectly to keep the commandments of God?

A. The Lord Jesus Christ was both able and also did perfectly keep the commandments of God; but he was not a mere man, being both God and man in one person. "He was in all points tempted like as we are, yet without sin."—Heb. iv. 15. "Whose are the fathers, and of whom, as concerning the flesh, Christ came, who is over all, God blessed for ever."—Rom. ix. 5.

Q. 4. Shall ever any mere man be able perfectly to keep God's commandments?

A. The saints, who are mere men, though not in this life, yet hereafter in heaven they shall be made perfect themselves, and be enabled perfectly to obey God in whatsoever it is that he shall require of them. "We are come to Mount Zion, to the heavenly Jerusalem, to an innumerable company of angels, to the general assembly and church of the first-born, and to the spirits of just men made perfect."—Heb. xii. 22, 23.

Q. 5. Do not the saints on earth keep the commandments of God?

A. The saints on earth do keep the commandments of God sincerely, but not perfectly: "For our rejoicing is this, the testimony of our conscience, that in godly sincerity we have had our conversation in this world."—2 Cor. i. 12. "If thou, Lord, shouldest mark iniquities, O Lord, who shall stand?"—Ps. cxxx. 3.

Q. 6. Do no saints attain perfection here in this life?

A. 1. All saints ought to endeavour after perfection, and that they may attain higher and higher degrees thereof. "Be ye therefore perfect, as your Father which is in heaven is perfect."—Matt. v. 48. 2. No saints on earth ever did attain absolute perfection, so as to obey God in all things, at all times, without any sin.

Q. 7. How do you prove that no saints ever did attain perfection in this life?

A. That no saints did ever attain perfection in this life may be proved—1. Because the best of saints, in this life, are renewed but in part, and have remainders of flesh and corruption, which do rebel and war against the Spirit and renewed part in them. "For the flesh lusteth against the Spirit, and the Spirit against the flesh; and these are contrary the one to the other; so that ye cannot do the things that ye would."—Gal. v. 17. 2. Because the Scripture telleth us expressly that none are without sin; and that such are deceivers of themselves, and make God a liar, that affirm the contrary. "For there is not a just man upon earth, that doeth good, and sinneth not."—Eccles. vii. 20. "For there is no man that sinneth not."—1 Kings viii. 46. "For in many things we offend all."—James iii. 2. "If we say that we have no sin, we deceive ourselves, and the truth is not in us. If we say that we have not sinned, we make him a liar, and his word is not in us."— 1 John i. 8, 10. 3. Because the Scripture hath recorded the sins of the most holy that ever lived. Abraham's dissimulation concerning his wife. "And Abraham said of Sarah his wife, She is my sister."—Gen. xx. 2. The like dissimulation of Isaac. "And he said, She is my sister; for he feared to say She is my wife."—Gen. xxvi. 7. Jacob's lie to his father. "And he said, Art thou my very son Esau? And he said, I am."—Gen. xxvii. 24. Joseph's swearing by the life of Pharaoh. "By the life of Pharaoh, ye shall not go hence, except your youngest brother come hither."—Gen. xlii. 15. Moses' unadvised speech. "They provoked his spirit, so that he spake unadvisedly with his lips."—Ps. cvi. 33. The Scripture recorded Noah's drunkenness; Lot's incest; David's murder and adultery; Job's and Jeremiah's impatience, and cursing their birth-day; Peter's denial of his Master with oaths and curses, and his dissimulation afterwards before the Jews; Paul and Barnabas' contention. And if such persons as these, who were filled with the Holy Ghost, and had as great a measure of grace as any whom we read of, either in the Scriptures or any history, were not perfect, without sin, we may safely conclude that no saints, in this life, have ever attained unto absolute perfection.

Q. 8. Doth not the Scripture tell us, " Whosoever is born of God doth not commit sin; for his seed remaineth in him; and he cannot sin, because he is born of God ?"—1 John iii. 9. And if the saints are without sin in their life, are they not perfect?

A. 1. If the sense of this place should be, that such as are born of God do not commit sin at all, then no regenerate persons which are born of God would ever be found committing sin; but the Scripture doth record the sins of many regenerate persons, as hath been shown, and experience doth evidence the same, that such as are born of God commit sin; and therefore that cannot be the meaning of the place, that such as are born of God do not commit sin at all. 2. Such as are born of God do not commit sin; that is, (1.) They do not commit sin with the full consent of their will, which is in part renewed; and which, so far as it is renewed, doth oppose sin, though sometimes it may be overpowered by the strength and violence of temptation. (2.) They do not live in a course of sin, as the unregenerate do. (3.) They do not commit sin unto death. " All unrighteousness is sin; and there is a sin not unto death. We know that whosoever is born of God sinneth not;" that is, not unto death.—1 John v. 17, 18.

Q. 9. Doth not God himself testify concerning Job that he was a perfect man? " Hast thou considered my servant Job, that there is none like him upon the earth, a perfect man?"—Job i. 8. Doth not Hezekiah also plead his perfection with the Lord when he was sick? " Remember now how I have walked before thee with a perfect heart."—2 Kings xx. 3. And doth not Paul also assert himself, and other Christians, to be perfect? " Let us, therefore, as many as be perfect, be thus minded."—Phil. iii. 15. And how, then, is perfection unattainable by the saints in this life?

A. 1. This perfection which is ascribed unto the saints in the Scripture, is not to be understood of absolute perfection and freedom from all sin, for the reasons already

given, which prove the contrary; but it is to be understood
of sincerity, which is evangelical perfection, or at the
farthest, of comparative perfection, not an absolute perfection.    2. Thus we are to understand the perfection which
God testifieth of Job.  " Hast thou considered my servant
Job, that there is none like him in the earth, a perfect
man?" that is, so perfect as he is, " a perfect and upright
man."   His perfection did consist in his uprightness and
sincerity; and that Job was not absolutely perfect doth
appear from his sin a little after, in his cursing his birth-
day.  " Let the day perish wherein I was born."—Job
iii. 3.   And after he is charged with sin. " He multiplieth
his words against God."—Job xxxiv. 37.    3. So also Hezekiah's perfection, which he pleadeth, was no more than his
sincerity.  " Remember I have walked before thee in truth,
and with a perfect heart."   And the Scripture doth note
his sin a little after, which is a clear evidence that he was
not absolutely perfect.  " But Hezekiah rendered not again
according to the benefit done unto him; for his heart was
lifted up: therefore wrath was upon him, and upon Judah
and Jerusalem."—2 Chron. xxxii. 25.    4. In the same
place where the apostle Paul doth assert himself and other
Christians to be perfect, he doth acknowledge that he was
not perfect.   "Not as though I had already attained, either
were already perfect; but I follow after, if that I may apprehend that for which also I am apprehended of Christ
Jesus.   Brethren, I count not myself to have apprehended,"
&c.—Phil. iii. 12, 13.   Therefore the perfection which he
had attained, which he speaketh of verse 15, is to be understood of evangelical perfection; the perfection which he
had not attained, is to be understood of absolute perfection.
It is evident, therefore, that no saints do attain absolute
perfection in this life; and such as do pretend unto it, it is
through their ignorance of themselves and of God, and the
extent of God's law.

Q. 10. Do all the children of men, and the saints themselves, break the commandments of God in this life?

A. The saints themselves, and much more such as are
no saints, do daily break the commandments of God in
thought, word, and deed.  " The imagination of man's

heart is evil from his youth."—Gen. viii. 21. "The tongue can no man tame; it is an unruly evil, full of deadly poison."—James iii. 8. "Men loved darkness rather than light, because their deeds were evil."—John iii. 19.

Q. 11. Are all thoughts of sin breaches of God's commandments, when they are without evil words or actions?

A. All thoughts of sin are breaches of God's commandments, without evil words or actions, when they are accompanied with evil inclinations, desires, and affections. "Whosoever looketh upon a woman to lust after her, hath committed adultery with her already in his heart."—Matt. v. 28. "Out of the heart proceed evil thoughts, murders, adulteries, fornications, thefts, false witness, blasphemies." —Matt. xv. 19.

Q. 12. May not the saints in this life be kept from sinful thoughts, words, and actions?

A. 1. The saints in this life cannot be wholly free from all sinful thoughts, words, and actions, because all, even the best of saints, through remaining corruption, are subject to daily infirmities and defects. 2. The saints in this life may be kept from all gross sins of thoughts, words, and deeds, and they are kept from the reigning power of any sin.

Q. 13. How are the saints kept from gross sins, and the reigning power of any sin?

A. The saints are kept from gross sins and the reigning power of any sin—1. By the reigning of Christ in their hearts. 2. The mortification of sin in the root of it through the Spirit. 3. By watchfulness against sin in the thoughts. 4. By avoiding occasion of sin, and resisting temptations unto it.

LXXXIII. Ques. *Are all transgressions of the law equally heinous?*

*Ans.* Some sins in themselves, and by reason of several aggravations, are more heinous in the sight of God than others.

Q. 1. What is it for sin to be heinous?

A. Sins are heinous, as they are grievous and offensive unto God.

Q. 2. Are not all sins heinous unto God?

A. All sins are heinous unto God, but all sins are not equally heinous; for some sins are more heinous in the sight of God than others.

Q. 3. How many ways are some sins more heinous in the sight of God than others?

A. Two ways. 1. Some sins are more heinous in themselves. 2. Some sins are more heinous than others in regard of their several aggravations.

Q. 4. What sins are more heinous in themselves than others?

A. 1. Sins against the first table of the law are more heinous than sins against the second table of the law: thus, idolatry is more heinous than adultery, sacrilege is more heinous than theft, blasphemy against God is more heinous than speaking evil of our neighbour, and so proportionably the highest sin committed against God more immediately, is more heinous than the highest sin committed more immediately against man; and the lowest sin committed immediately against God, is more heinous than the lowest sin committed against man. "If one man sin against another, the judge shall judge him: but if a man sin against the Lord, who shall entreat for him?"— 1 Sam. ii. 25. 2. Some sins against the second table of the law are more heinous in themselves than others against the same second table; as murder is more heinous than adultery, adultery is more heinous than theft, theft is more heinous than coveting thy neighbour's house; and here now may be added, that the same sins of any kind ripened into actions, are more heinous in themselves than those sins in the thoughts only and inclinations. This is evident from the greater displeasure which God doth express in Scripture for some sins than for others, against the second table of the law; and for sinful works than for sinful thoughts. 3. Sins against the gospel are more heinous of themselves, than sins against the law; sin against the gospel being committed against the greatest light that ever did shine upon men, and the greatest love and grace of God that ever was shown unto men, and therefore the punishment of gospel-sinners will be greater than the punishment of the most notoriously wicked heathens. "Then began he to upbraid the cities wherein most of his mighty works were done, because they repented not. Woe unto thee, Chorazin! woe unto thee, Bethsaida! it shall be more tolerable for Tyre and Sidon at the day of judgment, than for you. And thou, Capernaum, which art exalted unto heaven, shalt be brought down to hell: it shall be more tolerable for the land of Sodom in the day of judgment, than for thee."—Matt. xi. 20–24.

Q. 5. What are the aggravations which render some sins more heinous than others?

A. The aggravations which render some sins more heinous than others, are the circumstances which do attend them.

Q. 6. What is the first aggravation of sin?

A. The first aggravation of sin is from the persons offending: thus the sins of magistrates, ministers, parents, the aged, and all governors, are more heinous in the same kind than the same sins of subjects, people, children, the younger, and those that are under government, because of the ill example and ill influence of the sins of the one beyond the other. "And he shall give Israel up, because of Jeroboam, who did sin, and who made Israel to sin."— 1 Kings xiv. 16. "The prophets make my people to err." —Micah iii. 5. Thus the sins also of professors and God's people are more heinous than the sins of the wicked and ungodly in the same kind, because the name of God is hereby more blasphemed, and the wicked are hereby more hardened in their sins. "Thou that makest thy boast of the law, through breaking of the law dishonourest thou God? For the name of God is blasphemed among the Gentiles, through you."—Rom. ii. 23, 24.

Q. 7. What is the second aggravation of sin?

A. The second aggravation of sin is from the place: thus sins committed in a land of light are more heinous than the same sins committed in a place of darkness. "In the land of uprightness will he deal unjustly, and will not behold the majesty of the Lord."—Isa. xxvi. 10. Thus sins committed in a place of great deliverance and mercies are more heinous than the same sins committed in another place. "They remembered not the multitude of his mer-

cies, but provoked him at the sea, even the Red Sea."—
Ps. cvi. 7.   Thus also sins committed in a public place,
whereby others may be enticed and defiled, are more
heinous than the same sins committed in secret places.
"They spread Absalom a tent upon the top of the house;
and Absalom went in unto his father's concubines, in the
sight of all Israel."—2 Sam. xvi. 22.

Q. 8. What is the third aggravation of sin?

A. The third aggravation of sin is from the time: thus
sins committed on the Sabbath-day are more heinous than
the same sins committed on the week-day.   Drunkenness
and adultery are heinous and abominable on any day in the
sight of God ; but drunkenness or adultery, or any other
such sins, are more heinous before God on the Sabbath-
day.   Thus sins committed in or after the time of trouble
and affliction, are more heinous than the same sins committed at another time.   "In the time of his distress did
he trespass yet more against the Lord : that is that king
Ahaz."—2 Chron. xxviii. 22.   "Why should ye be stricken
any more? ye will revolt more and more."—Isa. i. 5.  Thus
sins committed after repentance and engagements to
be the Lord's, are more heinous than the same sins committed before repentance and such engagements ; so also
sins committed after admonitions and censures, are more
heinous than the same sins committed before such admonitions and censures.

Q. 9. What is the fourth aggravation of sin?

A. The fourth aggravation of sin is from the manner :
thus sins against knowledge are more heinous than sins
through ignorance; sins through wilfulness and presump-
tion are more heinous than sins through weakness and in-
firmity; sins through custom and with deliberation are
more heinous than sins through sudden passion and the
hurry of temptation; sins with delight and greediness are
more heinous than sins committed with regret and back-
wardness ; sins committed impudently and with boasting
are more heinous than the same sins committed with shame
and blushing; sins often repeated and long continued in,
are more heinous than sins but once or seldom committed,
and which are broken off by repentance.

**LXXXIV. Ques.** *What doth every sin deserve?*

*Ans.* Every sin deserveth God's wrath and curse, both in this life and that which is to come.

Q. 1. What is meant by God's wrath and curse, which every sin doth deserve?

A. By God's wrath and curse, which every sin doth deserve, are meant all those punishments which God in his wrath hath threatened to inflict upon sinners for their sins.

Q. 2. What are those punishments which God in his wrath hath threatened to inflict upon sinners for their sins?

A. The punishments which God in his wrath hath threatened to inflict upon sinners for their sins, are either in this life, such as all temporal and spiritual judgments here; or in the life which is to come, such as the punishment of hell; of both which we have seen before in the explication of the nineteenth answer.

Q. 3. Doth every sin deserve God's wrath and curse, both in this life and that which is to come?

A. Every sin doth deserve God's wrath and curse, both in this life and that which is to come, because every sin is committed against an infinitely holy and righteous God, and his justice doth require infinite satisfaction; and if some sinners do escape some temporal punishments, they cannot escape the eternal punishment of hell, which is the only satisfying punishment, unless they have an interest in the satisfaction made by Christ. "Cursed is every one that continueth not in all things which are written in the book of the law to do them."—Gal. iii. 10. "Then shall he say unto them on the left hand, Depart from me, ye cursed, into everlasting fire, prepared for the devil and his angels."—Matt. xxv. 41.

**LXXXV. Ques.** *What doth God require of us, that we may escape his wrath and curse, due to us for sin?*

*Ans.* To escape the wrath and curse of God, due to us for sin, God requireth of us faith in Jesus Christ, repentance unto life, with the diligent use of all the outward means whereby Christ communicateth to us the benefits of redemption.

Q. 1. How many things doth God require of us to escape his wrath and curse, due to us for sin?

A. God requireth three things of us, that we may escape his wrath and curse, due to us for sin—1. Faith in Jesus Christ. 2. Repentance unto life. 3. The diligent use of all the outward means whereby Christ communicateth to us the benefits of redemption.

Q. 2. Why doth God require of us faith in Jesus Christ, that we may escape his wrath and curse?

A. God requireth of us faith in Jesus Christ to escape his wrath and curse, because by faith in Jesus Christ we have an interest in Jesus Christ and his imputed righteousness, and the promise he hath made of remission and salvation unto us. " And be found in him, not having mine own righteousness, but that which is through the faith of Christ, the righteousness which is of God by faith."— Phil. iii. 9. " To him give all the prophets witness, that through his name, whosoever believeth in him shall receive remission of sins."—Acts x. 43. " By grace we are saved, through faith."—Eph. ii. 8.

Q. 3. Why doth God require of us repentance unto life, that we may escape his wrath and curse?

A. God requireth of us repentance unto life, that we may escape his wrath and curse, because the promise of forgiveness of sin is made to repentance, as a concomitant of faith; and it is not for God's honour to pardon and save any that go on still in their trespasses. " Repent ye, therefore, and be converted, that your sins may be blotted out."—Acts iii. 19. " Testifying both to the Jews and also to the Greeks, repentance toward God, and faith toward our Lord Jesus Christ."—Acts. xx. 21.

Q. 4. Why doth God require of us the diligent use of all outward means, that we may escape his wrath and curse?

A. God doth require of us the diligent use of all outward means to escape his wrath and curse, because although God could save without means, yet it is his will to appoint means, which, having his institution, we cannot expect the benefits of redemption and salvation should be communicated to us any other way. " It pleased God by the foolishness of preaching to save them that believe."— 1 Cor. i. 21. " Pray God, if perhaps the thought of thine heart may be forgiven thee."—Acts viii. 22.

LXXXVI. Ques. *What is faith in Jesus Christ?*
*Ans.* Faith in Jesus Christ is a saving grace, whereby we receive and rest upon him alone for salvation, as he is offered to us in the gospel.

Q. 1. How is faith a saving grace ?
A. Faith is a saving grace, not by the act of believing, as an act, for then it would save as a work—whereas we are saved by faith in opposition to all works; but faith is a saving grace, as an instrument apprehending and applying Jesus Christ and his perfect righteousness, whereby alone we are saved. " For God so loved the world, that he gave his only begotten Son, that whosoever believeth in him should not perish, but have everlasting life."— John iii. 16. " And they said, Believe on the Lord Jesus Christ, and thou shalt be saved."—Acts xvi. 31. " Even the righteousness of God which is by faith of Christ unto all and upon all them that believe."—Rom. iii. 22.

Q. 2. Who is the author of faith in Jesus Christ ?
A. The author of faith in Jesus Christ is God, whose gift it is, and who works this grace of faith in the soul by his Spirit. " Ye are saved through faith, and that not of yourselves, it is the gift of God."—Eph. ii. 8. " Ye are risen with him through the faith of the operation of God." —Col. ii. 12.

Q. 3. How doth God work this grace of faith in the souls of men ?
A. God doth work this grace of faith in the souls of men ordinarily by hearing of the word preached. " So, then, faith cometh by hearing, and hearing by the Word of God."—Rom. x. 17. " So we preach, and so ye believed."—1 Cor. xv. 11.

Q. 4. What is the object of this grace of faith?

A. The object of this grace of faith is the Lord Jesus Christ, and his righteousness, and the promises which are made through him in the covenant of grace. "He that believeth on him is not condemned."—John iii. 18. "For therein is the righteousness of God revealed from faith to faith : as it is written, The just shall live by faith."—Rom. i. 17. "The Scripture hath concluded all under sin, that the promise by faith of Jesus Christ might be given to them that believe."—Gal. iii. 22.

Q. 5. What is the subject of faith in Jesus Christ?

A. 1. The subject of denomination, or the persons in whom alone this grace of faith is to be found, are the elect only. "According to the faith of God's elect."—Tit. i. 1. "And as many as were ordained to eternal life believed." —Acts xiii. 48. 2. The subject of inhesion, or the parts of the soul in which faith is placed and doth inhere, is not only the mind and understanding, but also the will and heart. "These all died in faith, not having received the promises, but having seen them afar off, and were persuaded of them, and embraced them."—Heb. xi. 13. The persuasion of the truth of the promises is the act of the understanding; the embracement of the things promised is the act of the will. "With the heart man believeth unto righteousness."—Rom. x. 10.

Q. 6. What are the acts of faith in Jesus Christ?

A. The acts of faith in Jesus Christ are—1. A receiving of Jesus Christ. "As many as received him, to them gave he power to become the sons of God, even to them that believe on his name."—John i. 12. 2. A resting upon Christ alone for salvation. This is implied in all those Scriptures which speak of believing in Christ, and believing on his name.

Q. 7. How is Jesus Christ to be received by faith?

A. Jesus Christ is to be received by faith as he is offered to us in the gospel.

Q. 8. How is Jesus Christ offered to us in the gospel?

A. Jesus Christ is offered to us in the gospel, as priest, prophet, and king; and so we must receive him, if we would be saved by him.

Q. 9. When doth the soul rest upon him for salvation ?

A. The soul doth rest upon Christ for salvation when, being convinced of its lost condition by reason of sin, and its own inability, together with all creatures' insufficiency, to recover it out of this estate, and having a discovery and persuasion of Christ's ability and willingness to save, it doth let go all hold on the creatures, and renounce its own righteousness, and so lay hold on Christ, rely upon him, and put confidence in him, and in him alone, for salvation.

LXXXVII. Ques. *What is repentance unto life?*

*Ans.* Repentance unto life is a saving grace, whereby a sinner, out of a true sense of his sin, and apprehension of the mercy of God in Christ, doth, with grief and hatred of his sin, turn from it unto God, with full purpose of, and endeavour after, new obedience.

Q. 1. Why is repentance called repentance unto life ?

A. Repentance is called repentance unto life, because it is a saving grace, and a necessary mean for the attaining life and salvation; and that it might be distinguished from the sorrow of the world which worketh death. "Then hath God also to the Gentiles granted repentance unto life."—Acts xi. 18. "If the wicked will turn from all his sins," &c., "he shall surely live."—Ezek. xviii. 21. "For godly sorrow worketh repentance to salvation, not to be repented of; but the sorrow of the world worketh death." —2 Cor. vii. 10.

Q. 2. Can any repent of their sins by the power of nature ?

A. None can repent of their sins by the power of nature, because the hearts of all men and women by nature are like a stone, insensible of sin, and inflexible unto God's will; therefore there is need of the Spirit of God to work this grace in the heart, which he hath promised to do in the new covenant. "A new heart also will I give you, and a new spirit will I put within you; and I will take away the stony heart out of your flesh, and I will give you an heart of flesh: and I will put my Spirit within you, and cause you to walk in my statutes, and ye shall keep my judgments, and do them."—Ezek. xxxvi. 26, 27.

Q 3. Wherein doth repentance unto life consist?

A. Repentance unto life doth chiefly consist in two things—1. In turning from sin, and forsaking it. "Repent, and turn yourselves from all your transgressions; so iniquity shall not be your ruin."—Ezek. xviii. 30. "He that covereth his sins shall not prosper: but whoso confesseth and forsaketh them shall find mercy."—Prov. xxviii. 13. 2. In turning unto God. "Let the wicked forsake his way, and the unrighteous man his thoughts; and let him return to the Lord, and he will have mercy upon him, and to our God, for he will abundantly pardon." —Isa. lv. 7.

Q. 4. What is requisite unto the turning from sin in repentance?

A. It is requisite unto the turning from sin in repentance, that there be—1. A true sight of sin. 2. An apprehension of the mercy of God in Christ. 3. A grief for sin. 4. A hatred of sin.

Q. 5. Wherein doth the true sense of sin consist which is requisite in repentance?

A. The true sense of sin, which is requisite in repentance, doth consist in such an inward feeling of our miserable and low estate, by reason of the wrath and curse of God, and that eternal vengeance of hell, which for our sins we are exposed unto, as putteth us into great perplexity and trouble of spirit; so that our consciences being hereby pricked and wounded, can find no quiet, and take no rest in this condition. "When they heard this, they were pricked in their heart, and said unto Peter, and to the rest of the apostles, Men and brethren, what shall we do?" —Acts ii. 37.

Q. 6. What need is there of this sense of sin unto true repentance?

A. There is need of this sense of sin unto true repentance, because, without this sense of sin, sinners will not forsake sin, nor apply themselves unto the Lord Jesus for pardon and healing. "They that be whole need not a physician, but they that are sick. I am not come to call the righteous, but sinners to repentance."—Matt. ix. 12, 13.

Q. 7. What apprehensions of God's mercy are requisite in this repentance?

A. There is requisite in true repentance, that we have apprehensions of God's mercy, as he is both slow to anger and of great kindness; as he is most ready to forgive, and most ready to be pacified unto repenting sinners. " And the Lord passed by before him, and proclaimed, The LORD, The LORD God, merciful and gracious, long-suffering, and abundant in goodness and truth, keeping mercy for thousands, forgiving iniquity, and transgression, and sin."—Exod. xxxiv. 6, 7. " Or despisest thou the riches of his goodness, and forbearance, and long-suffering? not knowing that the goodness of God leadeth thee to repentance."—Rom. ii. 4.

Q. 8. Can we apprehend pardoning mercy in God only through Christ?

A. We can truly apprehend pardoning mercy in God only through Christ, because God is so infinitely just and jealous, and a consuming fire unto sinners out of Christ, and he is reconcilable unto sinners only through his Son, who hath given satisfaction unto his justice for sin. " All things are of God, who hath reconciled us to himself by Jesus Christ."—2 Cor. v. 18.

Q. 9. What need is there of the apprehension of God's mercy in Christ, in order to our repentance?

A. There is need of the apprehension of God's mercy in Christ in order to our repentance, because without the apprehension of this mercy of God, and willingness through his Son to be reconciled unto us, upon conviction of and contrition for sin, we shall either cast off our trouble, and run more eagerly unto the commission of sin than before; or, if we cannot cast off our trouble, we will sink under tormenting despair, and be in danger of making away with ourselves, as Judas did: whereas the apprehension of God's mercy in Christ is an encouragement to us to forsake our sins and to turn to him, and a mean to affect our hearts with kindly and godly sorrow for sin.

**Q. 10. Wherein doth true grief for sin consist?**

A. True grief for sin doth consist in our mourning and sorrowing for sin, not only as it is like to bring ruin upon ourselves, but chiefly as it hath brought dishonour upon God's name; not only as it hath wounded our consciences, but chiefly as it hath wounded our Saviour; not only as without repentance it is like to damn our souls, but also as it hath debased and defiled our souls. "I will declare mine iniquity: I will be sorry for my sin."—Ps. xxxviii. 18. "I acknowledge my transgressions; and my sin is ever before me. Against thee, thee only, have I sinned, and done this evil in thy sight."—Ps. li. 3, 4. "They shall look upon me whom they have pierced, and they shall mourn."—Zech. xii. 10. "We have sinned; we are all as an unclean thing, and all our righteousnesses are as filthy rags."—Isa. lxiv. 5, 6.

**Q. 11. May we not truly grieve for sin, though we do not weep for it?**

A. 1. If we can readily weep for other things, and cannot weep for sin, the truth of our grief is very questionable. 2. There may be true and great grief for sin without tears, in them that are of a dry constitution, and are not prone to weep upon any account; and as there may be in some many tears in the eye, where there is no grief in the heart, so in others there may be much grief in the heart, where there are no tears in the eye.

**Q. 12. Why is grief for sin needful in repentance?**

A. Grief for sin is needful in repentance, because it further works the heart unto a willingness to leave sin; because God doth require it, and hath promised mercy unto such as mourn for sin. "Be afflicted and mourn, and weep; let your laughter be turned to mourning, and your joy to heaviness."—James iv. 9. "I have surely heard Ephraim bemoaning himself thus, Thou hast chastised me, and I was chastised, as a bullock unaccustomed to the yoke; turn thou me, and I shall be turned: for thou art the Lord my God. Surely after that I was instructed, I smote upon my thigh; I was ashamed, yea, even confounded, because I did bear the reproach of my youth. Is Ephraim my dear son? is he a pleasant child? my bowels are troubled for him; I will surely have mercy upon him, saith the Lord."—Jer. xxxi. 18–20.

Q. 13. What is hatred of sin, which is requisite unto true repentance?

A. Hatred of sin, which is also requisite unto true repentance, is an inward deep loathing and abhorrence of sin, as the most odious thing in the world, which is accompanied with a loathing of ourselves, as being rendered by sin most loathsome and abominable in the eyes of God. "Then shall ye remember your own evil ways, and your doings which have not been good, and shall loathe yourselves in your own sight, for your iniquities and your abominations."—Ezek. xxxvi. 31.

Q. 14. Why is hatred of sin needful unto true repentance?

A. Hatred of sin is needful unto true repentance, because no affection of the heart will more engage us against sin than our hatred; and when grief for sin is much spent, hatred of sin will put weapons into our hands to fight against it.

Q. 15. What is that turning from sin which is part of true repentance?

A. The turning from sin which is a part of true repentance, doth consist in two things—1. In a turning from all gross sins, in regard of our course and conversation. 2. In a turning from all other sins, in regard of our hearts and affections.

Q. 16. Do such as truly repent of sin never return again unto the practice of the same sins which they have repented of?

A. 1. Such as have truly repented of sin do never return unto the practice of it, so as to live in a course of sin, as they did before; and where any, after repentance, do return unto a course of sin, it is an evident sign that their repentance was not of the right kind. 2. Some have truly repented of their sins, although they may be overtaken and surprised by temptations, so as to fall into the commission of the same sins which they have repented of, yet they do not lie in them, but get up again, and with bitter grief bewail them, and return again unto the Lord.

Q. 17. Wherein doth turning to the Lord (the other part of true repentance) consist?

A. Turning to the Lord doth consist—1. In making application of ourselves unto him for the pardon of sin and his mercy. "Have mercy upon me, O God, according to thy loving-kindness; according to the multitude of thy tender mercies, blot out my transgressions."—Ps. li. 1. 2. In our making choice of him for our God and chief good. "Behold, we come unto thee; for thou art the Lord our God."—Jer. iii. 22. "They shall call on my name, and I will hear them; I will say, It is my people; and they shall say, The Lord is my God."—Zech. xiii. 9. 3. In our delivering up ourselves unto his obedience. "I thought on my ways, and turned my feet unto thy testimonies."—Ps. cxix. 59.

Q. 18. What is that obedience which we must deliver ourselves up unto, in our returning to the Lord?

A. The obedience which we must deliver up ourselves unto, in our returning to the Lord, is the new obedience of the gospel.

Q. 19. Why is the obedience of the gospel called new obedience?

A. The obedience of the gospel is called new obedience, because it is required in the new covenant, and because it must proceed from newness of spirit, the new nature, or new principle of grace and spiritual life, which is put into the soul by the Spirit of God. "But now we are delivered from the law, that being dead wherein we were held, that we should serve in newness of spirit."—Rom. vii. 6.

Q. 20. When do we deliver up ourselves unto this new obedience?

A. We deliver up ourselves unto this new obedience—1. When we have full resolutions and purposes of it. "I have sworn, and I will perform it, that I will keep thy righteous judgments."—Ps. cxix. 106. "And exhorted them all, that with purpose of heart they would cleave to the Lord."—Acts xi. 23. 2. When we are diligent in our endeavours after it, that we may constantly walk in the ways of new obedience, without offence either to God or man. "And they were both righteous before God, walking in all the commandments and ordinances of the Lord blameless."—Luke i. 6. "And herein do I exercise myself, to have always a conscience void of offence toward God and toward men."—Acts xxiv. 16.

Q. 21. Do all that truly repent fully perform new obedience?

A. None that truly repent do here in this life perform new obedience fully, without any failure or defect, but they diligently endeavour to do it; and wherein they fall short, it is their grief and trouble. "For I am ready to halt, and my sorrow is continually before me."—Ps. xxxviii. 17.

LXXXVIII. Ques. *What are the outward means whereby Christ communicateth to us the benefits of redemption?*

*Ans.* The outward and ordinary means whereby Christ communicateth to us the benefits of redemption, are his ordinances, especially the Word, sacraments, and prayer; all which are made effectual to the elect for salvation.

Q. 1. What do comprehend all the outward and ordinary means whereby Christ communicateth to us the benefits of redemption?

A. The ordinances of the Lord do comprehend all the outward and ordinary means whereby Christ communicateth to us the benefits of redemption.

Q. 2. What are meant by the ordinances of the Lord?

A. By the ordinances of the Lord are meant those means of grace and salvation which are of the Lord's institution, which he hath appointed and commanded in his Word, and no other. "Teaching them to observe all things whatsoever I have commanded you."—Matt. xxviii. 20. "Be ye followers of me, even as I also am of Christ. Now I praise you, brethren, that ye keep the ordinances as I delivered them unto you; for I have received of the Lord that which also I delivered unto you."—1 Cor. xi. 1, 2, 23.

Q. 3. May we not make use of any ordinances which are of men's appointment only, in order to salvation?

A. We ought not to make use of any ordinances which are of men's appointment only, in order unto salvation, because this is will-worship, which is both vain and offensive; and we cannot groundedly expect the blessing of the Lord upon, or to receive any true benefit of any ordinances, but by those alone which are of his own appointment only. "Why are ye subject to ordinances, after the commandments and doctrines of men? which things have a show of wisdom in will-worship," &c.—Col. ii. 20, 22, 23. " But in vain they do worship me, teaching for doctrines the commandments of men."—Matt. xv. 9.

Q. 4. Why are the ordinances called the ordinary means whereby Christ communicateth to us the benefits of redemption?

A. The ordinances are called the ordinary means whereby Christ communicateth to us the benefits of redemption, because the Lord hath not wholly limited and bound up himself unto his ordinances; for he can in an extraordinary way bring some out of a state of nature into a state of grace; as Paul, who was converted by a light and a voice from heaven: but the ordinances are the most usual way and means of conversion and salvation, without the use of which we cannot, upon good ground, expect that any benefit of redemption should be communicated to us.

Q. 5. What are the chief ordinances of the Lord's appointment?

A. The chief ordinances of the Lord's appointment are the Word, sacraments, and prayer. "And they continued stedfastly in the apostles' doctrine and fellowship, and in breaking of bread, and in prayers."—Acts ii. 42.

Q. 6. To whom are the ordinances made effectual for salvation?

A. The ordinances are made effectual for salvation to the elect only. "And they continued with one accord in the temple, and breaking bread, praising God. And the Lord added to the Church daily such as should be saved."—Acts ii. 46, 47.

LXXXIX. Ques. *How is the Word made effectual to salvation?*

*Ans.* The Spirit of God maketh the reading, but especially the preaching of the Word, an effectual means of convincing and converting sinners, and of building them up in holiness and comfort, through faith, unto salvation.

Q. 1. What is the ordinance or appointment of the Lord, in reference unto the Word, that it may be effectual unto salvation?

A. The ordinance or appointment of the Lord, in reference unto the Word, that it may be effectual unto salvation, is—1. That we read the Word. "He shall read therein all the days of his life, that he may learn to fear the Lord his God, to keep all the words of this law, and those statutes to do them."—Deut. xvii. 19. "Search the Scriptures; for in them ye think ye have eternal life, and these are they which testify of me."—John v. 39. 2. That we hear the Word preached. "Incline your ear, and come unto me; hear, and your soul shall live."—Isa. lv. 3. "It pleased God by the foolishness of preaching to save them that believe."—1 Cor. i. 21.

Q. 2. How is the Word made effectual unto salvation?

A. The Word is made effectual unto salvation, First, In reference unto sinners and ungodly, as the Word is a mean—1. To convince them of sin, and to affect them with remorse for it. "But if all prophesy, and there come in one that believeth not, or one unlearned, he is convinced of all, he is judged of all; and thus are the secrets of his heart made manifest; and so, falling down on his face, he will worship God, and report that God is in you of a truth."—1 Cor. xiv. 24, 25. "For the word of God is quick and powerful, and sharper than any two-edged sword, piercing even to the dividing asunder of soul and spirit, and of the joints and marrow, and is a discerner of the thoughts and intents of the heart."—Heb. iv. 12. "Now, when they heard this, they were pricked in their hearts."—Acts ii. 37. 2. To convert them from sin, and join them unto Christ and his people. "The law of the Lord is perfect, converting the soul."—Ps. xix. 7. "Then they that gladly received his word were baptized; and there were added unto them about three thousand souls."—Acts ii. 41. "Howbeit many of them which heard the word believed; and the number of the men was about five thousand." — Acts iv. 4. Secondly, In reference unto those that are converted, the Word is effectual unto salvation, as it is a mean of building them up in holiness and comfort through faith unto salvation. "And now, brethren. I commend you to God, and to the word of his grace, which is able to build you up, and to give you an inheritance among all them which are sanctified."—Acts xx. 32. "And he gave some pastors and teachers; for the perfecting of the saints, for the work of the ministry, for the edifying of the body of Christ; till we all come in the unity of the faith, and of the knowledge of the Son of God, unto a perfect man, unto the measure of the stature of the fulness of Christ."—Eph. iv. 11-13.

Q. 3. How doth the Word build up the saints in holiness ?

A The Word doth build up the saints in holiness—1. As it is a mean to work them into a greater conformity unto the image of God, and to cause an increase of every grace in them. "We all with open face beholding as in a glass the glory of the Lord, are changed into the same image, from glory to glory."—2 Cor. iii. 18. "As new-born babes, desire the sincere milk of the word, that ye may grow thereby."—1 Pet. ii. 2. 2. As it doth reprove, correct, instruct in righteousness, and thereby perfect them more and more, and fit them for good works. "All Scripture is given by inspiration of God, and is profitable for doctrine, for reproof, for correction, for instruction in righteousness, that the man of God may be perfect, thoroughly furnished unto every good work."—2 Tim. iii. 16, 17. 3. As it is a mean of pulling down strongholds in the soul, and more and more subduing all thoughts and affections unto the obedience of Christ. "For the weapons of our warfare are not carnal, but mighty through God to the pulling down of strongholds, casting down imaginations, and every high thing that exalteth itself against the knowledge of God, and bringing into captivity every thought to the obedience of Christ."—2 Cor. x. 4, 5. 4. As it is a mean to strengthen the saints against the temptations of the devil and the corruptions of their own hearts. "Take to you the whole armour of God, that ye may be able to withstand in the evil day. Take the sword of the Spirit, which is the word of God."—Eph. vi. 13, 17. "Get thee hence, Satan; for it is written, Thou shalt worship the Lord thy God," &c.—Matt. iv. 10. "Wherewith shall a young man cleanse his way? by taking heed thereto according to thy word."—Ps. cxix. 9. 5. As it is a mean to establish the saints in the truths and ways of God, and to strengthen them against error and seduction. "Now to him that is of power to stablish you according to my gospel and the preaching of Jesus Christ," &c.—Rom. xvi. 25. "That we be no more children, tossed to and fro, and carried about with every wind of doctrine, by the sleight of men, and cunning craftiness, whereby they lie in wait to deceive."—Eph. iv. 14.

Q. 4. How doth the Word build up the saints in comfort?

A. The Word doth build up the saints in comfort—1. As it doth reveal and hold forth the chiefest grounds of comfort, such as the promises of pardon and eternal life. "Comfort ye, comfort ye, my people, saith your God. Speak ye comfortably to Jerusalem, and cry unto her, that her warfare is accomplished, that her sins are pardoned."—Isa. xl. 1, 2. "This is the promise that he hath promised, even eternal life."—1 John ii. 25. 2. As it is the means of conveying to the soul the most sweet and unutterable joy of the Holy Ghost. "And ye became followers of us, and of the Lord, having received the word in much affliction, with joy of the Holy Ghost."—1 Thess. i. 6.

Q. 5. Is the Word effectual unto salvation by any virtue or power in itself?

A. The Word is not effectual unto salvation by any virtue or power in itself, but by the operation of the Spirit of God, in and by the Word. "Who also hath made us able ministers of the New Testament, not of the letter, but of the spirit; for the letter killeth, but the spirit giveth life."—2 Cor. iii. 6.

Q. 6. How doth the Word work effectually unto salvation?

A. The Word doth work effectually unto salvation through faith. " Ye received it not as the word of men, but as it is in truth, the word of God, which effectually worketh also in you that believe."—1 Thess. ii. 13. " For I am not ashamed of the gospel of Christ; for it is the power of God unto salvation to every one that believeth." —Rom. i. 16.

XC. Ques. *How is the Word to be read and heard, that it may become effectual to salvation?*

*Ans.* That the Word may become effectual to salvation, we must attend thereunto with diligence, preparation, and prayer, receive it with faith and love, lay it up in our hearts, and practise it in our lives.

Q. 1. What is required before the hearing of the Word, that it may become effectual unto salvation?

A. Before the hearing of the Word, that it may become effectual unto salvation, two things are required—1. Preparation. 2. Prayer.

Q 2. What is that preparation that is required before the hearing of the Word?

A. The preparation which is required before the hearing of the Word is—1. That we consider the majesty of God, in whose presence we are to appear, and whose word we are to hear. " We are all here present before God, to hear all things that are commanded thee of God."—Acts x. 33. 2. That we examine ourselves, to find out, and lay aside, whatever may hinder the saving operation of the Word of God upon us. " I will wash mine hands in innocency, so will I compass thine altar, O Lord."—Ps. xxvi. 6. " Wherefore lay apart all superfluity of naughtiness, and receive with meekness the ingrafted word, which is able to save your souls."—James i. 21. " Wherefore, laying aside all malice, and all guile, and hypocrisies, and envies, and all evil speakings, as new-born babes, desire the sincere milk of the word, that ye may grow thereby." —1 Pet. ii. 1, 2.

Q. 3. What is that prayer which is required before hearing the Word?

A. The prayer which is required before hearing the Word, is prayer in secret, and in our families, for God's assistance of his ministers in preaching the Word to us, and for his blessing the Word, and making it effectual to us by his Spirit in our hearing of it. "Pray for us that the word of the Lord may have free course, and be glorified."—2 Thess. iii. 1.

Q. 4. What is required in reading and hearing the Word, to make it effectual unto salvation?

A. In reading and hearing the Word, that it may become effectual unto salvation, three things are required—1. Attention. 2. Faith. 3. Love.

Q. 5. What is that attention which is required in reading and hearing the Word?

A. The attention which is required in reading and hearing the Word, is a diligent inclining the ear, and bending the mind, that we may understand what we read and hear. " My son, if thou wilt receive my words, and hide my commandments with thee; so that thou incline thine ear unto wisdom, and apply thine heart unto understanding: then shalt thou understand the fear of the Lord, and find the knowledge of God."—Prov. ii. 1, 2, 5.

Q. 6. What is that faith which is required in reading and hearing the Word?

A. The faith which is required in reading and hearing the Word doth imply—1. In general, a believing assent unto the divine authority of the whole Scripture, that it is indeed the word of God; and however it was penned by divers holy men in divers ages, that yet the whole was indited, and they wrote nothing but as they were inspired by the Holy Ghost. "We thank God, because when ye received the word of God, which ye heard of us, ye received it not as the word of men, but as it is in truth, the word of God."—1 Thess. ii. 16. " All Scripture is given by inspiration of God."—2 Tim. iii. 13. " For the prophecy came not in old time by the will of man; but holy men of God spake as they were moved by the Holy Ghost."—2 Pet. i. 21. 2. The faith required in reading and hearing the Word, doth imply in particular—(1.) A believing assent unto the truth and excellency of all Scripture history, as that which most certainly was; especially the history of our Lord Jesus Christ, in his birth, life, death, resurrection, and ascension. (2.) A believing assent unto the truth and excellency of all Scripture prophecy, as that, so far as it is not yet fulfilled, which most certainly will be; especially the prophecy concerning the consummation of all things, and the general judgment of the world by Jesus Christ at the last day. (3.) A believing assent unto the truth and excellency of all Scripture doctrine, as that which is most high, and most worthy of understanding; especially the doctrine of the Trinity, and Christ's incarnation, and the way of man's redemption. (4.) A believing assent unto the truth and righteousness of all Scripture threatenings, whether in the law or gospel, and that in the most severe executions of them. (5.) A believing assent unto the holiness, righteousness, and goodness of all Scripture precepts; as also to the perfection of the Scripture rule for all things which concern our practice. (6.) A fiducial application of all Scripture promises, so far as they have a general reference unto all believers, as most firm, true, precious, and such as contain in them whatever is really for our good and happiness, both in this and in the other world.

Q. 7. What is that love which is required in reading and hearing the Word of God?

A. The love which is required in reading and hearing the Word of God, is love of the Word, because it is the word of God. "Consider how I love thy precepts. My soul hath kept thy testimonies; and I love them exceedingly."—Ps. cxix. 159, 167.

Q. 8. Wherein should our love to the Word of God show itself?

A. Our love to the Word of God should show itself—
1. In our high prizing the Word of God above things which are most necessary and precious in the world. "I have esteemed the words of his mouth more than my necessary food."—Job xxiii. 12. "The law of thy mouth is better unto me than thousands of gold and silver."—

Ps. cxix. 72. 2. In our earnest desires after the Word. "My soul breaketh for the longing it hath unto thy judgments at all times. I opened my mouth and panted; for I longed for thy commandments." — Ps. cxix. 20, 131. 3. In our delighting ourselves in the Word. "Thy testimonies are my delight, and my counsellors. Thy testimonies have I taken as an heritage for ever; for they are the rejoicing of my heart. I rejoice at thy word, as one that findeth great spoil."—Ps. cxix. 24, 111, 162.

Q. 9. What is required after the reading and hearing of the Word, that it may become effectual unto salvation?

A. There is required after the reading and hearing of the Word, that it may become effectual unto salvation— 1. That we lay it up in our hearts, making our hearts and memories store-houses of this heavenly treasure. "Thy word have I hid in my heart, that I might not sin against thee."—Ps. cxix. 11. 2. That we practise it in our lives, being ready to obey and do whatever we read or hear out of the Word to be our duty. "Be ye doers of the word, and not hearers only, deceiving your ownselves. Whoso looketh into the perfect law of liberty, and continueth therein, he being not a forgetful hearer, but a doer of the word, this man shall be blessed in his deed."—James i. 22, 25.

XCI. Ques. *How do the sacraments become effectual means of salvation?*

*Ans.* The sacraments become effectual means of salvation, not from any virtue in them, or in him that doth administer them, but only by the blessing of Christ, and the working of his Spirit in them that by faith receive them.

Q. 1. How, negatively, are the sacraments not effectual means of salvation?

A. The sacraments, negatively—1. Are not effectual means of salvation, by any virtue in themselves, to confer grace and salvation upon all the receivers, and by the work done, or bare receiving of them; for many may and do partake of the sacraments who are without true grace, and have no share in the salvation of the gospel. " And Simon himself was baptized.    But Peter said unto him, Thy money perish with thee: thou hast neither part nor lot in this matter; for thy heart is not right in the sight of God; for I perceive that thou art in the gall of bitterness and in the bond of iniquity."—Acts viii. 13, 20, 21, 23.   " Whosoever shall eat this bread, and drink this cup of the Lord unworthily, shall be guilty of the body and blood of the Lord."—1 Cor. xi. 27.   2. The sacraments are not effectual means of salvation through the intention of, or by any virtue in them that do administer them, there being no power in the most holy ministers themselves to give grace and to bring salvation unto any by their administration of the sacraments, or any other ordinance.    " So, then, neither is he that planteth any thing, neither he that watereth; but God that giveth the increase."—1 Cor. iii. 7.

Q. 2. How, positively, are the sacraments effectual means of salvation?

A. The sacraments positively are effectual means of salvation—1. By the blessing and presence of Christ, which do accompany the sacraments and other ordinances of his own institution.   " Where two or three are gathered together in my name, there am I in the midst of them." —Matt. xviii. 20.   " Teaching them to observe all things whatsoever I have commanded you: and, lo, I am with you alway, even unto the end of the world."—Matt. xxviii. 20   2. By the working of the Spirit (the effect and evidence of Christ's blessing and presence), whereby Christ doth put life, and virtue, and efficacy into his sacraments and ordinances, without which they would be wholly dead, and altogether ineffectual.   " For by one Spirit are we all baptized into one body, whether we be Jews or Gentiles, whether we be bond or free; and have been all made to drink into one Spirit."—1 Cor. xii. 13.

Q. 3. In whom doth the Spirit by the sacraments work effectually unto salvation?

A. The Spirit by the sacraments doth not work effectually unto the salvation of all that receive them, but of all that by faith receive them.

XCII. Ques. *What is a sacrament?*

*Ans.* A sacrament is a holy ordinance instituted by Christ, wherein, by sensible signs, Christ and the benefits of the new covenant are represented, sealed, and applied unto believers.

Q. 1. What is the proper signification of the word sacrament?

A. The proper signification of the word sacrament, as it was of old used, is a military oath, whereby the general did oblige himself to be faithful unto his soldiers, and the soldiers did engage themselves to be faithful unto their general.

Q. 2. Why are any of Christ's ordinances called sacraments, when we do not find the word sacrament used in any place of the Holy Scriptures?

A. Although the word sacrament be not used in the Scripture, any more than the word Trinity, yet, because the things signified by Sacrament and Trinity, and other words, are in the Scriptures, therefore we may lawfully make use of such words.

Q. 3. What is the thing signified by the word sacrament?

A. The thing signified by the word sacrament is a seal of the covenant of grace, whereby as the Lord doth oblige himself to fulfil the promise of the covenant unto us; so, by our receiving this seal, we oblige ourselves to be the Lord's, and to be true and faithful unto him.

Q. 4. Whose ordinance is the sacrament which we are to make use of?

A. The sacrament which we are to make use of is an ordinance, not of man's institution and appointment, but a holy ordinance of Christ's institution and appointment, who, being the only King of the Church, hath alone authority to appoint holy ordinances and sacraments.

Q. 5. How many parts are there in a sacrament?

A. There are two parts in a sacrament—1. The outward sensible signs. 2. The things signified by the signs.

Q. 6. How do the sensible signs and the things signified, in a sacrament, differ?

A. The sensible signs and the things signified, in a sacrament, do differ, as the sensible signs are an object of the understanding and faith, being represented by the outward signs.

Q. 7. What kind of signs are the sensible signs in a sacrament?

A. 1. The sensible signs in a sacrament are not natural signs, as the dawn of the morning is a sign of the approaching day, or as smoke is a sign of fire; but they are arbitrary signs, and by the appointment, not of men, but of Jesus Christ. 2. They are not bare signifying or representing signs, but withal exhibiting, conveying, and applying signs; as a seal unto a bond, or last will and testament, doth both signify the will of him whose bond or last will and testament it is, and doth also exhibit and convey, confirm and apply, a right unto the things promised and engaged therein. When the minister doth give forth the signs or outward elements, in the sacramental actions, the Lord doth give forth and convey the things signified unto the worthy receivers.

Q. 8. What are the things signified by the outward sensible signs in a sacrament?

A. The things signified by the outward sensible signs in a sacrament, are Christ and the benefits of the new covenant.

Q. 9. What is the use of a sacrament, in reference unto Christ and the benefits of the new covenant?

A. The use of a sacrament, in reference unto Christ, and the benefits of the new covenant, is—1. To represent Christ and the benefits of the new covenant. "This is my covenant which ye shall keep between me and you, and your seed after you: Every man-child among you shall be circumcised."—Gen. xvii. 10. 2. To seal and apply Christ, and the benefits of the new covenant. "And he received the sign of circumcision, a seal of the righteousness of the faith which he had being yet uncircumcised."—Rom. iv. 11.

Q. 10. To whom doth a sacrament represent, seal, and apply Christ, and the benefits of the new covenant?

A. A sacrament doth represent, seal, and apply Christ,

and the benefits of the new covenant, not unto all that partake thereof, but unto believers only; faith being the eye of the soul, to discern the things represented, and the hand of the soul, to receive the things sealed and exhibited in the sacrament.

XCIII. Ques. *Which are the sacraments of the New Testament ?*

*Ans.* The sacraments of the New Testament are baptism and the Lord's supper.

Q. 1. Were there ever any other sacraments used in the Church besides those of the New Testament?

A. Formerly, under the Old Testament, there were other sacraments of use amongst the Jews, and not those of the New Testament.

Q. 2. What were the ordinary sacraments of common use among the Jews under the Old Testament?

A. The ordinary sacraments of common use amongst the Jews under the Old Testament, were circumcision and the passover; which, since the coming of Christ, are abrogated and abolished, and are no more to be used in the Church under the gospel.

Q. 3. What are the sacraments, then, of the New Testament, which are to be used in the Church under the gospel?

A. The only sacraments of the New Testament, which are to be used in the Church under the gospel, are baptism and the Lord's supper;—baptism, which is to be received but once, instead of circumcision, for initiation; and the Lord's supper, which is to be received often, instead of the passover, for nutrition.

Q. 4. What is the doctrine of the Papists concerning the number of the sacraments of the New Testament?

A. The doctrine of the Papists concerning the number of the sacraments is, that there are seven sacraments under the New Testament. Unto baptism and the Lord's supper they add confirmation, penance, ordination, marriage, and extreme unction: which, though some of them are to be used, namely, marriage and ordination, yet none

of them in their superstitious way; none of them have the
stamp of divine institution, to be used as sacraments; none
of them are seals of the covenant of grace; and therefore
they are no sacraments, but Popish additions, whereby
they would seem to make amends for their taking away
the second commandment out of the decalogue, as contrary to their image-worship; whereas both such as add
and such as take away from God's laws and institutions
are under a severer curse than any of the anathemas and
curses of the Popish councils. " If any man add to these
things, God shall add unto him the plagues that are written
in this book: and if any man shall take away from the
words of the book of this prophecy, God shall take away
his part out of the book of life."—Rev. xxii. 18, 19.

## XCIV. Ques. *What is baptism?*

*Ans.* Baptism is a sacrament, wherein the washing with water, in the name of the Father, and of the
Son, and of the Holy Ghost, doth signify and seal
our ingrafting into Christ, and partaking of the benefits of the covenant of grace, and our engagement to
be the Lord's.

Q. 1. What is the outward sign or element in baptism?

A. The outward sign or element in baptism is water,
and that pure water; so that the addition thereunto of oil,
salt, and spittle, by the Papists in baptism, is an abominable profanation of the ordinance. " Can any man forbid
water, that these should not be baptized?"—Acts x. 47.
" Our bodies washed with pure water."—Heb. x. 22.

Q. 2. What is the thing signified by water in baptism?

A. The thing signified by water in baptism, is the blood
of our Lord Jesus Christ.

Q. 3. What is the outward action in baptism?

A. The outward action in baptism, is washing of the
body with water; which is all that the word baptism doth
signify, and which may be fitly done by pouring water
upon the face, to represent Christ's blood poured out for
us; or by sprinkling water upon the face to represent the

blood of sprinkling, with which the heart is sprinkled. "Having our hearts sprinkled from an evil conscience, and our bodies washed with pure water."—Heb. x. 22.

Q. 4. Is it not necessary to dip or plunge the body in the water in baptism, when the Scripture telleth us of several that went down into the water when they were baptized; and we are to be buried with Christ in baptism, and therefore plunged and covered with water in baptism, as Christ was covered with earth in the grave?

A. It is not necessary that the body should be dipped or plunged all over in baptism : For—1. When we read of some that went down into the water when they were baptized, we do not read that they were dipped or plunged over head and ears; they might be baptized by pouring or sprinkling the water upon their faces; yea, in some places where, the Scripture telleth us, persons were baptized, travellers tell us they were but ancle-deep, in which it was impossible they could be plunged all over; and Ænon, where it is said there was much water, the original words do not signify deep waters, but many streams, which are known to be shallow, and not fit to plunge the body into. 2. Though some went down into the water when they were baptized, yet the Scripture doth not say that all did so : but most probably water was brought into the house, when the jailer and all his household were baptized in the night; and not that he suffered the apostles (then prisoners) to go forth, and that he with them should go out with all his household, and leave all the other prisoners alone, to seek some river to be baptized and plunged into. 3. The burying with Christ by baptism, doth signify the burying of sin in the soul, by the baptism of the Spirit; and not the burying of the body, and covering it all over in the baptism of water. There is a baptizing or washing, as was said, in pouring or sprinkling water on the body; and as our Saviour told Peter, when he would have been washed all over by him, that the washing of the feet was sufficient, so the washing of the face is sufficient, especially for infants, who, in our colder climates, cannot be plunged in a river without manifest hazard of their lives, which none can prove by Scripture to be necessary.

Q. 5. What doth the washing of the body with water represent and signify?

A. The washing of the body with water in baptism doth represent and signify the washing of the soul from sin by the blood of Jesus Christ. "That loved us, and washed us from our sins in his own blood."—Rev. i. 5.

Q. 6. In whose name are persons to be baptized?

A. Persons are to be baptized in the name of the Father, and of the Son, and of the Holy Ghost. "Go ye, therefore, and teach all nations, baptizing them in the name of the Father, and of the Son, and of the Holy Ghost."—Matt. xxviii. 19.

Q. 7. What is to be understood by the baptizing in the name of the Father, and of the Son, and of the Holy Ghost?

A. By baptizing in the name of the Father, and of the Son, and of the Holy Ghost is to be understood, not only a naming of the Father, Son, and Holy Ghost, but a baptizing in the authority, and into the faith, profession, and obedience of the Father, Son, and Holy Ghost.

Q. 8. What are signified, sealed, and engaged on God's part, by our being baptized in his name?

A. There are signified, and sealed, and engaged on God's part, by our being baptized in his name—1. His ingrafting us into Christ. 2. His making us partakers of the benefits of the new covenant. "Know ye not that so many of us as were baptized into Jesus Christ, were baptized into his death?"—Rom. vi. 3.

Q. 9. What is meant by our ingrafting into Christ?

A. By our ingrafting into Christ, is meant our being cut off from our old stock of nature, and being joined unto Jesus Christ, whereby we come to draw virtue from him as our root, that we may grow up in him, and bring forth fruit unto him. "I am the vine, ye are the branches."— John xv. 5. "Thou being a wild olive tree, wert grafted in among them, and with them partakest of the root and fatness of the olive tree."—Rom. xi. 17.

Q. 10. What are the benefits of the covenant of grace, which by baptism we are made partakers of?

A. The benefits of the covenant of grace, which by baptism we are made partakers of, are—1. Admission into the visible Church. "Go, teach all nations, baptizing them," &c.—Matt. xxviii. 19. 2. Remission of sins by Christ's blood. "Be baptized every one of you in the name of Jesus Christ, for the remission of sins."—Acts ii. 38. 3. Regeneration and sanctification by Christ's Spirit. "According to his mercy he saved us, by the washing of regeneration, and renewing of the Holy Ghost." — Tit. iii. 5. 4. Adoption, together with our union unto Christ. "For ye are all the children of God by faith in Christ Jesus: for as many of you as have been baptized into Christ have put on Christ."—Gal. iii. 26, 27. 5. Resurrection to everlasting life. "If the dead rise not at all, why are they then baptized for the dead ?"—1 Cor. xv. 29. "We are buried with him by baptism into death," &c. "If we have been planted together in the likeness of his death, we shall be also in the likeness of his resurrection."—Rom. vi. 4, 5.

Q. 11. What is sealed and engaged on our part, by being baptized in the name of the Father, Son, and Holy Ghost?

A. By our being baptized in the name of the Father Son, and Holy Ghost, is sealed and engaged on our part, that we will be the Lord's: and that—1. Wholly; soul and body, with all our powers, faculties, and members, are to be employed by him as instruments of righteousness and new obedience. And, 2. Only the Lord's; and therefore we engage to renounce the service of the devil, and the flesh, and the world, and to fight under Christ's banner against these enemies of the Lord and of our souls. "We are buried with him by baptism into death; that like as Christ was raised up from the dead by the glory of the Father, even so we also should walk in newness of life. Reckon ye yourselves to be dead indeed unto sin, but alive unto God. Let not sin, therefore, reign, that ye should obey it in the lusts thereof: neither yield ye your members as instruments of unrighteousness unto sin; but yield yourselves unto God, as those that are alive from the dead ; and your members as instruments of righteousness unto God." —Rom. vi. 4, 11–13.

## XCV. Ques. *To whom is baptism to be administered ?*

*Ans.* Baptism is not to be administered to any that are out of the visible Church, till they profess their faith in Christ, and obedience to him; but the infants of such as are members of the visible Church are to be baptized.

Q. 1. Is baptism to be administered unto all?

A. Baptism is not to be administered unto all, nor to any that are out of the visible Church, because they, being out of the covenant, have no right unto the seals of the covenant. "At that time ye were without Christ, being aliens from the commonwealth of Israel, and strangers from the covenants of promise, having no hope, and without God in the world."—Eph. ii. 12.

Q. 2. May not heathens and infidels be baptized?

A. Heathens and infidels, who are without the Church whilst they continue infidels, ought not to be baptized; but if, upon the preaching of the gospel unto them, they repent and believe, and make profession of their faith and resolution of obedience, they are thereby virtually within the Church, and then have a right to this ordinance of baptism, and it ought not to be denied unto them. "And he said, Go ye into all the world, and preach the gospel to every creature. He that believeth, and is baptized, shall be saved," &c.—Mark xvi. 15, 16.

Q. 3. May not infants be baptized?

A. 1. No infants of heathens and infidels, whilst such, may be baptized, because both parents and children are out of the covenant. 2. The infants of Christians or believing parents, being visible Church members, may and ought to be baptized.

Q. 4. How do you prove that the infants of such as are visible Church members, may and ought to be baptized?

A. That the infants of such as are visible Church members may and ought to be baptized may be proved, because they are in covenant; and the promise of the covenant belonging unto them, this seal of the covenant doth belong to them also. "The promise is to you and to your children."—Acts ii. 39. It is upon account of the promise of the covenant that any have the seal; hence it was that not only Abraham, but all his seed, whilst in their infancy, received the seal of circumcision, because the promise of the covenant was made to both; and by the same reason, not only believing parents, but also their infants, are to receive the seal of baptism, the promise being made to both. "I will establish my covenant between me and thee, and thy seed after thee; to be a God unto thee, and to thy seed after thee. This is my covenant, which ye shall keep, between me and you and thy seed after thee; Every man-child among you shall be circumcised."—Gen. xvii. 7, 10.

Q. 5. How do you prove that because the infants of the Jews, under the law, had the promise and seal of the covenant of grace, namely, circumcision, whereby they were admitted to be visible Church members; therefore, that the infants of Christians, under the gospel, have the promise of the covenant of grace, and ought to have the seal of baptism, to admit them to be visible Church members also?

A. 1. That the infants of Christians have the promise of the covenant of grace made with Abraham is evident, because that covenant was an everlasting covenant. "I will establish my covenant for an everlasting covenant, to be a God to thee, and to thy seed after thee" (Gen. xvii. 7); which covenant Christ is the Mediator of, and it is renewed in the New Testament with all believers, and that as fully as under the law: and, therefore, if the infants under the law were included, the infants under the gospel are included too. 2. That the privilege of infants (being made Church members) under the law, doth belong to the infants of Christians under the gospel, besides the parity of reason for it, and equality of right unto it, is evident, because this privilege was never repealed and taken away under the gospel.

Q. 6. How do you prove that the privilege of infants being made visible Church members under the gospel was never taken away?

A. That the privilege of infants being made visible Church members was never taken away under the gospel is evident—1. Because, if this privilege were repealed, we would have some notice of its repeal in the Scripture; but we have no notice or signification of God's will to repeal this privilege throughout the whole book of God. 2. Because Christ did not come to take away or straiten the privileges of the Church, but to enlarge them; and who can, upon Scripture grounds, imagine that it was the will of Christ that the infants of the Jewish Church should be Church members, but the infants of the Christian Church should be shut out like heathens and infidels? 3. Because the Scripture is express, that the infants of Christians are holy. "Else were your children unclean, but now they are holy."—1 Cor. vii. 14. As the Jews are called in Scripture a holy nation, because by circumcision they were made visible Church members; so the infants of Christians, as well as themselves, are called holy; that is, federally holy, as they are by baptism made visible Church members.

Q. 7. How doth it appear that baptism doth make members of the visible Church?

A. That baptism doth make members of the visible Church under the gospel is evident, because it is the sacrament of initiation and admission into the Church, by which our Saviour gave his disciples commission to admit persons into his Church. "Go and teach all nations, baptizing them," &c. (Matt. xxviii. 19); or, make and admit disciples, as the Greek word signifieth *disciple them*.

Q. 8. But doth not Christ first require that people should be taught and believe, at least make a profession of their faith, before they be baptized; and therefore, all infants being incapable of being taught, and making profession of their faith, are they not hereby excluded from the privilege of baptism?

A. 1. That which our Saviour required of teaching, and an actual profession of faith, before baptism, is to be understood of the heathen nations, unto whom he sent his apostles to preach, who, without this, were not to be baptized; but there is not the same reason concerning the infants of such as are themselves members of the visible Church. 2. The infants of Church members being incapable of being taught and making an actual profession of faith, doth no more exclude them the privilege of baptism than their being incapable of working doth exclude them the liberty of eating, when the command is express, "If any work not, neither shall he eat."—2 Thess. iii. 10. Notwithstanding which command, infants being incapable of working, yet they may eat; and so infants, being incapable of professing their faith, may be baptized. 3. Infants, though they are incapable of being taught by men, and making an actual profession of their faith, yet they are capable of the grace of the covenant, by the secret work of the Spirit; "for of such is the kingdom of heaven." And who will say that all infants, dying in their infancy, are damned, as they must be, if they are incapable of the grace of the covenant? and if they be capable of the grace of the covenant, they are capable of this seal of baptism.

Q. 9. How can infants have right to baptism, when we do not find, throughout the whole New Testament, either precept or example for their baptism?

A. 1. The ordinance of baptism, as to the substance of it, is expressly appointed by our Saviour in the New Testament; but it is not needful that the circumstance of the time of its administration should be appointed too, when the time may be so clearly deduced by Scripture consequence. 2. We do not find, in the Scripture, any precept or example in the very words, that women shall partake of the Lord's supper; yet we believe that they did partake of the Lord's supper in Scripture time; and, they being Church members, and believers capable of the actual exercise of grace, have an undoubted right unto that sacrament. 3. We have proved from Scripture, that Christian infants have a right to be Church members, and therefore they have a right to baptism, which admits them thereunto, and that there is no Scripture repeal of this privilege. 4. We have no precept or example concerning the infants of such as were baptized themselves, that they should be, or that any of them were, kept unbaptized from their infancy, until they were grown up unto years of maturity, and did make an actual profession of their faith, and then did receive the ordinance of baptism; and why, then, will any do this which they have no Scripture precept nor example for? 5. There is great probability that the infants of believers, in some recorded cases of Scripture, were baptized in their infancy. Where whole households were baptized together, it is not said that the infants in such houses were excluded; and why, then, should we exclude infants from the ordinance, whom God hath nowhere excluded?

XCVI. Ques. *What is the Lord's supper?*

*Ans.* The Lord's supper is a sacrament, wherein, by giving and receiving bread and wine, according to Christ's appointment, his death is showed forth; and the worthy receivers are, not after a corporal and carnal manner, but by faith, made partakers of his body and blood, with all his benefits, to their spiritual nourishment, and growth in grace.

Q. 1. How many things are most considerable in the Lord's supper?

A. There are eight things most considerable in the Lord's supper—1. The nature of it. 2. The author of it. 3. The outward elements and actions. 4. The internal mysteries, or the things signified. 5. The subject of it, or the persons that have right to receive it. 6. The manner how it is to be received. 7. The benefits of it. 8. The end of it.

Q. 2. What is the Lord's supper as to the nature of it?

A. The Lord's supper, as to the nature of it, is a sacrament and seal of the covenant of grace, wherein the mutual obligations, both on God's part and on our part, which are made in baptism, are renewed and confirmed.

Q. 3. Who is the author of the Lord's supper?

A. The Lord's supper is a sacrament, not of man's invention, but our Lord Jesus Christ is the author of it; and it is of his appointment and institution. "For I have received of the Lord that which also I delivered unto you, that the Lord Jesus took bread," &c.—1 Cor. xi. 23.

Q. 4. When did the Lord Jesus institute and appoint this sacrament of his supper?

A. The Lord Jesus did institute and appoint this sacrament of his supper the same night in which he was betrayed. "The Lord Jesus, the same night in which he was betrayed, took bread."—1 Cor. xi. 23. It was at night, because it was to succeed and come in the room of the passover: it was the same night in which he was betrayed, because it was to be a commemoration of his death.

Q. 5. Are not Christians bound to receive this sacrament at night, when our Saviour did first institute and administer it, and the apostles did first receive it at night?

A. We are no more bound from this example to receive this sacrament at night, than we are bound to receive it in an upper room, and but twelve in company, which was the practice in the first institution. We have not the same reason for receiving it at night as the apostles had, who were then to eat the passover before: and although the time of receiving it be an indifferent thing, yet the noon (the time when our Saviour gave up the ghost) seemeth to be the most suitable time for the receiving of it; especially since at that time both body and mind are ordinarily in the best disposition for receiving it with the greatest activity, and the least faintness and weariness.

Q. 6. In what posture should the sacrament be received?

A. The table posture seemeth to be the most decent, and not to be esteemed irreverent, when Christ himself was present and did so administer it to them.

Q. 7. By whom is the sacrament of the Lord's supper to be administered?

A. The sacrament of the Lord's supper, as also the other of baptism, is to be administered by none but such as are the ministers of Jesus Christ, called and installed in this office, according to the Scripture rule: such are Christ's ambassadors; and none but such have authority to exhibit or apply the broad seals of the kingdom of heaven.

Q. 8. What are the outward signs and elements in the Lord's supper?

A. The outward signs and elements in the Lord's supper are bread and wine.

Q. 9. What bread is to be used in the Lord's supper?

A. Ordinary bread is to be used, and not wafers, after the manner of the Papists; and it is most decent that it be white bread.

Q. 10. What wine is to be used in the Lord's supper?

A. Any kind of wine may be used in the Lord's supper. We read that Christ drank of the fruit of the vine with his disciples, but what sort of wine is not said; yet it seemeth most suitable, and most lively to represent the blood of Christ, when the wine is of a red colour, such as tent or claret wine.

Q. 11. May and ought all that receive the Lord's supper to receive it in both elements, the bread and the wine too?

A. All that receive the Lord's supper may and ought to receive it in both elements, the bread and also the wine. This is evident from the directions which the apostle doth give unto the Corinthians in general about the receiving this sacrament, wherein he joins the cup and the bread together, as belonging to all that did receive. "As often as ye eat this bread, and drink this cup, ye do show the Lord's death till he come. Let a man [that is, any man, and not the minister only] examine himself, and so let him eat of that bread, and drink of that cup."—1 Cor. xi 26, 28. And therefore the practice of the Papists, in tak ing away the cup from the people, is unwarrantable and injurious.

Q. 12. What are the outward actions in this sacrament of the Lord's supper?

A. The outward actions in this sacrament of the Lord's supper—1. On the minister's part, are, his blessing the elements, and setting them apart for this sacramental use by reading the words of the institution, with thanksgiving, and prayer unto God for his blessing; his taking the bread, and breaking it; his taking the cup, and distribut ing both the bread and wine unto the people, in the words of our Saviour, when he first did institute the sacrament. 2. On the part of the people, the outward actions are, their taking the bread and wine, and eating the one and drinking the other.

Q. 13. What are signified and represented by the bread and wine in this sacrament?

A. By the bread and wine in this sacrament are signified and represented the body and blood of Christ. "Take, eat; this is my body. This cup is the new testament in my blood."—1 Cor. xi. 24, 25.

Q. 14. Is not the bread in this sacrament transubstantiated and turned into the real body of Christ, when our Saviour telleth his disciples expressly, "This is my body?"

A. The bread in this sacrament is not transubstantiated and turned into the real body of Christ, but is only a sign and representation of Christ's body.

Q. 15. How do you prove that the bread in this sacrament is not turned into the real body of Christ?

A. That the bread in this sacrament is not turned into the real body of Christ, may be proved by divers arguments.

Arg. 1. It is evident, both unto sense and reason, that the bread, after consecration, remaineth bread as it was before. (1.) It is evident unto sense, the quantity or bigness of bread remaineth, the figure of bread remaineth, the locality or place of bread remaineth, the colour, taste, and smell of bread remain ; and nothing in the world is more evident unto sense than the bread in the sacrament, no alteration in the least, unto the sense, being made by its consecration. (2.) It is evident unto reason that the bread cannot be turned into another substance, and the accidents not to be at all changed or altered. When our Saviour turned water into wine, the water, as it lost its substance, so also it lost its colour, taste, smell, and other accidents; and the wine made of water, had the colour, taste, and smell of wine, as well as the substance of wine : but in the sacrament there is no other colour, taste, figure, or any accident, out of bread; and therefore, in reason, there is no other substance but of bread. In the sacrament we must either clothe the body of Christ with the accidents of bread, and say that his body is of such a figure, taste, and colour, as the bread is, which would render him ill-favoured, ill-shapen, and debase his body (so glorious now in heaven) into the likeness of bread, which is such an absurd blasphemy that none will affirm; or else, if the accidents of bread cannot be attributed unto Christ's body, and yet the substance of bread be gone and the substance of Christ's body come into its room, then the accidents of bread do exist without a subject, which is most absurd and contradictory to reason. We perceive by our senses such a colour, taste, and figure: it cannot be the body of Christ that is of such a colour, taste, and figure; and if there be no other substance in the room that hath these accidents, hence it follows, that it is *nothing* which hath this colour, taste, and figure; and that in the sacrament, there is a white *nothing*, a sweet *nothing*, a loaf of *nothing*, a piece of *nothing*, which is a ridiculous absurdity. Nothing is more evident unto reason, than that the substance of the bread remaineth unchanged, while the accidents remain unchanged.

Arg. 2. If the bread in this sacrament be turned into the real body of Christ, then either there are so many bodies of Christ as there are pieces of bread eaten in all sacraments, or else they are all one and the same body. (1.) It cannot be that there should be so many bodies of Christ as there are pieces of bread eaten in all sacraments; because, first, Christ would then be a monster with many thousands, yea, millions of bodies. Secondly, It would lie in the power of any minister to make as many bodies of Christ as he pleased, or that God should be bound to work a miracle every time the bread is consecrated. Thirdly, This cannot consist with Christ's unity. Fourthly, None of Christ's bodies, but one, would be the body which was born of the Virgin Mary, and that died upon the cross. Fifthly, All these bodies, but the one he hath in heaven, would be without a soul, and so altogether insufficient to save the soul, or to confer any spiritual life or grace by the feeding upon them in the sacrament. Therefore it cannot be that there should be so many bodies of Christ as there are pieces of bread eaten in all sacraments. (2.) Neither can it be one and the same body of Christ which the bread in the sacrament is turned into; for then it would follow, first, That Christ's body is both visible and invisible: visible in heaven, and invisible in the sacrament. Secondly, That one and the same body of Christ is present in divers places at the same time, in heaven and in divers places of the earth; and to say that one and the same body, which is circumscribed by one place, is at the same time present in a thousand other places, is abhorrent unto all reason: and it is in effect to say—It is where it is not, and is not where it is, which is an absurd contradiction. If Christ's body be in heaven, it is not in the sacrament; if it be in the sacrament, it is not in heaven. Christ's body is not divided, and so by parts in one place and in another at the same time; neither is Christ's body infinite, and so present in divers places together, as God is present; for then his body would cease to be a body: therefore Christ's body cannot be in divers places together; therefore, being in heaven, it is not present in the sacrament.

Arg. 3. If the bread in the sacrament be turned into the real body of Christ, then, after the eating of it, either it returneth to heaven (which it cannot do, because it is there already), or else it remaineth with them that eat it; and if so, then Christ's body in part would be turned into the substance of our bodies; and if we are wicked, when these same bodies are raised, it would be tormented for ever in hell; part also of Christ's body would go into the draught, and be subject to corruption; either of which to affirm is most horribly blasphemous: therefore the Popish tenet of transubstantiation is to be abominated by all Christians.

Arg. 4. If the bread in this sacrament were turned into the real body of Christ, both the nature and end of the sacrament would be destroyed. The nature of the sacrament is to be a sign, the end of it is to be a remembrance of Christ; both which suppose Christ's body to be absent, which this sacrament is a sign and remembrance of: whereas, if the bread were turned into Christ's body, it would be present.

Arg. 5. It is bread which is eaten in this sacrament, and not the body of Christ; and so it is termed by the apostle. "As often as ye eat this bread;"—not this body of Christ. —" Whosoever shall eat this bread unworthily," &c.— " Let a man examine himself, and so let him eat of that bread."—1 Cor. xi. 26–28. And if it be bread which is eaten in this sacrament, surely the bread is not turned into the real body of Christ.

Q. 16. But are not the words of our Saviour plain in his

institution of this sacrament—" This is my body?" and
would he have said it, had not the bread been turned into
his real body?

A. If all Scripture expressions besides were to be understood literally, then there would be some reason that this
expression should be so understood too; but we frequently
find figurative expressions in the Scripture, and that concerning Christ. "That rock was Christ."—1 Cor. x. 4.
"Jesus Christ himself being the chief corner-stone."—
Eph. ii. 20. Is Jesus Christ, therefore, turned into a rock
or stone? In the same sense as, in the Jewish sacrament,
the paschal lamb is called the passover, the bread in the
Christian sacrament is called the body of Christ: the
paschal lamb could in no proper sense be the passover,
which was the action of the angel in passing over the
houses of the Israelites, when he destroyed the first-born
of the Egyptians. What absurdity is it to say, that the
paschal lamb was turned into this action of the angel!
Surely a present substance could not be turned into an
accident or action which was long before; but it was a
sign or commemoration of that action: so the bread in this
sacrament is not properly the body of Christ, and so one
body turned into another without its accidents; but the
bread is a sign of the body of Christ, and a commemoration
of Christ's body which was crucified for us.

Q. 17. But cannot God, by his infinite power, turn the
bread into the real body of Christ? and if he can do it,
why may we not believe that he really doeth it, when Christ
saith, " This is my body?"

A. Although God, by his infinite power can do all things
which are possible unto true power, yet we may safely say
that God cannot do any which implieth imperfection and
weakness, such as to make contradictions true, and to introduce ridiculous absurdities and blasphemous consequences: which he should do, if he should turn the bread
in the sacrament, but without the transmutation of its
accidents, into the real body of Christ.

Q. 18. How do the bread and wine in this sacrament
represent the body and blood of Christ?

A. The bread and wine in this sacrament do represent

the body and blood of Christ, in that as the bread and wine do nourish, strengthen, and refresh the body, and satisfy the natural appetite; so the body and blood of Christ, received in this sacrament, do nourish, strengthen, and refresh the soul, and satisfy the spiritual appetite.

Q. 19. What is·represented by the actions of the minister, in the taking the bread and breaking it, and taking the cup and giving both unto the people?

A. By the actions of the minister, in taking the bread and breaking it, and taking the cup, and giving both unto the people, is represented God's taking his Son, and giving him to be broken and crucified upon the cross for us; and withal, his giving him in this sacrament unto us to be our Redeemer and Saviour.

Q. 20. What are represented by the actions of the people in receiving the bread and wine, and feeding upon them?

A. By the actions of the people in receiving the bread and wine, and feeding upon them, are represented their receiving of Jesus Christ, given them by the Father, and feeding upon him in the sacrament.

Q. 21. Do all that receive this sacrament partake really of the body and blood of Christ, with the benefits of the new covenant?

A. None but worthy receivers do receive and partake really of the body and blood of Christ, with the benefits of the new covenant.

Q. 22. How do worthy receivers really partake of the body and blood of Christ, with all its benefits?

A. The worthy receivers do really partake of the body and blood of Christ, with all its benefits—1. Not after a corporal and carnal manner, and by conjunction of his real body and blood unto their body, as meat and drink are really joined unto them in their eating and drinking thereof: But, 2. It is by faith that Christ's body and blood are really, but spiritually, joined unto their souls; and the virtue and efficacy, the fruits and benefits of his death, are applied by them, whereby they receive spiritual nourishment and growth in grace. "The cup of blessing which we bless, is it not the communion of the blood of Christ?

The bread which we break, is it not the communion of the body of Christ?"—1 Cor. x. 16.

Q. 23. How do believers receive spiritual nourishment and growth in grace in and by this sacrament?

A. Believers receive spiritual nourishment and growth in grace in and by this sacrament—1. As they draw virtue from Christ's death, for the crucifying of the flesh, for mortifying and purging away sin, which doth hinder their spiritual nourishment and growth. 2. As the Lord doth convey by his Spirit, and they do receive in this sacrament by faith, further supplies of his grace, which, by his death, he hath purchased for them, and which, in his covenant of grace (whereof this sacrament is a seal), he hath promised unto them.

Q. 24. What is the end of this sacrament of the Lord's supper?

A. The end of this sacrament of the Lord's supper is the showing forth of Christ's death, by the receiving of which Christians do publicly own, and give testimony of their belief in, and hopes of salvation by, a crucified Lord. "For as often as ye eat this bread, and drink this cup, ye do show the Lord's death till he come."—1 Cor. xi. 26.

## XCVII. Ques. *What is required to the worthy receiving of the Lord's supper?*

*Ans.* It is required of them that would worthily partake of the Lord's supper, that they examine themselves of their knowledge to discern the Lord's body, of their faith to feed upon him, of their repentance, love, and new obedience; lest, coming unworthily, they eat and drink judgment to themselves.

Q. 1. What is it to receive the Lord's supper worthily?

A. 1. To receive the Lord's supper worthily, is not to receive it meritoriously, as if we were to bring any merit or worth of our own thereunto; for so none can be worthy of Christ or any of his benefits. 2. We receive the Lord's supper worthily when we receive it with due preparation before we come to it, and with suitable behaviour when we are at the table of the Lord.

Q. 2. What is that preparation which is required to the worthy receiving of the Lord's supper?

A. There is required to the worthy receiving of the Lord's supper—1. Habitual preparation, that the persons who receive it be in a state of grace. 2. Actual preparation, that their graces be drawn forth into exercise.

Q. 3. What is requisite for the obtaining of this habitual and actual preparation, in order to our worthy receiving?

A. It is requisite, for the obtaining of this habitual and actual preparation, in order to our worthy receiving, that we examine ourselves. "But let a man examine himself, and so let him eat of that bread, and drink of that cup."— 1 Cor. xi. 28.

Q. 4. Wherein are we to examine ourselves in order to our preparation for this sacrament?

A. We are to examine ourselves, in order to our preparation for this sacrament—1. In our knowledge to discern the Lord's body, which is represented by the bread. "Not discerning the Lord's body."—1 Cor. xi. 29. 2. In our faith to apply Christ and feed upon him, and so to draw virtue and spiritual nourishment from him. "Examine yourselves, whether ye be in the faith."—2 Cor. xiii. 5. 3. In our repentance, self-judging, and godly sorrow for our sins, which have brought sufferings upon our Lord. "For if we would judge ourselves, we should not be judged."—1 Cor. ix. 31. 4. In our love to Christ, who in his death expressed such love to us; and in our love to one another, who are redeemed by the same blood. 5. In our new and sincere obedience to the gospel, which we must engage in, and be fully resolved, in the strength of the Lord, to perform, before we can worthily receive this sacrament. "There-fore, let us keep the feast, not with old leaven, neither with the leaven of malice and wickedness, but with the unleavened bread of sincerity and truth."—1 Cor. v. 8.

Q. 5. What is requisite by way of preparation for this sacrament, besides self-examination?

A. By way of preparation for this sacrament, besides self-examination, there is requisite, prayer to God for his presence, blessing, and assistance of his Spirit; and meditation, in order to the exciting of our affections and the drawing forth of our graces into exercise.

Q. 6. Who are they that come to the Lord's table unworthily?

A. 1. Such come to the table of the Lord unworthily, as have no habitual preparation, being in a graceless and Christless state; who, having no faith, can neither discern the Lord's body, nor spiritually feed upon him; who, being without repentance, love, and new obedience, can neither bring glory to the Lord, nor enjoy communion with him by receiving this sacrament. 2. Such also come to the table of the Lord unworthily, who, although they are gracious, and have habitual preparation, yet take no care, by self-examination, prayer, and meditation, to attain actual preparation, whereby they displease God, and lose also the benefit of the ordinance.

Q. 7. If such as are gracious do take pains in self-examination, and other duties, to get their hearts prepared, and yet they are still out of frame, would they not be unworthy receivers, should they come to the Lord's table?

A. When such as are gracious do, by self-examination and other duties, endeavour to get their hearts prepared, though they be out of frame, they ought to come to the Lord's table, because God may bring them into frame in and by the ordinance; however, they must wait there, and attend upon God out of obedience, when they cannot do it with sensible, melting, warm, and delightful affection, and their sincerity through Christ will be accepted.

Q. 8. When we doubt and fear whether we be truly gracious, may we come to the Lord's table?

A. We may and ought to come to the Lord's table, although under doubts and fears, if we have a sense of our need of, and hungering desires after, Jesus Christ, together with resolutions to give up ourselves in covenant to the Lord—this sacrament being a mean of getting evidences of God's love; and when we cannot come with assurance, we may come for assurance.

Q. 9. What must be our behaviour at the table of the Lord, that we may be worthy receivers?

A. That we may be worthy receivers, our behaviour at

the table of the Lord must be humble and reverent, as to the outward gestures of our bodies and inward frame of our hearts. We must seriously mind the outward elements and actions, looking chiefly to the things signified, represented, and exhibited in the ordinance. We must meditate upon Christ's death, so disgraceful and painful, for us—grieving for our sins, the cause of it—hungering and thirsting after him, and the benefits purchased by his death—applying the promises of the covenant and New Testament, which is of full force through the death of the Testator—drawing nourishment and all needful spiritual supplies from him, in whom all fulness doth dwell—rejoicing in his love—giving thanks for his grace—renewing our covenant—and mingling all especially with faith and most endeared love to the Lord, and with love in him one to another.

Q. 10. What is required of worthy receivers after they come from the table of the Lord?

A. It is required of worthy receivers, after they come from the table of the Lord, that they examine themselves as to their carriage and success. If they have not met with God, and have been out of frame, that they inquire into the cause, mourn for their defects, be earnest for a pardon, and, by after pains, labour to get the benefit of the ordinance, and withal, endeavour to mend for the future. If they have met with God, and been enlarged and sweetly refreshed, they must be very thankful for assistances and enlargements, labour to retain the sweet relish they have had still upon their spirits—they must endeavour to draw more and more virtue from Christ, for the crucifying of the world and the flesh—they must be very watchful against Satan, sin, and carnal security—they must be careful to perform their vows, and keep the covenant which they have renewed.

Q. 11. What is the sin of unworthy receiving the Lord's supper?

A. The sin of unworthy receiving the Lord's supper is, that such are guilty of the body and blood of the Lord; that is, they are guilty of an affront and indignity which they offer to the Lord's body and blood. " Whosoever shall eat this bread, and drink this cup of the Lord unworthily, shall be guilty of the body and blood of the Lord."—1 Cor. xi. 27.

Q. 12. What is the danger of our unworthy receiving the Lord's supper?

A. The danger of our unworthy receiving the Lord's supper, is the eating and drinking judgment to ourselves; that is, provoking the Lord, by our unworthy receiving, to inflict temporal, spiritual, and eternal judgments upon us. " For he that eateth and drinketh unworthily, eateth and drinketh damnation to himself, not discerning the Lord's body. For this cause many are weak and sickly among you, and many sleep."—1 Cor. xi. 29, 30.

## XCVIII. Quest. *What is prayer?*

*Ans.* Prayer is an offering up of our desires unto God for things agreeable to his will, in the name of Christ, with confession of our sins, and thankful acknowledgment of his mercies.

Q. 1. How many parts are there in prayer?

A. There are three parts in prayer—petition, confession, and thanksgiving; but most properly, prayer doth consist in petition.

Q. 2. What kind of petition is prayer unto God?

A. The petition of the lips, without the desire of the heart, may be accounted prayer by men, but it is not acceptable prayer unto God, which is an offering up of the desires unto him, and pouring forth of the heart before him. " Trust in him at all times; ye people, pour out your hearts before him."—Ps. lxii. 8.

Q. 3. Unto whom are we to direct our prayers?

A. We are to direct our prayers to God only. " Hearken unto the voice of my cry, my King and my God! for unto thee will I pray. My voice shalt thou hear in the morning, O Lord; in the morning will I direct my prayer unto thee, and will look up."—Ps. v. 2, 3.

Q. 4. Why are we to direct our prayers only unto God?

A. We are to direct our prayers only unto God—1. Because prayer is a part of religious worship, and God is the only object of religious worship. " Thou shalt worship the Lord thy God, and him only shalt thou serve."—Matt. iv. 10. 2. Because God only is everywhere present to see his people, and to hear their prayers. " The eyes of the Lord are upon the righteous, and his ears are open unto their cry."—Ps. xxxiv. 15. 3. Because God only can answer our prayers by fulfilling our desires, and giving the things which we pray for and stand in need of. " The Lord is nigh unto all them that call upon him. He will fulfil the desire of them that fear him: he also will hear their cry and save them."—Ps. cxlv. 18, 19.

Q. 5. For what things may we pray unto God?

A. 1. We may not pray for the fulfilling of any sinful desires. " Ye ask and receive not, because ye ask amiss, that ye may consume it upon your lusts."—James iv. 3. 2. We may and ought to pray unto God only for such things as are agreeable unto his will. " And this is the confidence that we have in him, that if we ask anything according to his will, he heareth us. And if we know that he hear us, we know that we have the petitions that we desired of him."—1 John v. 14, 15.

Q. 6. What are the things agreeable unto God's will which we may pray for?

A. The things which we may pray for, are not all things which are agreeable unto his secret will; for thus all things which come to pass, even the worst of sins which are committed, are agreeable unto God's secret counsel and eternal determination; but all things which are agreeable unto God's revealed will in his Word, we may pray for; such as the pardon of our sins, the supplies of his grace, spiritual life and strength here, eternal life and glory hereafter, deliverance from spiritual and eternal evils; also whatever temporal good things we stand in need of, and all those things which either expressly or inclusively he hath promised in his covenant unto us.

Q. 7. In whose name ought we to pray unto God?

A. We ought to pray unto God only in the name of the Lord Jesus Christ. " Whatsoever ye shall ask in my name, that will I do, that the Father may be glorified in the Son. If ye shall ask any thing in my name, I will do it."—John xiv. 13, 14.

Q. 8. What is it to pray unto God in the name of Christ?

A. To pray unto God in the name of Christ, is not barely to mention the name of Christ with our lips in the conclusion, or any part of our prayers; but it is by faith to mention his name, depending upon Christ alone for admittance and access unto God in prayer, for acceptance, audience, and a gracious return unto our prayers. "In whom we have boldness and access with confidence by the faith of him."—Eph. iii. 12.

Q. 9. Why must we pray unto God in the name of Christ?

A. We must pray unto God in the name of Christ, because God being so infinitely holy and jealous, so infinitely just and righteous, and we being so unholy and sinful, and our prayers at best so imperfect, and so mingled with defilement, that neither our persons would find acceptance, nor our prayers any audience with God, without the name and mediation of Christ, and the mixture of the sweet incense of his merits with our prayers, to take away the ill savour of them, and the using of his interest with the Father, upon his account alone, to give an answer unto them. "And another angel came and stood at the altar [that is, the Lord Jesus Christ, who is the Angel of the Covenant], having a golden censer; and there was given unto him much incense, that he should offer it with the prayers of all saints upon the golden altar, which was before the throne. And the smoke of the incense, which came with the prayers of the saints, ascended up before God, out of the angel's hand."—Rev. viii. 3, 4.

Q. 10. May we not make use of the name of angels, and the Virgin Mary, and other saints, in prayer, directing our prayers unto them to help us, at least to improve their interest in heaven for us, as the Papists do teach and practise?

A. 1. It is idolatry to direct our prayers unto any creature, God being the alone object of this and all other religious worship; therefore we ought not to direct our prayers unto angels (who have refused worship), much less unto any saints. "Let no man beguile you of your reward, in a voluntary humility, and worshipping of angels."—Col. ii. 18. "And I fell at his feet to worship him: and he said unto me, See thou do it not; I am thy fellow-servant," &c.— Rev. xix. 10. 2. There is but one Mediator and Intercessor in heaven for us, namely, the Lord Jesus Christ, and it is an affront to him to make use of any angels or saints as our intercessors. "There is one God, and one Mediator between God and men, the man Christ Jesus."—1 Tim. ii. 5. "If any man sin, we have an Advocate with the Father, Jesus Christ the righteous."—1 John ii. 1. 3. We have neither precept nor example in Scripture for, nor any promise unto any prayers which we shall make either unto or by either angels or saints. 4. The chiefest saints in heaven are ignorant of our condition on earth; neither can they, where they are, hear, much less give answer unto our prayers, and therefore are unfit to be the object of our prayers, or to make particular intercession for us. "Doubtless thou art our Father, though Abraham be ignorant of us, and Israel acknowledge us not."—Isa. lxiii. 16. Therefore the doctrine and practice of the Papists herein is both unallowable and abominable.

Q. 11. How must we pray unto God, that our prayers may be acceptable unto him, and answered by him?

A. That our prayers may be acceptable unto God, and answered by him, we must pray—1. With sincerity. "Let us draw near with a true heart."—Heb. x. 22. 2. With humility. "Lord, thou hast heard the desire of the humble."—Ps. x. 17. 3. With faith. "Let him ask in faith."—James i. 6. 4. With fervency. "The effectual fervent prayer of a righteous man availeth much."—James v. 16. 5. With perseverance. "Men ought always to pray, and not to faint."—Luke xviii. 1. 6. We must look after our prayers, and wait for a return. "Therefore I will look unto the Lord: I will wait for the God of my salvation; my God will hear me."—Micah vii. 7.

Q. 12. Can we ourselves pray thus acceptably unto God?

A. We cannot of ourselves pray thus acceptably unto

God, without the Spirit of God to help our infirmities, and to teach us both for what and how to pray. "Likewise the Spirit also helpeth our infirmities; for we know not what we should pray for as we ought; but the Spirit maketh intercession for us with groanings that cannot be uttered. And he that searcheth the hearts, knoweth what is the mind of the Spirit, because he maketh intercession for the saints according to the will of God."—Rom. vii. 26, 27.

Q. 13. Doth God accept and answer all the prayers that are offered unto him?

A. 1. God doth not accept and answer the prayers of the wicked. "The sacrifice of the wicked is an abomination to the Lord; but the prayer of the upright is his delight."—Prov. xv. 8. 2. God doth not accept the prayers of his own people when they regard iniquity in their hearts. "If I regard iniquity in my heart, the Lord will not hear my prayers."—Ps. lxvi. 18. 3. God doth accept the prayers of his people which are offered up unto him in the name of Christ, and by the help of the Spirit, and which are for things agreeable unto his will; so that he either giveth the things unto them which they pray for, or else something that is equivalent or better for them.

Q. 14. What is the second part of prayer?

A. The second part of prayer is confession of our sins, with which our petitions for pardon and supply of our wants should be introduced.

Q. 15. What sins should we make confession of in prayer?

A. In prayer, we should make confession of our original and actual sins against law and gospel; of omission and commission, in thought and heart, of lip and life, with aggravations of them; acknowledging withal our desert of temporal, spiritual, and eternal judgments and punishments for them. "I acknowledged my sin unto thee, and mine iniquity have I not hid."—Ps. xxxii. 5. "Against thee, thee only, have I sinned, and done this evil in thy sight. Behold, I was shapen in iniquity, and in sin did my mother conceive me."—Ps. li. 4, 5. "O Lord, to us belongeth confusion of face, because we have sinned against thee.—Dan. ix. 8.

Q. 16. How ought we in prayer to confess our sins?

A. We ought in prayer to confess our sins humbly, fully, freely, with grief for them, and hatred of them, with full purpose and full resolution, in the strength of the Lord, not to return again to the practice of them.

Q. 17. What is the third part of prayer?

A. The third part of prayer is, thankful acknowledgment of God's mercies, temporal and spiritual, here, and the promises of life and happiness in the other world; which we ought to acknowledge with admiration, faith, love, joy, and all kind of suitable affections. "By prayer and supplication, with thanksgiving, let your requests be made known unto God."—Phil. iv. 6.

XCIX. Ques. *What rule hath God given for our direction in prayer?*

*Ans.* The whole Word of God is of use to direct us in prayer; but the special rule of direction is that form of prayer which Christ taught his disciples, commonly called *The Lord's Prayer*.

Q. 1. What is generally useful for our direction in prayer?

A. The whole Word of God is generally useful for our direction, as it containeth plenty of matter for prayer, guideth us to the manner of it, and aboundeth with variety of expressions which most fitly may be used in it.

Q. 2. What is the special rule for our direction in prayer?

A. The special rule for our direction in prayer is that form of prayer which Christ taught his disciples, commonly called The Lord's Prayer. "After this manner therefore pray ye: Our Father which art in heaven, hallowed be thy name," &c.

Q. 3. How many parts are there in the Lord's prayer?

A. There are three parts in the Lord's prayer; the preface, the petitions, and the conclusion.

C. Quest. *What doth the preface to the Lord's prayer teach us?*

*Ans.* The preface of the Lord's prayer, (which is, " Our Father which art in heaven,") teacheth us to draw near to God with all holy reverence and confidence, as children to a father, able and ready to help us; and that we should pray with and for others.

Q. 1. What is the preface of the Lord's prayer itself?

A. The preface of the Lord's prayer itself, is in these words, " Our Father which art in heaven."

Q. 2. What do the words, " Our Father," in the preface, teach us?

A. These words, " Our Father," in the preface, teach us —1. To draw near-unto God with confidence, both of his all-sufficiency and his readiness to help us; as also with a filial affection of desire, love, and delight, as children to a Father. " For ye have not received the spirit of bondage again to fear; but ye have received the Spirit of adoption, whereby we cry, Abba, Father."—Rom. viii. 15. " Him that is able to do exceeding abundantly above all that we ask or think."—Eph. iii. 20. " If ye, then, being evil, know how to give good gifts unto your children, how much more shall your Father which is in heaven give good things to them that ask him?"—Matt. vii. 11. 2. To pray to God with and for others, he being a common Father unto all his people. " Praying always with all prayer and supplication for all saints."—Eph. vi. 18.

Q. 3. Are we to pray unto God only for the saints and such as are his children?

A. We must pray unto God, not only for the saints and his children, but also for all men : we must pray, not only for the Church in general, but also for the nation wherein we live—for magistrates, and for ministers; and not only for our friends, but also for our enemies. " Pray for the peace of Jerusalem."—Ps. cxxii. 6. " I exhort, therefore, that, first of all, supplications, prayers, intercessions, and giving of thanks, be made for all men; for kings and for all that are in authority, that we may lead a quiet and peaceable life in all godliness and honesty."—1 Tim. ii. 1.

2. " Love your enemies, and pray for them that despitefully use you and persecute you."—Matt. v. 44.

Q. 4. What do these words, " Which art in heaven," teach us?

A. These words, " Which art in heaven," teach us to draw near unto God with all holy reverence, because of our great distance, God being not our earthly Father, but our Father which is in heaven. " Be not rash with thy mouth, and let not thine heart be hasty to utter anything before God: for God is in heaven, and thou upon earth."—Eccles. v. 2.

CI. Ques. *What do we pray for in the first petition?*

*Ans.* In the first petition, (which is, " Hallowed be thy name,") we pray, That God would enable us, and others, to glorify him in all that whereby he maketh himself known; and that he would dispose all things to his own glory.

Q. 1. What is the second part in the Lord's prayer?

A. The second part in the Lord's prayer is petitions.

Q. 2. How many petitions are there in the Lord's prayer?

A. There are six petitions in the Lord's prayer.

Q. 3. What is the first petition in the Lord's prayer?

A. The first petition in the Lord's prayer is in these words, " Hallowed be thy name."

Q. 4. What is meant by the name of God?

A. By the name of God is meant, God's titles, attributes, ordinances, word, and works, whereby God is pleased to make himself known. See the explication of the fifty-fourth answer.

Q. 5. What is it to hallow God's name?

A. To hallow God's name, is, to sanctify, honour, and glorify God in all things whereby he maketh himself known. " Sanctify the Lord of hosts himself, and let him be your fear and your dread."—Isa. viii. 13. " Give unto the Lord the glory due unto his name; worship the Lord in the beauty of holiness."—Ps. xcvi. 8, 9.

Q. 6. What do we pray for in the petition, "Hallowed be thy name?

A. In the petition, "Hallowed be thy name," we pray —1. That God would hallow and glorify his own name, by magnifying himself in the world, and by disposing all things for his own glory. "Let thy name be magnified for ever."—2 Sam. vii. 26. "Fill their faces with shame, that they may seek thy name, O Lord: that men may know that thou, whose name alone is JEHOVAH, art the Most High over all the earth."—Ps. lxxxiii. 16, 18. 2. That God would enable us to hallow and glorify his name, by confessing and forsaking our sins, which rob him of his glory; by admiring and adoring him in his glorious titles and attributes, in his infinite excellences and perfections; by believing, loving, and obeying his word; by observing and attending upon his worship and ordinances; by magnifying him in his works, and making use of his creatures for his glory; by sincere, diligent, zealous, and constant endeavours to promote his honour and interest in our places and relations; and that the chief design of our thoughts, words, and actions, may be the glory of God, and that he would enable others also thus to hallow and glorify his name. "God be merciful unto us, and bless us; and cause his face to shine upon us; that thy way may be known upon earth, thy saving health among all nations. Let the people praise thee, O God; let all the people praise thee."—Ps. lxvii. 1–3. "For of him, and through him, and to him, are all things; to whom be glory for ever."—Rom. xi. 36.

CII. Ques. *What do we pray for in the second petition?*

*Ans.* In the second petition, (which is, "Thy kingdom come,") we pray, That Satan's kingdom may be destroyed; and that the kingdom of grace may be advanced, ourselves and others brought into it, and kept in it; and that the kingdom of glory may be hastened.

Q. 1. What is meant by the kingdom of God, which, in this petition, we are to pray for the coming of?

A. By the kingdom of God, which, in this petition, we are to pray for the coming of, is meant—1. The kingdom of God's grace here in this world. "The kingdom of God is within you."—Luke xvii. 21. 2. The kingdom of God's glory in the other world. "Know ye not that the unrighteous shall not inherit the kingdom of God?"—1 Cor. vi. 9.

Q. 2. What do we request, in our praying that God's kingdom of grace may come?

A. We request, in our praying that God's kingdom of grace may come—1. That the kingdom of Satan, and all the professed enemies of God's kingdom, may be destroyed; and that all the power also of sin in ourselves and others, whereby Satan hath dominion, may be subdued. "Let God arise, let his enemies be scattered: let them also that hate him flee before him."—Ps. lxviii. 1. "He that committeth sin is of the devil. For this purpose the Son of God was manifested, that he might destroy the works of the devil."—1 John iii. 8. 2. In general, that the kingdom of God's grace might be advanced in the world, above all other kingdoms. "And it shall come to pass in the last days, that the mountain of the Lord's house shall be established in the top of the mountains, and shall be exalted above the hills, and all nations shall flow unto it."—Isa. ii. 2. 3. In particular, that ourselves and others might be brought into this kingdom of God's grace, by the power and efficacy of God's work and Spirit in our conversion. "Finally, brethren, pray for us, that the word of the Lord may have free course and be glorified, even as it is with you."—2 Thess. iii. 1. "The Gentiles to whom I now send thee, to open their eyes, and to turn them from darkness to light, and from the power of Satan unto God."—Acts xxvi. 17, 18. "Brethren, my heart's desire and prayer to God for Israel is, that they might be saved."—Rom. x. 1. 4. That ourselves and others, who are brought already into the kingdom of grace, may be kept in it by strengthening and establishing grace. "The God of all grace, who hath called us unto his eternal glory by Christ Jesus, after that ye have suffered a while, make you perfect, stablish, strengthen, settle you."—1 Pet. v. 10.

Q. 3. What do we request in praying that the kingdom of God's glory may come?

A. We request, in our praying that the kingdom of God's glory may come, that his kingdom of glory may be hastened, which will appear and be manifested unto the whole world at the second coming and appearance of the Lord Jesus to judgment. " He which testifieth these things, saith, Surely I come quickly. Amen. Even so, come, Lord Jesus."—Rev. xxii. 20.

CIII. Ques. *What do we pray for in the third petition ?*

*Ans.* In the third petition, (which is, "Thy will be done in earth as it is in heaven,) we pray, That God, by his grace, would make us able and willing to know, obey, and submit to his will in all things, as the angels do in heaven.

Q. 1. What is meant by the will of God, which we are to pray that it might be done?

A. By the will of God, which we are to pray that it might be done, is meant—1. The will of God's precept, or that which he is pleased to require of us. " Not every one that saith unto me, Lord, Lord, shall enter into the kingdom of heaven; but he that doeth the will of my Father which is in heaven."—Matt. vii. 21. 2. The will of God's providence, or that which he is pleased to do with us, and unto us. "If I might have a prosperous journey, by the will of God, to come unto you."—Rom. i. 10. " It is better if the will of God be so, that ye suffer for well-doing, than for evil-doing."—1 Pet. iii. 17.

Q. 2. What do we request, when we pray that the will of God's precept be done?

A. When we pray that the will of God's precept be done, we request—1. That ourselves and others, who naturally are dark and ignorant of his will, may, by his Word and Spirit, be enabled to know and understand it. "Ye were sometimes darkness, but now ye are light in the Lord. Be not unwise, but understanding what the will of the Lord is."—Eph. v. 8, 17. " We cease not to pray for you, and to desire that ye might be filled with the knowledge of his will, in all wisdom and spiritual understanding."—Col. i. 9. 2. That ourselves and others, who naturally have in our hearts an enmity against God's law, might be inclined and enabled to obey and do whatever it is the will of God to command. "The carnal mind is enmity against God; for it is not subject to the law of God, neither indeed can be."—Rom. viii. 7. "Incline my heart unto thy testimonies."—Ps. cxix. 26. "Teach me to do thy will; for thou art my God: thy Spirit is good." —Ps. cxliii. 10. "I will put my Spirit within you, and cause you to walk in my statutes, and ye shall keep my judgments and do them."—Ezek. xxxvi. 27.

Q. 3. What do we request, when we pray that the will of God's providence may be done?

A. When we pray that the will of God's providence may be done, we request that ourselves and others might have compliance of will with the will of God, so as thankfully to accept merciful providences, and patiently submit unto afflictive providences. "And Mary said, Behold the handmaid of the Lord; be it unto me according to thy word." —Luke i. 38. "And when he would not be persuaded, we ceased, saying, The will of the Lord be done."—Acts xxi. 14.

Q. 4. How are we to pray that God's will may be done by ourselves and others?

A. We are to pray that God's will may be done by ourselves and others on earth, universally, readily, unweariedly, constantly, even as it is done in heaven. "Bless the Lord, ye his angels, that excel in strength, that do his commandments, hearkening unto the voice of his word. Bless the Lord, all his works, in all places of his dominions: bless the Lord, O my soul."—Ps. ciii. 20, 22.

CIV. Ques. *What do we pray for in the fourth petition?*

*Ans.* In the fourth petition, (which is, "Give us this day our daily bread,") we pray, That, of God's free gift, we may receive a competent portion of the good things of this life, and enjoy his blessing with them.

Q. 1. What is meant by "our daily bread?"

A. By "our daily bread," is meant all outward provision for our daily sustenance. "I will abundantly bless her provision: I will satisfy her poor with bread."—Ps. cxxxii. 15.

Q. 2. What do we ask in praying for "our daily bread?"

A. In praying for "our daily bread," we do not ask plenty, but a competent portion of the good things of this life, such as God seeth to be necessary and most convenient for us. "Give me neither poverty nor riches; feed me with food convenient for me."—Prov. xxx. 8.

Q. 3. May we not have convenient outward provisions without our asking?

A. We may have convenient outward provisions without our asking, but we cannot have them without God's giving. "Thou givest them their meat in due season."—Ps. cxlv. 15.

Q. 4. Why need we ask of God daily outward provisions, if we may have them without asking?

A. We ought to ask for our daily outward provisions— 1. Because God requireth that we should ask for these things; and he hath promised only unto such, that they should not want them. "The young lions do lack, and suffer hunger; but they that seek the Lord shall not want any good thing."—Ps. xxxiv. 10. 2. Because, in asking aright our daily outward provisions, we ask and obtain the blessing of God with them; and without asking, if we have these things, we have them with God's curse. "And ye shall serve the Lord your God, and he shall bless thy bread, and thy water."—Exod. xxiii. 25.

CV. Ques. *What do we pray for in the fifth petition?*

*Ans.* In the fifth petition, (which is, "And forgive us our debts as we forgive our debtors,") we pray, That God, for Christ's sake, would freely pardon all our sins; which we are the rather encouraged to ask, because by his grace we are enabled from the heart to forgive others.

Q. 1. What is meant by " our debts ?"

A. By " our debts," is meant our sins against God, whereby we are indebted unto his justice, which we can no otherwise satisfy than by undergoing eternal punishment.

Q. 2. Have all need of forgiveness, and may any debt be forgiven ?

A. All, being sinners, have need of forgiveness, and any sins (excepting the sin against the Holy Ghost) may be forgiven. " If thou, Lord, shouldest mark iniquities, O Lord, who shall stand ? But there is forgiveness with thee, that thou mayest be feared."—Ps. cxxx. 3, 4.

Q. 3. May we pray unto God for the forgiveness of our sins upon the account of our own merits ?

A. We have no merit, in the sight of God, of our own; and therefore we must pray that God would freely pardon all our sins, of his own mercy and loving-kindness. " Have mercy upon me, O God, according to thy loving-kindness; according unto the multitude of thy tender mercies, blot out my transgressions."—Ps. li. 1.

Q. 4. May we hope by prayer to obtain forgiveness, of God's mercy, without any merits ?

A. God being infinitely just, as well as merciful, we must bring merit before him, that we may obtain forgiveness of him ; but because we have it not of our own, and he has provided it for us in his Son, we must pray for pardon for the merits' sake of Christ, who hath purchased forgiveness for us with his blood. " In whom we have redemption through his blood, the forgiveness of sins."—Eph. i. 7.

Q. 5. What may encourage us to ask forgiveness from God ?

A. We may be encouraged to ask forgiveness from God, when, by his grace, we are enabled with our hearts to forgive others. " For if ye forgive men their trespasses, your heavenly Father will also forgive you."—Matt. vi. 14.

CVI. Ques. *What do we pray for in the sixth petition?*

*Ans.* In the sixth petition, (which is, "And lead us not into temptation, but deliver us from evil,") we pray, That God would either keep us from being tempted to sin, or support and deliver us when we are tempted.

Q. 1. What do we request in praying, "Lead us not into temptation?"

A. In praying, "Lead us not into temptation," we request that God would keep us from being tempted unto sin.

Q. 2. How doth God keep us from being tempted unto sin?

A. God keepeth us from being tempted unto sin, either when he restraineth the devil (the great tempter of mankind) from assaulting us with his prevailing temptations; or else restraineth us from coming into those ways where temptations are waiting for us, and where we should be tempters unto ourselves. "Watch and pray, that ye enter not into temptation."—Matt. xxvi. 41. "Keep back thy servant from presumptuous sins; let them not have dominion over me."—Ps. xix. 13.

Q. 3. What do we request in praying, "Deliver us from evil?"

A. In praying, "Deliver us from evil," we request, that when we are tempted by the devil, or the flesh, or the world, unto sin, that we may be supported and strengthened to resist and overcome the temptations, so as to be delivered, by the power of God's sufficient grace, from falling into the evil of sin. "Resist the devil, and he will flee from you."—James iv. 7. "God is faithful, who will not suffer you to be tempted above that ye are able."—1 Cor. x. 13. "There was given to me a thorn in the flesh, the messenger of Satan, to buffet me. For this thing I besought the Lord thrice, that it might depart from me. And he said unto me, My grace is sufficient for thee."—2 Cor. xii. 7–9.

**CVII. Ques.** *What doth the conclusion of the Lord's prayer teach us?*

*Ans.* The conclusion of the Lord's prayer, (which is, "For thine is the kingdom, the power, and the glory, for ever, *Amen*,") teacheth us to take our encouragement in prayer from God only; and in our prayers to praise him, ascribing kingdom, power, and glory to him; and in testimony of our desire and assurance to be heard, we say *Amen*.

Q. 1. What is the conclusion of the Lord's prayer itself?

A. The conclusion of the Lord's prayer itself is in these words, "For thine is the kingdom, the power, and the glory, for ever, Amen."

Q. 2. What is the first thing which this conclusion of the Lord's prayer doth teach us?

A. The first thing which this conclusion of the Lord's prayer doth teach us, is, to take our encouragement in prayer, not from ourselves, or any worthiness of our own, but from God only, who having the kingdom and eternal sovereignty, the power and eternal all-sufficiency, the glory for ever, and therefore incomparably glorious in his faithfulness, goodness, and most tender mercy, we may persuade ourselves that he is both able to give what we ask, and that he is willing, and will give what he hath promised unto us. "We do not present our supplications for our righteousness, but for thy great mercies. O Lord, hear; O Lord, forgive; O Lord, hearken, and do; defer not, for thine own sake, O my God."—Dan. ix. 18, 19. "Hearken unto the voice of my cry, my King, and my God; for unto thee will I pray."—Ps. v. 2. "Now unto him that is able to do exceeding abundantly above all that we ask or think, according to the power that worketh in us, unto him be glory in the Church by Christ Jesus, throughout all ages, world without end. Amen."—Eph. iii. 20, 21.

Q. 3. What is the second thing which this conclusion of the Lord's prayer doth teach us?

A. The second thing which this conclusion of the Lord's

prayer doth teach us is, in our prayers to God to praise him, ascribing kingdom, power, and glory unto him. "Blessed be thou, Lord God of Israel our father, for ever and ever. Thine, O Lord, is the greatness, and the power, and the glory, and the victory, and the majesty; for all that is in the heaven and in the earth is thine; thine is the kingdom, and thou art exalted as head above all. Now, therefore, our God, we thank thee, and praise thy glorious name."—1 Chron. xxix. 10, 11, 13. "Now unto the King eternal, immortal, invisible, the only wise God, be honour and glory, for ever and ever. Amen."—1 Tim. i. 18.

Q 4. Why are we to say, "Amen?"

A. We are to say, "Amen," which signifieth *so be it*, or, *so shall it be*, in testimony of our desires and assurances to be heard. "Amen. Even so, come, Lord Jesus."—Rev. xxii. 20.

THE END.